The PETER LAWFORD Story

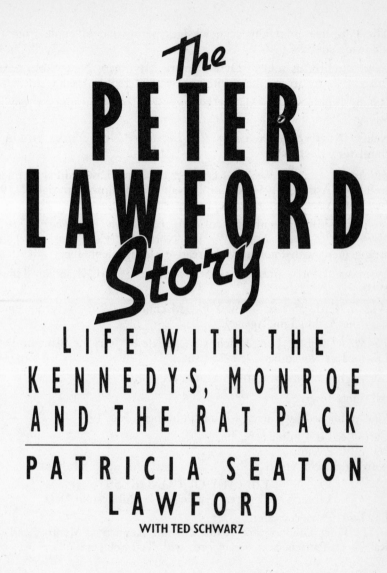

The PETER LAWFORD Story

LIFE WITH THE KENNEDYS, MONROE AND THE RAT PACK

PATRICIA SEATON LAWFORD

WITH TED SCHWARZ

Carroll & Graf Publishers, Inc.
New York

The Publisher gratefully acknowledges permission to quote from the following sources:

Exner, Judith, as told to Ovid Demaris, *My Story*, New York, Grove Press, 1977 by arrangement with the Scott Meredith Agency, Inc.

Galon, Buddy, *Bitch*, Massachusetts, Branden Publishing, Brookline Village, 1986.

Kelley, Kitty, *Elizabeth Taylor: The Last Star*, New York, Simon & Schuster, 1981.

The New York Daily News. Coverage of the Peter Lawford/Pat Kennedy wedding. (April 25, 1954). Credit to Nancy Randolph. Copyright © 1954 *New York News, Incorporated*, reprinted with permission.

Sullivan, William, with Brown, Bill, *The Bureau: My Thirty Years in Hoover's FBI*, New York, W. W. Norton & Co., Inc., 1979. By arrangement with International Creative Management, Inc.

Swanson, Gloria, *Swanson on Swanson*, New York, Random House, 1980.

Wilson, Earl, *Sinatra*, New York, Macmillan, 1976, by arrangement with the Arthur Pine Agency.

The Press-Telegram, Long Beach, CA. Article by Jerry Le Blanc on Peter Lawford in November 19, 1972 issue.

First published by Carroll & Graf Publishers, Inc. 1988

Carroll & Graf Publishers, Inc.
260 Fifth Avenue
New York, NY 10001

LIBRARY OF CONGRESS
Library of Congress Cataloging-in-Publication Data

Lawford, Patricia Seaton.
  The Peter Lawford story : life with the Kennedys, Monroe, and the Rat Pack / Patricia Seaton Lawford, with Ted Schwarz.
    p.   cm.
  ISBN: 0-88184-434-9 : $17.95
  1. Lawford, Peter, 1923–1984.   2. Motion picture actors and actresses—United States—Biography.   I. Schwarz, Ted, 1945–
II. Title.
PN2287.L287L3   1988
791.43'028'09—dc19
[B]   88-20974
                                                                    CIP

Manufactured in the United States of America

For Daniel K.,
who gave me encouragement
and showed me I could love again.

Acknowledgments

To Gloria Luchenbill, with thanks for her many kindnesses and generous assistance.

To Seymour Grush, who provided the facilities of the Best Western Sunset Plaza Hotel as a base for the research for this book.

To Jackie Gayle, for his assistance both with interviews and with lodging.

To Lee Briggs of U.S.A. ComputerTech of Canoga Park, California, for providing the computer equipment for both authors of this book, enabling us to meet what would otherwise have been an impossible deadline.

To Kent Carroll, for his sensitivity as an editor, both to the often delicate subject matter and to my needs in trying to come to grips with what I have for so long suppressed.

To James Mason for his invaluable assistance.

To Susan Hill, who was the first to believe in this book and who worked to shape it into a project of which I am extremely proud.

To Ted and Leslie Schwarz who were always there when I needed support.

And to P.K., Peabody, and Sherman, who had to get into this book somewhere or I'd never hear the end of it.

Contents

Foreword

IF I KNEW THEN WHAT I KNOW NOW, NOT A THING WOULD I change. In spite of all the difficulties one encounters by living with a performer, that life is by far the greatest teacher. Peter was a great believer in learning from negative situations, a belief he permanently instilled in me. Throughout all the pain of drug and alcohol abuse, the man's personality was so powerful that I found myself blinded to the horror I was experiencing. It wasn't until I developed as a woman and as an adult that I realized he did not have all the answers. Then I sought help for this person who shaped my life and gave to me more love than I had ever known.

After he died on Christmas Eve (he always did have great timing), the team of doctors attending him for the last year of his life took me into a conference room and said, "Mrs. Lawford, we want you to know that you prolonged Peter's life by many years and you should have no guilt about his passing." Guilt I don't have, but one always feels "God, I wish I could have saved him."

Throughout our ten years together, Peter shared with me the intimate details of his life. He was planning an autobiography before he died and told me "If anything should ever happen to me, Patricia, for chrissakes, do the book. I've told you everything." He had experienced great trepidation about many subjects to be covered in his book—for example, the Kennedys and Marilyn Monroe. To the end he remained loyal to one of Hollywood's great mysteries. I feel there are stories that should be told about this man and his life among Hollywood's elite and America's royalty.

It is with his blessing that I embark upon this project.

Patricia Seaton Lawford
Los Angeles, California

viii

Prologue

I suppose it was inevitable that Peter Lawford and I would eventually become both lovers and husband and wife during the last decade of his life. We both grew up misfits, abused at home, shunted from area to area, involved with show business from the time we were young.

Peter stayed with show business, of course. MGM made him a star in the 1940s and he had great success in the early days of television. If anything, it might be said that he grew "too big," eventually informing a producer that the character he wanted Peter to play in a new film was not one that could succeed. Peter realized that the character was based on his late brother-in-law's favorite fictional hero. He understood that it might lead to a series of films. But Peter's personal manager, Milt Ebbins, was certain that the part was a loser and that's why he refused to let Peter become James Bond.

I ended my career at a young age. A talent scout came to my elementary school when I was five years old and chose me to be the prize girl for the "Billy Barty Show." Billy Barty was a skilled actor who also happened to be a dwarf. His first big success was as one of the Munchkins in the movie *The Wizard of Oz*, a film that made Judy Garland a major star. Eventually he had his own children's show, and I was chosen to be the child who would stand around in a pretty dress and give prizes to other children. The trouble was that I was a bigot. There was no way I was going to appear on television with a grown-up who was shorter than me, especially since I was just a little kid. When the talent scout insisted I would have fun, I insisted on throwing a temper tantrum until they chose another little girl from my class.

I got a little further with "Bob Baker's Marionette Theater." Once again I was chosen to give out prizes—this time having to

9

endure putting on Mary Janes and some little lace socks—and I actually tolerated two appearances. Only then did I decide that the actor's life was not for me. So I started to cry and carry on until they agreed to make someone else a "star."

My mother immediately took me out of public elementary school and enrolled me in a strict Catholic parochial school, Immaculate Heart of Mary. She thought it would tame my rebellious attitude, but instead it nurtured it. The nuns still used rulers to crack our knuckles, and mine were frequently reddened, though I usually received the ultimate punishment—being locked in the storage closet.

It was not that the punishment was undeserved. I used to make up notes that read: "Drop your books on the floor when the clock reads 10:10. If you don't, you're dead!" I would either type them at home or disguise my handwriting, then pass them around when I thought the nuns weren't looking.

The books would be dropped by some of the kids (and I made sure I saw which ones didn't, because they would not be my friends) and class would be disrupted. The nuns couldn't prove anything against me, but when you're known as a troublemaker and are practically rolling on the floor with laughter over a juvenile prank, it's not too hard to place the blame. I would immediately be ordered into the closet by Sister Marie Claudette, banished to the darkness while class continued.

I would like to tell you a dramatic story about the trauma I endured within those black walls while I listened to the teaching of spelling and arithmetic in the classroom. But the truth is that the closet was also where all our lunch bags were stored. I went from bag to bag, eating all the good cookies—the chocolate chips, the Oreos—and switching sandwiches at random. Then, when I was allowed out and we all went to the playground to eat, I would listen to such cries as "My mom gave me bologna for lunch and this is a cheese sandwich!" or "I know she put some cookies in here. They're my favorites and I watched her do it!"

It should have been obvious to everyone what had happened, especially since I was too stuffed to eat my own sandwich, but no one was that wise. I regularly made return trips to the closet.

I think the only reason I survived those years was because I was "adopted" by Monsignor Charles O'Donnell, who was aware of the abuse I was experiencing at home. He knew I was being emotionally abused at home and tried to get me to talk about it. When my life became too rough, he would put on his formal robes, then walk into class. All of us children would stand and say "Good morning, Monsignor O'Donnell." He would smile, greet us, then tell Sister Marie Claudette that he needed to see me.

"Pat Seaton," the nun would solemnly announce, "you are excused for the rest of the day."

Then the monsignor and I would solemnly walk down the hall. He had his formal robes and I wore the school uniform of navy-and-green beret, blazer, and jumper; a white blouse; a navy man's tie in a Windsor knot; and black-and-white saddle shoes. No one questioned that I was probably going to be punished on a much greater scale than anyone else had ever endured with the rulers and the closet. What they did not see was our continuing around the corner, out the door, and into the church's limousine. We would immediately drive to the El Padrino Room of the Beverly Wilshire Hotel, where he would order me Irish coffee. I drank cup after cup, thinking it was a drink made in Ireland. I talked more and more freely about my home life and my problems, never realizing that the monsignor had ordered me seemingly endless rounds of an alcoholic beverage until I was quite drunk.

It is one of those ironies of my life with Peter that there is a good chance he might have seen me with the monsignor on one of these excursions. Peter regularly had lunch in the El Padrino Room, and the monsignor was the man who baptized each of Peter's four children. However, if he did see the odd couple with the robes and the uniform, the memory of the experience did not linger in his mind.

Part of my family was in show business when I was growing up, though I was never encouraged one way or another toward such a career. Instead, one relative, a writer and producer, delighted in having me around. He gave me seemingly endless gifts—dresses, a Lionel train set, toy trucks that could dump real dirt—and encouraged my creativity, yet he never tried to bring me on the sets and I was still a child when he died.

I did go to parties at one wealthy relative's mansion. I remember seeing Jimmy Stewart there, and Cary Grant was introduced to me. But I was not impressed. All that concerned me was how quickly I could get out of my stupid dress, let down my hair, and dive into his swimming pool.

Oddly, though I never was an actress, I had a strong interest in stage lighting and constantly asked questions about it until I was fairly knowledgeable about the techniques. It was a skill that surprised Peter, though it was the only one I had.

Like Peter, I lived in a variety of cities, seldom having friends, and constantly exposed to a variety of cultures and social strata. In fact, it was while I was in England with my father when I was around twelve years old that I first saw Peter. He was making a film there, and we spotted him on the street. I had no idea that he was an actor, had never seen his work, yet there was something striking about him. He caught my attention, my eyes riveted on his handsome, sophisticated style. He had the presence in real life that a man such as Cary Grant was only able to develop for the screen, and I asked my father who he was. "That's Peter Lawford, the actor," he said.

I thought nothing further of the incident. Then, five years later, I actually met the man who had been a curiosity on the London streets that day. We moved in together almost immediately, and we were together until his death more than a decade later. During those years he shared stories of growing up throughout the world, the horrors of his early abuse at the hands of his mother, his delight in working for MGM, his friends such as Nancy Davis Reagan, the Kennedys, Marilyn Monroe, Elizabeth Taylor, and others, many of whom became my friends as well. And then, two years before his death, he decided to write the story of his life.

Eventually Peter began working on his book with Sterling Lord, the well-known New York literary agent, and Wayne Warga, a writer for "Entertainment Tonight," and was on the verge of signing a contract with a major New York publisher. However, his health gave out and he could not work. Just before he entered the hospital for the last time he asked me to complete the book, using the outline he had developed, the extensive notes he had made, our many hours of intimate conversations, and interviews he wanted me to conduct with his friends. However, when he died I was too overwrought to think about such things, despite the urgings of both Sterling Lord and the publishing company, which offered Peter's contract to me. I put everything off for many months until I thought I could do what Peter wanted.

Eventually I was ready to go to work. I contacted author Ted Schwarz and, together, we began the project Peter asked me to complete. We followed his outline. We worked with the extensive notes he left. Separately and together we conducted dozens of interviews with major stars, studio officials, behind-the-scenes personnel, and numerous others. This, then, to the best of our ability, is Peter's story.

1
The Early Years

"The first time I met Peter Lawford it was the mid-1940s and he was already the hot new actor in town. My father was doing a radio show called "Sealtest Village Store" with Joan Davis at NBC and it was live on the air. Peter was the guest star that week and had been fine at rehearsal. However, the show was about to air and he was late.

"I was a twelve- or thirteen-year-old kid, and I remember being bored and wanting to get out of everyone's way because they were freaking out that Mr. Peter Lawford was not arriving. I stood at the back of the building, looking out at the parking lot, thinking that maybe I'd see him first or something.

"All of a sudden there was a honking and Peter pulled into the parking lot. He was driving an open-topped convertible filled with four girls, all of them in bathing suits. He had gotten caught in traffic coming from Malibu and didn't realize how late it was.

"It was like watching Errol Flynn. Peter stopped the car in the middle of the lot, leaped over the side without opening the door, and started running toward the studio. He was very fit, well-muscled and tanned, and was wearing a bathing suit, sweater and sandals. He ran down the hall, sending the pages flying, and went inside the studio, which had a live audience, and did the show that way."

—Jack Haley, Jr.
Actor, Producer, Studio Executive

MY LATE HUSBAND, PETER LAWFORD WAS BORN INTO CONTROversy, a fact that would foreshadow a life in which his name would be linked with the alleged murder of Marilyn Monroe; the Kennedy White House; the era of burned-out, drug-abusing movie stars; and even the beginning of the sun-and-surfing California beach bum era. Luck and natural good looks brought him a successful career in movies. The influence of his father-in-law, Joseph Kennedy, at one time reputed to be one of the wealthiest and most powerful men in the world, allegedly brought him a career in television. And his insecurity, self-doubt, and dependence on drugs and alcohol resulted in four wives, great debts, and deep emotional pain.

May Aylen was living in India with her husband, Colonel Ernest Aylen, a member of the British forces commanded by General Sir Sydney Lawford, a handsome, regal leader known behind his back as "Swanky Syd." The general was all military, one of the most highly decorated British soldiers in World War I, eventually knighted in the field. His world was one of power, influence, and high position. When he dressed in formal uniform, his chest was covered with medals and battle ribbons, a swagger stick at his side. He had great bearing and delighted in being in the company of beautiful women. This included his colonel's wife, with whom he had an affair that would have remained discreet had May Aylen not become pregnant.

May explained to the colonel that she was going to divorce him. Her reasons were quite obvious: she was pregnant with another man's child. The colonel was a proud man who could not handle the emotional reality that came from learning that the wife he loved was pregnant by the leader he most admired.

What happened next may have profoundly affected May Aylen's

sanity. The colonel summoned her to his office, meeting her at the door when she arrived. The first thing she noticed was his regal bearing, his full dress uniform, and the military posture he adopted when he faced her. Then she saw that his feet were bare and that a shotgun was at his side.

Without saying a word, the colonel angled the shotgun so the barrel was pointing toward his face. He slipped a toe onto the trigger, carefully balanced the weapon, then saluted May, almost simultaneously using his toe to fire the gun. His head exploded right in front of her—blood, brains, and bits of skull splattering against the wall. The trauma of seeing this was so great that when Peter was born at home, according to the nurse in attendance, it was a breach birth, his body weight was low, and the umbilical cord was wrapped around his neck. He was named Peter Sydney Vaughn Aylen, the last link with the colonel whom he would never know. He became Peter Sydney Lawford, the only name he would use throughout his life, after his mother married the general.

The shock may have started May's deterioration into mental illness. Certainly it accounted for the love/hate relationship she developed with her son, a relationship that caused her to constantly try to find ways to humiliate the boy.

May never would admit to the truth of Peter's conception, despite the evidence from Peter's birth certificate, friends' statements, and other documentation over the years. When she wrote her autobiography (*Bitch!—The Autobiography of Lady Lawford as Told to Buddy Galon*), she told a story of having her first husband die without leaving her any money. She claimed that he left it all to his girlfriend, a woman who was probably a figment of May's imagination. She created the fiction that she went to live with her father and thought nothing of dating. The general was a friend of her father's who she claimed approached her only when she was in young widowhood. The marriage was allegedly as passionless as if it had been arranged.

She commented: "Peter was an awful accident! I did everything to prevent such an accident . . . including the cause of such accidents. After I married, I used to lie awake and make up excuses to my husband to keep from having to endure that horrible, messy, unsanitary thing that all husbands expect from their wives. If only the Bible had not said, 'Wives, submit yourselves unto your husbands.'

"I can still remember slipping to the kitchen and getting uncooked meat which I rubbed against my nightdress. I was *always* having my period! But, oh, that horrible time when I really did not have my period. I rushed to Lord Evans to hear my fears confirmed—I was two-and-a-half months pregnant. Oh, God! Even too late for an abortion—of course, I don't believe in that anyway—it's murder. I've never approved of abortion. Yet I never wanted Peter.

"I can't stand babies! They run at both ends; they smell of sour milk and urine. I never saw Peter until he was washed and perfumed. Ugh! Peter was such a mistake! No, I don't think Peter knows he was an accident. It might hurt him if he knew. But I made the general promise that there would be no more babies—*ever!*"

The pregnancy may have been upsetting, and May probably did not wish to have children. However, there was intense passion at the start of the relationship with the general. Peter was the result of an extramarital affair with a man who delighted in having sex with beautiful women. If she ever did come to despise sex, something quite doubtful while Sir Sydney was alive, then it was as the result of guilt and was a radical change from her earlier feelings.

It was September 7, 1923, when Peter was born (May Lawford admitted to being married in 1924, not realizing that Peter's birth certificate was a public record that would reveal the truth), a time of relative peace for the British Empire and the world. World War I was over. The Russian revolution had taken place. Nations such as India were solidly ruled by the English, and the general lived peacefully with his family in various countries of the world. Much of the time they would be on ships or staying in luxury hotels and apartments, citizens of the world with a son whose citizenship was British yet whose first language, because of the travels, became French.

Peter enjoyed all the trips, experiencing many of the world's cultures and meeting people from all walks of life. I think this was why he had no pretensions about others, accepting everyone for what they were. This was also why he had such an easy time adjusting to Hollywood, an area filled with pretensions, dishonesty, deceit, and superficial relationships. Hollywood was just another culture to Peter, just another place where he arrived with no friends and little knowledge of the area, then had to adapt so he appeared as though born to that world. His high intelligence and his experiences as a lonely child gave him that ability.

Peter Lawford, aged 6 years, son of Lady Lawford, demonstrates in mind and body the benefits of a New Health upbringing. Educated as yet entirely by his mother, he is quick at learning, speaks French and Spanish well, and shows ability as

an actor and impersonator. —Caption under a small photograph
run in the November 1930 issue of *New Health*.

My future in-laws, the Lawfords were wealthy, well able to
afford both necessities and luxuries for Peter. Yet May was uncomfortable with the son who was the focal point for so much
conflict and pain. She humiliated him in any way she could,
dressing him as a girl in all the latest styles for that opposite sex
for the first nine years of his life. His family album contains
photographs of one of the most adorable "flappers" ever to be
raised in what Americans called the Jazz Age of the Roaring
Twenties. The horror of the photograph is the knowledge that the
"flapper" is actually a boy, Peter, who was kept relatively isolated
from other children during those early years.

There were other indignities as well. Peter was not educated,
though he did have nannies who cared for him, teaching him the
basics of reading, writing, and language. May, knowing that her
preventing Peter from learning would be considered abusive by
her friends, created the myth that there were tutors traveling with
them to educate their son. But the existence of the tutors was a lie
meant to avoid personal embarrassment. Peter later commented:
"The biggest mistake which I was to find out was that, because of
not going to school, I would feel inferior for a long time." He felt
himself to be a fraud despite his sophistication, a brilliant mind,
and a fluency in several languages, an attitude that led, in part, to
his self-destructiveness in later years.

The importance of learning was not lost to Peter, though. He
became a slow but avid reader, keeping a dictionary always close
at hand. As an adult, he bragged that there was a period in his life
when he took a dictionary to bed, teaching himself the meaning
and proper use of two new words each night. In that way he was
able to increase both his vocabulary and his understanding of the
world around him.

The paper seems unusually full of instructions for children's
discipline. So pathetic! When all that is required is strict adher-
ence to the instructions of the Almighty, which can be found in
the Bible, the use of example and instinct.

Since women took over the world most children have become
impudent, mannerless, noisy little horrors; shunned by land-
lords, the terror of shopkeepers!

A little less career and a little more home, a good flexible
slipper and permitting the father to have some say in their
upbringing is the answer to the rot that is eating up the modern

children of all nations. —Letter to the editor by Lady May
Lawford, *Los Angeles Examiner*, July 31, 1949

May Aylen became Lady May Lawford, wife of a man who
walked with royalty. She had a great desire for public attention
and first achieved it by joining what was called the British Empire
party during the time the family lived in the Mayfair district of
London. The political movement was a conservative one gaining
great exposure in the press. May became an active campaigner on
behalf of their candidates, speaking frequently, though as much to
get her name into the papers as to support a cause in which she
believed. She carefully clipped all articles in which her name
appeared, tacking them to the wall for a while, then filing them in
a scrapbook.

May's flamboyance led her to become interested in the movies,
still a young entertainment industry in England and the United
States. The family was once on a tour of a studio in Shepherd's
Bush, then the heart of the British film industry. A movie called
Poor Old Bill was being made by director Monty Banks, the
husband of Gracie Fields, one of the first of the great European
movie stars. The film was not going well.

This was a time when child stars, such as America's Jackie
Coogan, were quite popular, so a child was being used in the
Banks picture as well. The scene being shot was supposed to be a
simple one. The little boy who had been hired was cutting a pair
of pants to fit his pet dog. Then he was to put the clothing over
the dog's paws, add his father's glasses, and get "caught" by his
irate parent. It was an action everyone thought could be achieved
in one or two takes. The dog seemed to be cooperative but the
boy was unable to play his part correctly. Scene after scene was
being ruined, hundreds of feet of film wasted. Banks was frustrated, yelling at the child, shouting "It's no good! Do it again!"

Finally the director called for a break in the shooting while he
tried to compose himself. He walked over to where the Lawfords
had been watching and was introduced to the family. Banks
looked at Peter and said, "That's the kind of boy I need."

Peter was not impressed with the director's comment concerning his potential as an actor. In later years he remembered Banks's
frustration and felt that had his parents been accompanied by a
dog instead of a child, the director would have declared "That's
the kind of dog I need," replacing the animal instead of the actor.
He simply wanted to do something different and Peter became the
focus of that desire.

Banks hired him on the spot, and suddenly, at age seven, Peter was in his first movie. He was given a contract, a week's work, and seven British pounds for his efforts. Although not even Peter realized it then, he was also given a career.

The first surprise for Peter was how much he enjoyed the smell of the production studio. Actors frequently speak of the "smell of the greasepaint" when they are involved with stage plays. They talk of the dressing room odor that is a mix of sweat, makeup, and cold cream. A different, yet distinct odor was found on the old movie lots, reinforcing the fantasy world of the filmmaker. It was one that remained in the boy's consciousness, something he wanted to experience again.

Peter also enjoyed the separation from his mother. He had become extremely introverted, playing by himself or dominated by Lady May. On the set, though she was present, the director was king. For one week and a total of five scenes, he was not a withdrawn little boy. Even when the director yelled at him the first day on the set, he felt as though he had broken through his mother's control.

Oddly, when Peter finally saw himself on the screen for the first time, he was embarrassed. "I thought that I really looked like a bloody fool. I thought, 'What am I doing up there?' " Yet despite all this, he had to admit it was fun.

"It was fun because it was different," he said later. Then he asked his parents, "Am I going to do another one?"

May Lawford was delighted with her son's interest. Jackie Coogan was a big child star whose proud mother was regularly interviewed by the press. If Peter became England's new child star, Lady May would be a great celebrity. As a result, she readily agreed to let Peter work later that year when Monty Banks called once again.

Although Peter made the second movie, the London County Council decided that acting was not a healthy profession for a child, who should be in school during those formative years. Child stars in the United States were being given sleeping pills at night and stimulants in the morning in order to keep them working. They had tutors on the movie lots, yet it was obvious that the children were being exploited. The London County Council did not want to repeat such horrors and thus wrote what came to be known in both the United States and England as the "Coogan Law." This ensured that children doing any work on films would have their schooling and their health placed ahead of the work.

Peter was not being given an education, despite the Coogan Law, so his involvement would theoretically not have mattered. However, Lady May never fought the issue, becoming bored with the industry when it was obvious that no one was going to fulfill her wishes for her child.

The change in the law was not a serious disappointment for Peter. Instead of escaping his mother by making movies, he began fleeing from her by attending them. There were always Saturday shows for children, but Peter also attended every day of the week that he was allowed to go. He was still young enough that there was a mixture of fantasy and reality on the screen. As he later explained the situation: "I think in a funny way I was probably hoping to see myself up there.

"The make-believe [of movies] was like a game. It is hide-and-seek on a higher level. I mean I didn't sit down at age seven or eight and lay out my future, but it obviously had an effect. And when I was older, I started to get idols."

There was one adult pastime to which the young Peter Lawford was introduced that did stay with him over the years. This was sex, and his teacher was the German nanny who lived with the family when they moved to Monte Carlo. (Many of these moves made little sense to him either as a child or, upon reflection, as an adult. He went along with whatever was happening, never able to form close associations with any area or children his age.)

"In this arena I consider myself most fortunate," Peter later wrote. "I did not learn about it on the streets, or from grubby little boys with hair in their palms, or from playing the popular game of 'Doctor!' I was, as I recall, about ten years old. We were in the south of France. My parents were away and, as I mentioned before, I always had a nanny. This particular one was teaching me German among other things. She was German herself, about thirty-five, and even I, at an early age, could tell that she was a sure nine on a scale of one to ten.

"One lovely day she suggested we take a picnic basket and go off into the country, which was quite close by. 'What fun,' I said to myself, and off we went.

"Let me make it quite clear that up to now there been no mention, even in jest, of anything pertaining to sex. We found this lovely spot in a meadow under a tree, there were some beautiful flowers growing wild all around us. We had our sandwiches and some fruit.

"I was comfortably full and felt relaxed and happy. She was sitting against the tree with her eyes closed, when she gently put her arm around my shoulder and pulled me toward her, saying, 'Rest your head in my lap.' There seemed to be nothing wrong with that so I complied.

"In a few minutes I was half asleep, when I felt her hand gently rubbing my stomach. The next thing I knew she had slipped inside my little short pants and was caressing my penis. My God, it felt good and, for some reason, most natural.

"Meanwhile, with her other hand she had unbuttoned her blouse and was pulling my head toward her breasts. She told me I was such a good boy that she wanted me to kiss them. 'Will you?' she said, as she put her nipple in my mouth. In French she said, 'Doucement,' gently. She was becoming aroused and made me suck them both while holding the back of my head. She wouldn't let me up.

"Unbeknownst to me, because my eyes were closed, she had been playing with herself during all this and must have had her own climax, because she suddenly rose up, flipped me on my back, my pants suddenly vanished, and she was eating me alive! Needless to say, with the erection I was sporting, my arrival couldn't have taken more than a minute and a half.

"Well! In my life I never experienced such a feeling! To try and describe where my head went would be futile. I was to learn later on that that was the beginning of my sexual addiction. The opposite sex would be, was, and is still being chased. The season is always open."

Other picnics in the park followed this early initiation into sex. Peter, his nanny, and a woman friend of the nanny would sit in the shade of a tree, eating lunch and mutually fondling one another. There were no threats, no violence, yet Peter sensed that if his mother found out, she would be irate.

The sexual relationship was an extremely complex one because of the way in which Peter was raised. The nanny had a unique role in the British household of that day. A nanny took over all the functions of an American mother, cleaning the child, taking care of it, and not letting the child into the presence of his parents until he was suitably presentable, usually at mealtimes. Then, when the dinner was over, the child would be taken away by the nanny so as not to disturb the adults' activities.

This close relationship with the nanny was so similar to that of mother and child that the sex acts caused sexual problems similar to those that can be caused by incest. Peter came to fear intimacy yet desire frequent sexual relations, preferring the impersonal approaches of ménage à trois and oral sex with as many different partners as possible.

(The following poem, written by the adult Peter Lawford, is an ode to the memory of the early sexual experiences.)

Patricia Seaton Lawford
Connaught Square

Connaught Square—a lazy square
Where gardens intertwine.
With privilege to play in
if born of social kind.

It's reaching chestnuts,
tailored lawns.
The bramble bushes,
so full of thorns.

Running through
with mirthful glee.
Herbaceous borders
tall as me.

The rush of traffic
on the fringe.
The whirling sprinklers
on a binge.

The famous tree
from whence I fell.
Which I avoid
like holy hell.

The grocer boy would
like to play.
Not aloud [*sic*] he's black
they say.

Then my nanny
I loved her skirt.
An early start
for such a squirt.

Diaper changes
on the hour.
With penises about
to flower.

A crack of thunder
makes us flee.

My mother screaming
time for tea.

Nanny takes me
by the hand.
I visualize
a wedding band.

My fondest memories
my exclusive lair.
I shall always
remember Connaught Square.

Peter never told anyone what was happening with the nanny over the months he enjoyed her pleasure. However, he did tell his parents about an uncle who tried to sexually molest him. He was staying with the uncle one night when he awakened to find a pillow being pushed over his head. The uncle was trying to suffocate the boy just enough to stop resistance while he sexually fondled him. Peter would never say whether or not he escaped unmolested, but he told his parents immediately and they banished the uncle from their home from that day forward. The incident also turned Peter against the idea of homosexual relationships for himself, though he, like most of the other members of the movie colony, was not biased against men and women who enjoyed same-sex pleasure with consenting partners.

Peter frequently told me that when the nanny stopped working for the Lawfords he was crushed. This was the first love of his life and he never wanted it to stop. He later claimed that every little boy should be introduced to sexual experience in this manner, so pleasurable had it been for him. Yet the truth was that he was corrupted in subtle ways that affected both my relationship with him and his relationships with numerous previous lovers.

Because of his experiences with the nanny and her friend, oral sex and multiple partners became Peter's focus of attention in later years. When he reached Hollywood, his name would be linked with the wilder actresses of the 1940s—Lana Turner, Judy Garland, Nancy Davis, and numerous others.

Even as Peter aged, oral sex and multiple partners were his pleasures of choice. I was the fourth woman to be married to him, and I came into his life when heavy drug use had made him almost impotent. He was incapable of having intercourse, and his rare orgasms came through prolonged oral sex, usually with two partners.

I can remember a time in Los Angeles when Peter sent me out shopping for some things he said he needed while he stayed at home, relaxing alone, or so I thought. I had just purchased a couple of beautiful negligees that were in my drawer, with the tags still on them. In my bathroom was an array of expensive cosmetics as well as a new bottle of Joy perfume, the only perfume I liked in those days. But none of this was a concern as I naively left the house.

When I returned home, I discovered two girls in the bathroom, each wearing one of those new negligees, smelling of my perfume, and applying my makeup. As I watched, they leaped onto the bed and began fooling with Peter's cock.

I was irate, but if Peter was shocked or embarrassed by my return, he never showed it. Instead he expressed annoyance with what he called my "common Catholic upbringing."

Looking back on Peter's past and our relationship I can say that I understand how his childhood sexual experiences influenced him, especially when he lost his sex drive through heavy drug use. Yet I am equally surprised that I loved him so much and myself so little that I accepted his desires in our relationship. For six and a half years, I had only oral sex with Peter, sometimes alone with him and sometimes with another woman he wanted to watch having sex with me before bringing us both to orgasm. Finally I sought regular intercourse outside of our relationship, having a series of affairs with various celebrities we knew.

But that life was years away from young Peter. All he knew at the time was the pleasure of his "loving" nanny and her friend. As Peter moved into adolescence he firmly believed that his early sexual experiences had been among the happiest times of his life.

There was also tragedy during those early years, accidents that would physically scar Peter for life. The first, and the least visible, came when he was three years old. His parents were spending the winter in Monte Carlo; Peter was being cared for by a rather incompetent nanny. The woman liked to use the kitchen for bathing Peter, taking advantage of a large sink next to a double-burner device for making coffee.

The routine the nanny used was always the same. She would wash Peter in the sink, rub him down, then hold him over the hot burner to dry his back. Usually the rubdown made Peter easy to handle. However, one day he was still slippery from the soapy water, a fact she did not realize until she was trying to hold him over the hot burner. The child slipped from her grasp, his body falling onto the burner and suffering severe skin damage. Lady May, hearing the screams, rushed in, fired the woman on the spot, then looked to see what could be done to help Peter. These scars, though greatly faded, were always with him.

The second injury occurred a few years later in a small town in France. Peter was playing with some children in the bungalow his parents had rented. He was near a French window containing numerous small panes of glass. "I tripped," he later recalled. "And to save myself, I stuck my hand out and went through it. The mistake I made was in pulling back. That's when the damage was done."

Peter's artery began gushing blood. "I looked down and the flap was laid back, and I could see bone, muscle, everything. I cut muscles, tendons. . . . But my first reaction was, 'Give me a Band-Aid.' "

The other children had run away, terrified that they might have pushed him, something Peter did not think had occurred. He went over to the bathroom sink, applied a Band-Aid, put on his shirt, and decided that nobody would ever know what happened. "But then self-preservation and instinct told me, 'That ain't going to handle it,' so I started to run because I started to feel a little queasy."

Peter was in danger of dying, though he did not realize it. Modern open-heart surgery is routinely accomplished with blood loss that is less than a pint. By the time he reached professional help, he had lost over two pints of blood.

The child raced to the concierge desk, then sat on the floor, too weak to move. The concierge said, "What are you doing bleeding on my carpet?"

It was tea time and a bloody carpet would be unappetizing to the guests of the posh hotel where the family had their bungalow. A few people were disgusted, others realized that something was not normal.

Embarrassed, Peter mumbled an apology. Only then did the concierge realize that the child was in serious trouble.

The concierge shouted for a doctor. The hotel had a large atrium rising several floors, the concierge desk at the bottom. A man on the fifth floor leaned over the railing and explained that he was a doctor. Then, seeing what was happening, he raced downstairs, removed his necktie, and made a tourniquet to stop the bleeding.

Moments later General Lawford appeared, kneeled down, and said, "Good God, what did you do?"

Peter explained what had happened, then said that it was lucky it wasn't his left arm since he was left-handed. Meanwhile he was carried to the hotel bus to be transported to the clinic that was located back by the golf course.

If the general was calm, his mother was even more so at first. She looked at her son and said, "Peter, couldn't you have done it in the springtime?" Her reasoning was unclear, though the question seemed to make sense to her, Peter choosing to not respond. Lady May showed no fear, no emotion, as they drove to get help.

The damage was so severe that the doctor wanted to amputate. Lady Lawford very quietly explained, "You don't have my permission to cut his arm off. You will do the best you can and try to save the arm, and we will see what happens." However, the doctor kept insisting that cutting off the arm was the only thing to do. Finally, exasperated, Lady Lawford looked at the man indignantly and, in perfect French, said, "Fuck off." A second doctor came in, took Peter to the hospital, and stitched him together.

The repair was relatively successful despite the warnings of the first doctor. All the nerves had been severed on the arm, an injury that was not treatable until new surgical techniques were discovered during World War II. Yet despite that fact, gangrene did not set in and he eventually had approximately 75% use of the arm. Only his hand was twisted and withered, and he kept it hidden in a pocket most of the time. When he did use it, it was much like a hook into which he inserted a cigarette, a liquor glass, or anything else. Should he forget a cigarette was in the hand, he would not feel the pain when the lighted end burned his flesh. Instead, he would suddenly grasp his shoulder in agony, the shoulder being the first location where nerves were sensitive to the burn.

Peter often told me that his most vivid memory of his mother's toughness came when the family was staying in a hotel in France. May was alone in their upper-story suite when she heard a burglar at the balcony window. He had apparently either climbed down from above or made his way across the balconies from another suite on the same floor. Whatever the case, May calmly went to where the general kept his service revolver, made certain it was loaded, then returned to the window the burglar was forcing open. She aimed the weapon, fired, the bullet killing him instantly and the impact sending him back off the balcony, careening to the ground. She eventually went downstairs, explaining to the French police what had happened. There was no emotion— neither fear, nor anger, nor remorse. A man was trying to break into her room and the only proper response was to kill him. It was all so very simple that she could not understand why there was any fuss. She was not charged with any crime.

The biggest problem for young Peter came during the recovery period. Standard nursing treatment then included using stone water bottles packed around the ankles to keep the body warm. The containers, looking a little like pottery, were actually stone. Boiling water was placed inside, heating the container to a temperature approximately equal to that of the water. Then the bottle had to be wrapped in towels until the insulation of the towels was sufficient to lower the level of heat to a manageable temperature. The nurse once did the wrapping improperly and the full heat of the bottle was placed against Peter's feet, causing third-degree burns and blisters.

Peter's right hand started to atrophy, something the doctor counteracted by physically forcing it open during the postsurgical checkups. The pain of the forced separation of his fingers from his palm was intense, Peter becoming nauseated and nearly passing out. Yet the action saved him for acting. The hand would never again be quite so disfigured, his grip wide enough open so that when he had to use the hand, such as for saluting, it could be propped into position. He was also taught how to grasp a tennis ball to keep the hand as supple as possible, though it never had any strength.

Peter was always quite close to his father. He trusted the older man completely, a fact that saved Peter's life when they were traveling in Ceylon (now called Sri Lanka). The incident occurred one evening after Peter had prepared for bed.

The general, wearing a side arm as was his habit, walked into Peter's bedroom to say good-night. The mattress for the bed was made from feathers tightly stuffed into the material. Peter had taken off his clothing, pulled back the covers, and was sitting on the bed when his father said, "Peter, don't move." Then he drew his service revolver and fired into the mattress until the gun was empty. When Peter could look to see what happened, there was a dead snake, a Russel's viper, next to him. The snake his father had killed was one of the deadliest in the world, a snake whose bite brings excruciating pain and death within a few hours.

There were fairly frequent trips to the United States during the next few years, especially to Hawaii, California, and, later, Florida. May Lawford suffered from arthritis, and the doctor had said that the warmer climates would help Peter's healing.

Prior to the accident, a military career was a foregone conclusion for Peter. He would have an appointment to the Queen's Guards, then go on to a life that would take him to whatever heights his skills might allow. The only person who objected to these career plans was Peter, who was relieved when he realized that the accident would give him the freedom to pursue acting without family hostility.

May Lawford made the adjustment quite easily, then was surprised by the way she was treated as she tried to enter the world of film production to help her son. When Peter was around eleven years old, the family was on the cruise ship *Mariposa*, just off Hawaii. The cruise ships were popular at the time, actors and actresses frequently using them to relax between film projects. One such actor spotted the Lawfords and became seemingly impressed with May and the general. He told them that they had to come to his home for lunch when they reached Hawaii, an invitation May thought was serious. As Peter explained: "We were staying at the Ambassador Hotel and she called his house a couple of times, but he never called back, so that was my first smell of 'Let's have lunch next week.' He really meant, 'Don't call me; I'll call you.'

"She said, 'Those movie people are uncouth, don't answer telephone calls,' and it got her so pissed off that we got on the next boat and went to the Panama Canal."

From the Panama Canal, the Lawfords went to New York, where another culture shock was waiting. Peter, though no longer dressed as a girl, was still being dressed as a little boy. He frequently wore short pants and white socks, both considered grave social errors by the prepuberty set. As they walked down a Manhattan street, ". . . suddenly a rock lands at my feet from across the street. 'Hey, white socks!' And there was a near riot. I react right away. . . . Instinct. . . . Somebody threw a rock at me and I threw it back.

"My parents were trying to get me out of there. I was into it. Ten to one with these kids against me. They would have eaten me alive."

The Lawfords managed to get Peter back to the hotel room, where May's attitude was "They don't know how to dress children over here." The general, on the other hand, was pleased with his son for fighting back. "Good work," he whispered. Then he convinced May that perhaps it was time for Peter to be dressed like older American boys.

The one area where Peter was able to be active without ridicule from other kids or problems with his mother was athletics. Henry Lawford, Sir Sydney's brother, had been a champion tennis player and had won the first Wimbledon Tournament. Peter became so skilled that when the family moved permanently to the United States, Peter, despite the handicap of his deformed hand and arm, gained a position on the Junior Davis Cup Team. However, he was not allowed to compete in the finals because the matches required that a participant be a citizen of the country he represented. Since Peter remained a British subject at that time, he had to be replaced by a man of lesser ability.

I can remember one time when Peter and I were in London and he decided to show me the clubhouse at Wimbledon. As much as Peter was hurt by being dressed differently from the other children when he was growing up, as an adult he came to believe that a man had "style" by the way he held himself, not what he wore. He knew that you could look elegant in faded jeans and a T-shirt just as much as you could in a tuxedo if you had the style to carry it off. Peter did, dressing to please himself. However, when we arrived at Wimbledon, it was made very clear that Peter's extremely casual clothing was not appropriate.

Peter would not tolerate being kept from the club. He explained who he was as an actor and in relation to the Kennedy family. He stood up to the pompous attitude he was facing and we got inside, much to the disgust of the employee who agreed to show us the portraits of past champions.

As we climbed the winding stairway to the top, we passed such recent stars as Connors, Borg, and all the others. The employee, a horrible snob, became haughtier in his attitude as he read us each passing name. Then, at the top, he looked down at Peter and commented, "And that, sir, is the gentleman who won the very first Wimbledon championship, H. F. Lawford. . . ." Suddenly he looked at Peter, realizing for the first time that the man in front of him was the nephew of a player he revered. Peter just smiled and said, "Yes, I know."

Peter's first film after his hand became deformed was a movie called *Lord Jeff*. He was one of several boys who supposedly attended a naval academy. The boys wore sailor suits, and Peter got to say such inspiring dialogue as "Yes, sir." He received less camera attention than in his first movie. However, it did rekindle his interest in being an actor.

Sons of Bus Driver and General Are Hollywood "Finds" by Our London Correspondent

Sons of a London bus driver and a British general are chief supporting players to Freddie Bartholomew in the film *Lord Jeff*, which has just gone into production in Hollywood and will be seen in England in about four months.

The film is about the work of Dr. Barnardos Homes, and eleven-year-old Terry Kilbourne, whose father, Thomas

Kilbourne, won a newspaper competition some months ago and gave up bus-driving to go to Hollywood, plays the part of a Lancashire boy.

Terry's story was told me at the Metro-Goldwyn-Mayer office today.

"It was a busman's holiday that put him on the road to film fame.

"When he was appearing at a busmen's concern in London it happened that a Los Angeles lawyer, in England for a holiday heard him. The lawyer was impressed and offered Terry an introduction for film directors if he ever visited Hollywood.

"There did not seem much chance of that until his father won the competition and decided to take a chance. He and Terry went to America and the lawyer introduced them to Hollywood.

"Terry's first job was to give dialect studies in a broadcast with Eddie Cantor.

"Sam Wood, who is directing *Lord Jeff*, heard him and signed him to play the Lancashire boy in the film.

Wood has just sabled [*sic*] to London that in his opinion Terry has the most radiant smile of any boy actor he has seen.

"The other boy is Peter Lawford, fifteen-year-old son of Lieutenant-General Sir Sydney Lawford, who went to live in Hollywood five months ago," said the MGM representative.

"Young Peter has travelled all over the world with his father, to France, Brazil, Australia, Tahiti, Colombia, Panama. He speaks five languages.

"Peter started his film career when he was eight and living at Shepperton-on-Thames. He saw a camera unit taking shots and he pestered his father until he was allowed to ask for a part.

"He got a part in the film, and he was in *Gentleman of Paris* and *Poor Old Bill*. When General Lawford's work took him to Paris Peter played French boys in films there without a trace of accent.

"When they arrived in Hollywood five months ago, Peter wrote to Sam Wood, without his father knowing, and suggested himself for the main part in *Lord Jeff*, but Mr. Wood explained that it was already booked for Freddie Bartholomew.

"He offered the part of the Cockney boy instead and Peter accepted.

"These two are looked upon in Hollywood as great finds."
—*The Manchester Evening News*, May 11, 1938.

(Not everything in this article was entirely accurate, especially the story of how Peter gained his first role. It is the first
known example of a film company's publicity mill creating the
myth of Peter Lawford, the actor.)

The movies and the constant travel ended in 1939. War was
raging in Europe and, on September 3, England was officially
fighting with Germany. The Lawfords were in New York when
the Irving Trust Company, the bank where his father kept a
portion of his wealth, informed him that all accounts were frozen
in England. The cash he had in the United States, plus what
possessions he retained, would be all he could have if he stayed in
America.

General Lawford had come to the United States with sizable
wealth, enough to have allowed the family to weather the war
years despite most of their holdings being in England. However,
he had made some bad investments, including becoming involved
with an outlandish scheme to use sugar beet plants in the con-
struction of model homes. The general had no business sense,
though he thought he had enough money to be able to absorb the
losses. The war proved him wrong.

The family decided against going back to England. The general
was quite elderly and in retirement. May was much younger but
had no fondness for Britain and had a need for a warmer climate.
And Peter, because of the way in which he had been raised, was a
citizen of the world. He had no particular ties with any country,
had neither the interest nor the physical ability to go to war.

What Peter did not know until later was that the general had
lost everything he had in England. It is uncertain whether assets
were destroyed during the blitz or if the holdings he had were
used as collateral for his many bad investments. Whatever the
situation, it was only the money the family had in hand in the
1940s that remained the Lawford estate. Without Peter's financial
support, the Lawfords would have been impoverished.

There were several options, including taking the train to California. But the cheapest approach seemed to be selling what they
could, buying a secondhand Lincoln, and driving to Florida,
where they had friends. The climate would be warm and they
could financially survive.

Florida was yet to be developed; even the major cities were
relatively small and housing was inexpensive. The general borrowed money from friends and rented a small house at the end of
West Palm Beach. It was an unsavory area, but the cost of living
was low.

Peter cared little about the loss of the family fortune. He grabbed his tennis racket when they moved into their house and went immediately to the courts. He became part of a local tennis team, proving his skill enough to be accepted for a seat on the Junior Davis Cup Team. He also obtained a job parking cars for twenty-five dollars a week at a lot in Miami.

The lot was in an area that had clubs, stores, and businesses. Many of the customers paid by the month, and Peter was assigned to act as manager, collecting the rents and overseeing what took place.

Two other young men, whose names were Frank and Ham, also worked at the lot. They were both black, one an extrovert, the other rather quiet, and both quite friendly with Peter.

This was a period when Florida was typical of the southern states. Racial separation was normal and it was not unusual to see drinking fountains with signs marked WHITE and COLORED. Many restaurants were required by law to use separate dishes for blacks and whites—in those circumstances where blacks were served at all. Violence against blacks was not uncommon, yet Peter knew none of this. Having been raised throughout the world, he had become friendly with people of all races and never gave anyone's color a second thought. The two young black men were friendly, so the three of them ate lunch together, played "pigeon" poker (in which the dealer would cheat if not watched closely), and generally had a good time.

The main area where Peter was naive while working at the parking lot was in not recognizing the racism of some of the long-term, regular customers. They found the sight of a white boy being friendly with "niggers" offensive. Eventually they complained to the man who had gotten Peter the job, a man who ironically was Jewish and had been subjected to bigotry himself.

The man was gentle with Peter. He tried to explain to him the social climate in the United States. Then he said that when the three of them were together, it didn't look as though anyone was working, even though Peter explained that one of them jumped up to help whenever a car came into the lot. Finally the man simply had to tell Peter to stop being so friendly with the blacks because there were complaints from people who might take their business elsewhere.

There was no threat to fire Peter. There was also no threat against the other employees. However, the man did get the courage to explain to all three that their actions did not look good to the customers, something Peter was forced to accept.

Peter stayed at the lot for two years, enjoying the money he was making, which he later estimated was probably nine dollars a week more than the job should have paid. The man who hired him was apparently trying to help the Lawfords any way he could.

The only problem with the man's intentions was Peter's love for poker and his two new friends. He knew they cheated. He knew that he was a poor player even in an honest game. Yet he liked his new friends and delighted in the games, during which he lost most of his earnings.

The idea that Peter knew his family was in serious financial trouble yet enjoyed gambling with friends who regularly took him for at least a portion of his pay seems odd, yet I learned that this was typical of Peter. He had no sense of saving money. If he had money, he was both a generous and a self-indulgent man. I can remember many times when he would give financial assistance to both friends and strangers. We also rode regularly in limousines, chartered jets, and helicopters. I never knew the source of what seemed to be vast wealth and I never cared. I assumed that he knew what he was doing, could afford our life-style, and that he planned for the future.

It came as a shock to me when our accountant became annoyed with me for our high living. He said that the money Peter earned was almost gone and that we could not afford our indulgences. I immediately changed those aspects of how we lived that I could control, such as cooking more at home instead of always eating out. Yet Peter never understood the need to plan ahead.

As we discussed those Florida years, it was quite obvious that his attitude toward life was a paradox. He took a job to help supplement the family income, receiving a higher-than-normal pay from an employer who wanted to help him. At the same time, he chose to gamble with that money, reducing his ability to aid his parents. He wasn't the naive, compulsive gambler for whom betting is a seemingly uncontrollable sickness. He gambled for fun just as he worked hard for money to help his family. He simply lacked the sense to understand his own folly. It was only by chance that he made so much money while young that he could gamble, spend lavishly when he so chose, and still adequately support his parents.

During that Florida period, Peter began experiencing a phenomenon that would continue throughout his life. He would have encounters with people in ways that seemed innocuous at the time, yet would become a common ground for something more important later on. This happened with his connection to me and Monsignor O'Donnell and the El Padrino Room, as I mentioned earlier. And it happened at the parking lot with one extremely rich man who occasionally used the lot and tipped well for services— twenty-five cents instead of the usual dime. The man's name was Joseph Kennedy, and he was known to the attendants as a "heavy cat." He was considered extremely friendly, always stopping to talk with anyone, no matter how humble that person's position.

Peter later learned that Joe Kennedy had been the major reason that Peter was told to avoid his new friends. "It doesn't look good to see the niggers sitting under the tree with the white boy," the older man was alleged to have complained. Yet regardless of the accuracy of the statement, the attitude in Florida and other parts of the South was such that the issue would have been raised one way or another. And later still, Peter would have Joe Kennedy as his father-in-law.

Despite Peter's job and the money his father had borrowed, the family's life was becoming increasingly grim. He had received a small fee for *Lord Jeff*, and that money was spent. He had not impressed anyone enough to be offered additional parts, and so Peter's only contributions to the family funds came from parking cars. The Lawfords still followed such conventions as tea time, but they now had to watch their spending, learning to comparison shop in the grocery stores.

Finally, by chance, the daughter of a family friend told Peter that nothing was happening in Miami. She was upset with the conditions there and planned to drive out to California. She knew someone connected with the movie business and, if Peter wanted to go with her, she would introduce him.

Peter had never lost his delight with making movies and readily agreed, staying with the girl's family after they arrived. The general and Lady Lawford followed soon afterwards, taking a small apartment on Ophir Drive while Peter found work as a movie theater usher. What they did not know was that all of their lives were about to change in ways that would involve some of the most prominent entertainers, power brokers, and politicians in the United States.

2
The MGM Years

"Of course we shall have sex. As long as we have men and women in the world, we'll have sex. And I approve of it. We'll have sex in motion pictures, and I want it there.

"But it will be normal, real beautiful sex—the sex that is common to the people in the audience, to me and to you. A man and a woman are in love with one another. That's sex and it's beautiful."

—Louis B. Mayer of MGM Studios

PETER LAWFORD OWED HIS HOLLYWOOD CAREER TO WORLD War II. He arrived in California a handsome nineteen-year-old kid whose greatest desire in life was to ride the waves on a surfboard. He was wild, delighting in the sun, the beach, and every willing girl he could find. He had no training as an actor, no special skills that electrified a room the moment he entered. He was just a newly poor kid with an English accent and a desire to break into the movies. Except for his accent, he was no different from hundreds of other young men and women who flocked to California in an effort to be discovered. At least not until the war began.

Peter's first job was as an usher for the Village Theater in Westwood. Knowing that he had to work, yet not wanting to work too hard, he began altering the work to suit his temperament. First came an assignment to place the letters advertising the new shows on the marquee. It required using a ladder and a letter-holding device that Peter hated to use. He managed to convince Richard Anderson, an usher at the Bruin Theater across the street (and later an actor in his own right), that putting up the letters was impossible because of his shriveled hand. He paid Anderson to handle the task for him, a price he felt was worth the expense even though he was perfectly capable of doing the work himself.

Peter also did not see why his friends should have to pay to see the movies. He began sneaking them through the back exit, supplying both himself and his friends with bonbons. Eventually his generosity was discovered, and Peter was fired from his job. Before that, though, he had managed to keep the position even as he began gaining an occasional part in films, the usher's job being the only employment he could count on. He went from the set of

36

Mrs. Miniver back to the theater, for example, well aware that a single line in a film was not so secure a career as showing movie-goers to their seats.

There was no money for a car, so Peter took streetcars to auditions. Many were "cattle calls," where any actors could appear. Others were more specific, a limited number of actors being asked to appear so just the chance to audition meant he was a step ahead of many of his rivals for the same parts.

The part Peter played in *Mrs. Miniver*, a film starring Greer Garson, was more important that he realized. He had an almost meaningless role, his total speaking performance involving the saying of one line: "The Germans are coming!" The best young male part in the film was the one that actor Richard Ney had. He played Greer Garson's son (and later married Garson), but many people in the film industry confused Peter and Ney, thinking that Peter had played the son. The skill Ney showed was so good that producers who heard of the performance but had not seen the film auditioned Peter by mistake.

The importance of *Mrs. Miniver* was unknown at the time the idea first made the rounds of Hollywood. It began with the discovery of newspaper essays by Jan Struther, a British mother of three children. Mrs. Struther had written the essays to try to explain what it was like to endure the German blitz. She told of life in the shelters, the fear, the efforts to survive and carry on as normal an existence as possible. She brilliantly captured the lives of everyday people caught up in extraordinary circumstances. The only problem was that no one in the movie industry felt audiences could truly relate.

The essays became of greater interest after they were combined in book form and sold well in the United States. Kenneth MacKenna, story editor for Metro-Goldwyn-Mayer, had turned down the project when he read the essays separately, but decided to buy the project after reading them in book form. A price of $30,000 was paid.

Several other factors were developing at this time. The White House was interested in bringing America into the war with Germany and encouraged any project that would help Americans understand the Battle of Britain. Also, before the picture could go into production, Japan bombed Pearl Harbor, making a movie relating to war all the more likely to succeed.

The script was not true to the essays; additional scenes were added for dramatic effect. Among these was one of Mr. and Mrs. Miniver sitting with their children in a bomb shelter, reading *Alice in Wonderland* to them as they waited out a raid.

Greer Garson was also a problem. She had been employed by MGM since 1937, and had been universally disliked when she arrived. Garson was British and flaunted her upbringing, wearing white gloves and insisting on formalities such as afternoon tea. Mayer had informed her that her attitude would not be tolerated and she toned down her actions, but not before she had alienated many of the other actors.

When the film had to be cast, Norma Shearer was the first person asked to play Mrs. Miniver. Shearer turned it down at once because the part was too old for her. (Hollywood women even then knew that youth and beauty mattered in building a career.) Mrs. Miniver was an older woman, almost matronly.

Greer Garson recognized this fact as well, and, being thirty-three, she knew she did not have that many more years before age would reduce her options. However, she was not then a star and had little choice when Mayer asked her to take the role.

The situation was made more difficult because William Wyler was the director. He had little tact and definite ideas about the film. For example, one of the more touching scenes in the movie comes when Mrs. Miniver encounters a German pilot in her garden. The youth is wounded, scared, and little more than a boy. It is a scene that is poignant and was meant to show that not all people in wartime are bad, regardless of their roles. However, Wyler wanted to make the youth tough and vicious.

"If I have a lot of Germans, I can show one nice one. But if I have only one German, and one of Herman Göring's Luftwaffe monsters, at that, I've got to make him typical."

Wyler was forced to compromise and almost lost his job. Then, after that near fiasco, he was approached by Greer Garson, who said, "Should I have the makeup department put little lines in my face and gray my hair?"

Wyler replied, "Oh, no. You look just right as you are."

Garson was ready to explode. She had read the essays. She knew the age of the woman she was playing and had the usual actress's fear of getting older. She was ready to quit when Wyler covered himself by adding, "I mean, I want you to look young and vital, a youthful woman. The audience will make allowances, you may be sure."

The movie was extremely powerful despite numerous inconsistencies, including Garson's insistence upon wearing a sexy negligee during a bedroom scene where a plain flannel nightgown would have been more appropriate. When Franklin Roosevelt saw an early print at the White House, he asked Louis B. Mayer to rush the film into the theaters instead of waiting for the usual publicity buildup. He felt that it would show American women what their British counterparts were being forced to endure. Even Winston Churchill applauded the release, sending Mayer a message that read: "*Mrs. Miniver* is propaganda worth a hundred battleships."

The film went on to earn Greer Garson an Oscar as best actress of 1942. Other awards included best picture and honors for the director, supporting actress Teresa Wright, the cinematographer, and the scenarists. Peter gained publicity by association with such greatness, though his part was, to say the least, limited.

The war helped Peter in other ways. First there was his accent. The British were heroes before America entered World War II because they were standing alone against Hitler. Once we were in the war, they were crucial allies. Thus, many films required English actors, who were in extremely short supply. Anyone with a genuine British accent who was not in the war was pressed into films. Many of the movies had one or two British natives and numerous Americans trying desperately to produce believable English accents.

Another factor in boosting Peter's career was that because of his hand injury he was not in the army. Other actors who were 4-F (the classification for men who were physically unfit) or too old also found that they had a chance for stardom that had previously been denied. After all, the real stars were gone. Clark Gable enlisted after his wife of twenty-two months, Carole Lombard, was killed in Nevada when the plane carrying her on a tour to sell war bonds crashed. James Stewart and Robert Montgomery entered the service, as did Mickey Rooney and numerous others.

At first Mayer took these departures angrily, feeling that the patriotic duty of Hollywood was to make movies. However, after Pearl Harbor was attacked, he fired actor Lew Ayres for refusing to serve. Ayres was the star of the popular Doctor Kildare series of films and a man who declared himself to be a conscientious objector. He was quoted as saying, "I'll praise the Lord, but I'll be damned if I'll pass the ammunition."

Only older stars or those with health problems, such as Spencer Tracy and Walter Pidgeon, remained. New blood, no matter how thin, was desperately needed. A handsome, young, legitimately 4-F youth with a British accent seemed made in heaven for Mayer. In reality, the two would clash violently.

To understand the conflict between the young Peter Lawford and the aging L. B. Mayer, it is important to understand how the studios were being run in the early days. There had been scandals, of course, and some studio heads were known for their egomania. For example, Harry Cohn ran a studio where it was rumored that you could not be nurtured into becoming a great star under his tutelage unless you had sex with Cohn. This edict existed for all actors, male and female.

Likewise, some of the stars were known for their excesses. They were rich, hero-worshipped, able to have any man, woman, or physical or sensual pleasure they desired. But the men who ran the studios had strict standards, standards that could not be broken without retribution against the people involved. This attitude would eventually hurt Peter when it came to his relationship with Louis B. Mayer.

The attitude of management becomes much more understandable when you know a little of the history of MGM and Mayer, its most powerful head.

Louis B. Mayer was born into poverty. His family was living in a small Russian town that was experiencing a famine. Mayer, himself, was never clear about his date of birth; he was born in either 1882 or 1885.

The Mayers were Jews who were living in the wrong place at the wrong time. Czar Alexander III had taken control of the country and he created policies based on the advice of Constantine Pobyedonostzev, a deadly anti-Semite who had a theory for handling the "Jewish problem." Under this plan, a third of all Russian Jews would be encouraged to emigrate to other countries, a third would be converted to Christianity, and the remaining third would be slaughtered. This plan resulted in the first mass exodus of Russian Jews to the United States, among them the Mayer family.

The pogroms against the Jews began in 1881, but it was not until 1888 that Jacob Mayer, Louis's father, was able to afford the thirty-dollar steerage passage for each member of his family. They arrived in New York, stayed long enough for Sarah Mayer to have two more sons, then moved to Canada. The family had not been able to establish a business in New York, and Canada seemed to offer greater opportunity.

By 1895 Jacob Mayer was working as a peddler in Saint John, New Brunswick, a small town on the Bay of Fundy.

Jacob went from selling household supplies and dress goods to opening a junk business. A scrap metal operation quickly followed. Yet despite his hard work, Jacob had the reputation for being a scholarly man who revered the traditional Jewish life-style that stressed the religious life. By contrast, his wife, Sarah, was a natural entertainer. She liked to tell stories of old times, to sing folk songs and holy music. She encouraged her children to use their imagination in an effort to grow as individuals.

Louis understood the importance of hard work and making money, quitting school shortly after his twelfth birthday in order to work for his father as a collector of scrap metal. By the time he was fourteen the sign in front of his father's shop read J. MAYER & SON.

By 1900 J. Mayer & Son acted as the northeastern representative of a national salvaging operation, a fact that allowed Louis to travel through New England. He found that he loved the Boston area and relocated there in 1904, settling in a boardinghouse in the South End. This was a Jewish ghetto filled with tenements, shops, and small businesses. It was there that he met Margaret Shenberg, the daughter of a cantor for Knesseth Israel synagogue, which Louis attended. They were married in June, less than six months after he arrived in Boston. They had little money and moved into her parents' home.

Mayer, despite being based in Boston, attempted to enter the scrap business in New York but was wiped out by the recession of 1906 and 1907. Then he began working at a nickelodeon called the Hub on Dover Street. The business was one that fascinated him, and he made an effort to learn all that he could about it.

The Hub was one of approximately three thousand nickelodeons that existed in 1907. The entertainment was crude by modern standards, short silent dramas and scenes of everyday events. However, the price was low and the films could be understood by everyone, including the large immigrant population that did not yet understand the language or the customs of its new country. It was one of the few businesses that prospered when times were bad.

Mayer studied the films and the public's reaction to them until he was able to predict which ones would be popular with the patrons of the Hub. Once he was certain that he understood the public's taste, he invested in a theater of his own, the Gem, located in Haverhill, Massachusetts.

Mayer prospered, expanding until he had several theaters featuring programs that included such live entertainers as Harry Houdini, the famous magician and escape artist. Then he added vaudeville acts, showing the films at the end as "chasers," the signal to the audience to leave so a new audience could take their seats.

Mayer experimented with different forms of entertainment in the theaters he ran. In March of 1912 Mayer arranged for Alice Neilsen and the Boston Opera Company to perform *Madame*

Butterfly for one day in Haverhill. Later the Boston Symphony would appear, all performances being sellouts. He also began going to other towns to put together a chain of theaters under his ownership.

Mayer wanted to do more in the entertainment business than just have theaters. In 1912, while staying at New York's Knickerbocker Hotel, he met Ben Stern. Stern had been the general manager for producer Henry Harris, one of the victims of the sinking of the *Titanic*. He needed money to become a producer in his own right, and Mayer needed a man with expertise in production to teach him that end of the business. Together they offered not only original entertainment but also touring editions of Broadway shows. Oddly, though there was a successful first year, the partnership was dissolved.

During this same period, Adolph Zukor, a Hungarian immigrant who had also started in show business with his own nickelodeon, developed the idea of filming special programs. He wanted to take the great stage actors of the day and film them in their most triumphant roles. Toward this end he created Famous Players, a company that was extremely successful despite the fact that the films were poorly made even by the standards of the day. The cameramen had not yet learned how to effectively handle the medium under such circumstances. The actors were uncomfortable performing in a different manner than they had in plays. And the total effect was rather wooden compared with both what could be seen on Broadway and the filmed productions of some of the rival companies.

Mayer's genius came from looking at the film industry as a whole rather than as three separate, interdependent businesses. There were exhibitors of films, distributors of films, and producers of films. The producers were in the best position in some ways because they controlled the length and type of product available. The distributors also had great power, determining the prices to be charged for the work shown. The exhibitors were the least in control, having to settle for whatever product was available at whatever rental rates were asked.

Mayer's next step was to form the Louis B. Mayer Film Company, which started by buying the rights to three-reel comedies starring Stan Lupino, then a British music hall comedian. Then Mayer agreed to handle the work of another company, a partnership run by former glove manufacturer Samuel Goldfish (later to be known as Samuel Goldwyn); Jesse Lasky, an ex-vaudevillian; and Cecil Blount deMille, a playwright and actor of little repute. Together they ran the Jesse Lasky Feature Film Company, which planned to imitate Zukor's idea of filming Broadway plays. The first two films—*The Squaw Man*, directed by deMille, and *Brewster's Millions*—were rather poor quality productions. However, the latter was extremely popular with the public and made everyone quite a bit of money.

Mayer's financial base for future operations came from the film *The Birth of a Nation*, D. W. Griffith's film that was sold by region throughout the United States. Mayer formed a separate company, Master Photoplays, which agreed to the charge of $50,000 plus ten percent of the net profits for the right to show the picture. The company cleared $600,000 profit after all fees were paid. Mayer's share ensured that he could expand.

By 1915 Mayer had become the secretary for a new distribution company called Metro Pictures Corporation. The company franchised pictures in different regions, Mayer receiving the New England franchise as well as a salaried job with the company. He thus had become involved with several aspects of the film business, giving him the background he would eventually need to call upon when he relocated with the majority of the film industry to California.

It was in 1907 that film companies first started moving west. The city of Los Angeles actively pursued them, stressing the quality and consistency of the weather. Great amounts of light were critical when working with the relatively insensitive films of the day. Variations in scenery were needed for different pictures, and weather had to be generally mild. The facts in the promotional material sent by the city fit these needs so well that California seemed like an Eden.

Mayer and his wife joined the exodus from the east in 1918, moving into the Garden Court Apartments on Hollywood Boulevard. The city was actually nothing more than clusters of neighborhoods with dusty, disorganized streets. Yet the weather was right for the film industry and that was what mattered.

During this same period, other companies were forming and would be influential in Mayer's life. Samuel Goldfish joined with the Selwyn brothers, Edgar and Archibald, to form Goldwyn Pictures Corporation. The name came from the first half of Goldfish and the last half of Selwyn but would eventually be adopted by Goldfish as his own last name. The arrangements were such that Goldfish put up the working capital and the Selwyn brothers, producers of Broadway shows, put up the motion picture rights to the numerous highly successful plays they had produced in New York.

Goldfish was a marketer who understood how to reach the

public. He pioneered the type of advertising efforts that have become so familiar today but that were new at the time.

The first effort Goldfish made was to take a series of full-page advertisements in the *Saturday Evening Post*, then one of the largest and most popular magazines in the nation. The *Post* was a family magazine that was considered extremely high class, a magazine not normally associated with the film industry. Thus, Goldfish's ads, in keeping with this image, emphasized the quality of the work. His company offered "Pictures Built upon the Strong Foundation of Intelligence and Refinement." This was also the time when the trademark of the Goldwyn company was first used, a lion resting in profile and framed with a flowing loop of film bearing the motto *Ars Gratis Artis* (Latin for "Art Is Beholden to the Artists").

The same year that the Mayers went to California, Goldwyn also came west, leasing the Culver City studio of Triangle Productions. The various companies were positioning themselves for an important merger, though none of them realized that at the time.

The choice of Culver City was an easy one because of promotional moves by Harry Culver, the man for whom the community was named. Culver City is located between Los Angeles and the seaside community of Venice. Culver, a real estate expert, erected a hotel at a midway point, then offered free land to any movie studio that wanted to go into business there. The area had already been used for a number of one-reel westerns, but the land was rather desolate and worth next to nothing on the open market. However, in 1915, when Culver started his development of the area, the movie companies were familiar with the location and the sunlight. They were happy to get the free land, just as Culver was delighted to have the actors and support personnel start to build homes and develop the area. His offer of free land gave the community an economic base, and his territory prospered because so many people connected with the industry wanted to live close to where they worked.

Mayer had finally achieved a level of success where he could begin acting in the manner that would eventually bring him into conflict with Peter Lawford. He had started life being despised for no reason other than the fact that his family followed religious practices that were despised by their government. He had emigrated to a strange land where the language, the customs, and the manner of dress were all unfamiliar to him. Then he entered the scrap metal business, a field that involved hard physical labor plus the "gift of gab" in order to buy and sell effectively. Yet no matter how successful he was in business, he recognized that he was crude by American standards.

Mayer seemed to long for an image of sophistication. He was brilliant, financially successful, and an astute businessman. He was earning large sums of money, living in luxurious surroundings, and creating films that would eventually set the tone for what Americans perceived as "style" and the good life. He felt that he needed to mold his employees in the image that he, himself, wanted to achieve.

The actors and actresses might have been exciting on the screen, but Mayer knew them for what they were. Acting was not a respected profession, the public assuming that performers had loose morals, a belief that many stars reinforced by their personal lives. Yet this reality did not mean that change could not be brought to the industry.

Mayer was determined to produce the finest family entertainment possible. He felt that family pictures were best made by stars who typified properly nurtured, properly guided family members. He became determined to be a benevolent dictator/ father figure for his employees, setting standards for their dress, their conduct, and their care. And he would do it in any way that worked.

Mayer's ideas helped change the image of acting in the United States. Eventually his studio would control all photographs taken of his stars, all publicity, and even all public dating. The stars would only be seen in proper dress and engaged in morally uplifting activities when they dated one another. They would be given quotes such that the public might think that an actress spent all her time, when not working on the set, reading the Bible, sewing, and going to fine restaurants with actors who would not so much as kiss her good-night. The fact that the actress might prefer getting drunk and having sex with the son of a gangster who was financing her latest picture was never known. Mayer, who had pretensions rather than class, determined that he would not allow anyone to work for him unless they went along with his publicity campaigns.

The price the actors paid for this was not bad, though. Peter and others who were interviewed for this book who worked for Mayer over the years told of having everything they could want on the set. There were studio dentists and doctors available without charge. There was legal assistance and schools for both children and adults. The latter offered courses in singing, dancing, speaking, performing, and all the other skills necessary for success. It was as though all you had to do was be hired by Mayer and you were given the key to the candy store. Everything you needed for your career was available to you for the asking—if you towed the line.

Yet the truth was that Mayer remained crude, especially in the manner in which he tried to get his way. He would do anything to win an argument, including resorting to personal theatrics.

Mayer was an extremely emotional man. He would often cry when watching one of his more dramatic films. He would also use any ploy when losing an argument with someone to get his way.

His ability to cry during the viewing of one of his own films was a joke within the industry, but the trait was typical of his character. Mayer was a genuine sentimentalist, his taste touching the nerves of the American public. He delighted in films such as *The Child Thou Gavest Me* and *The Song of Life*. Typical plots would involve a heroine who was from a poor, honest, hardworking background, her family exploited by the rich. Such a woman would profess that love was the answer to all problems, then prove it by marrying one of the wealthy men in the story. It was a popular theme and, in a sense, reflected his own and his wife's background.

Mayer's temperamental side was carefully nurtured, an acting job as skilled as that of professionals. For years, whenever he seemed to be losing an argument with one of his stars, he would suddenly faint. The star would be terrified that he or she had pushed too far. Obviously Mayer was in frail health. Obviously Mayer felt very strongly about the issue. And equally obvious, any further arguing could be dangerous for the studio executive.

The period of "unconsciousness" would last long enough to strike terror in the heart of the person who was arguing. Then Florence Browning, Mayer's secretary, would come rushing in, throw cold water in his face, and "revive" him. He would mutter "Where am I?", be helped to his feet, and continue the discussion with his opponent well under control.

The phoniness of Mayer's fainting spells eventually disgusted his staff. Finally, unable to stand the situation any longer, Florence Browning positioned herself in the doorway with a pitcher of cold water immediately after sending in a star with whom an argument was inevitable. The star was seated in such a manner that the secretary was not visible. However, Mayer saw what was happening and realized that his game was over.

Mayer may have been pretentious, but he was also streetwise, a man who knew when to land the first punch in a confrontation he couldn't win through fair methods. The most famous such incident involved Mildred Harris Chaplin, an eighteen-year-old girl who had briefly been married to the famous comic actor Charlie Chaplin. Mildred Harris was not a great star or a skilled actress. There was no reason for the public to come to see her in *Polly of the Storm Country*, which Mayer was producing. But by utilizing her married name of Chaplin, Mayer knew that he could create a strong market for the film.

Charlie Chaplin was irate about his name being indirectly exploited. There was nothing illegal about what was taking place, yet Chaplin wanted to do something to stop Mayer. Finally, when both men were at a party in the Alexandria Hotel, Chaplin challenged Mayer to a fight. The comic star was in top physical condition, athletic, and well able to devastate the sedentary Mayer. However, Mayer was the more cunning of the two. When Chaplin ordered the producer to remove his glasses, Mayer did just that, using one hand to reach for the lenses and the other to sucker punch Chaplin on the jaw.

It was on April 17, 1924, that the merger that would affect so many stars of the 1940s took place. Loew's Inc. purchased Goldwyn Pictures Corporation, then merged it with Metro Pictures to form Metro-Goldwyn Pictures. Then Louis B. Mayer and his partners in what was known as the Mayer group were brought in to manage the operation. Mayer was named vice president and general manager at a salary of $1,500 a week. His partner, Irving Thalberg, was named second vice president and supervisor of production at $650 a week, and his other partner, Robert Rubin, was named secretary (with a New York office) at $600 per week.

Mayer insisted upon having a separate identity from the company and was offered the option of having screen credit that would read "Produced by Louis B. Mayer for the Metro-Goldwyn Corporation." He turned down this opportunity, selecting instead to have the pictures bear the credit "Produced by Metro-Goldwyn-Mayer." From that point forward, the MGM trademark would become the most important in the industry.

With this importance, Mayer felt he had license to try to influence politics and society. For example, in 1934 the writer Upton Sinclair decided to run for governor of California. Sinclair was a Socialist whose career had been spent exposing injustices to the working poor. One of his novels, *The Wet Parade*, was bought by MGM. It was the story of Prohibition and alcoholism, not a particularly good work, but by the time it hit the screen it had a script written in the typical MGM uplifting manner, and the star of the film, a then-unknown actress named Myrna Loy, had her first big hit.

Sinclair declared that he wanted to "end poverty in California" (a slogan that was contracted to EPIC). He was aware that many of the Depression poor were coming into the state because physical survival was easier in the warm climate. These were men and women who were without jobs, shelter, food, or a future. They wanted jobs and needed financial help to stay alive until they could find employment. EPIC, among other things, would tax all the movie studios and use the money to help the homeless.

The tax would not have been a major burden, but the idea that a governor might interfere with private enterprise in such a manner infuriated Mayer. First he and other studio heads threatened to leave the state and move to Florida, an idle threat that made great copy to people who did not know better. Not only would the expense have been great for such a move, the high humidity and swamplike conditions found in Florida would have made working conditions intolerable. The studio heads cringed at the thought of a major star being bitten by mosquitoes and thus unable to pose for close-ups until the bites had healed.

Mayer was the head of one of the most important studios in California and thus, to Sinclair, he was as evil as the Antichrist. Didn't the people realize that there were more than three hundred thousand known homeless in the Los Angeles area alone, people who could be helped by just a portion of the money being made at MGM?

Outraged, Mayer began a campaign to reelect Republican governor Frank Merriam. He used every dirty trick MGM personnel could create. Employees earning more than $100 per week were handed blank checks made out to Louis B. Mayer and ordered to make a contribution that would be used for Merriam.

Irving Thalberg began making fake newsreels to be shown in the state's theaters. One had a poorly dressed man talk of his support for Sinclair, explaining that the writer would do much for California. After all, look at what Sinclair had done for Russia.

Another showed extremely well dressed individuals talking in favor of Merriam while slovenly men with foreign accents spoke in favor of Sinclair. And another showed trainloads of hoboes on their way to California to take advantage of the EPIC program Sinclair was going to put into effect if he was elected.

Thalberg later discussed his actions with Fredric March. He commented: "I had those shorts made. Nothing is unfair in politics. I used to be a boy orator for the Socialist party on the East Side in New York. Do you think Tammany ever gave me a chance to be heard?"

The Hearst chain of newspapers also conducted a smear campaign, though whether or not it was coordinated with Mayer and

Thalberg has never been ascertained. However, in the end, Merriam was reelected, though just barely. He received 1,138,620 votes to Sinclair's 879,537. A third-party candidate, Raymond Haight, came away with 302,519.

It is interesting to note that despite Sinclair's loss, his EPIC platform made so much sense during the Depression years that it was essentially adopted by both Governor Merriam and, later, Franklin Roosevelt. Specific items, including increased inheritance taxes, graduated individual and corporate income taxes, and a gift tax, entered into law. The *Argonaut*, a longtime San Francisco newspaper, looked at the situation and the brilliant Sinclair and the not-so-bright Governor Merriam and commented: "Would Sinclair have done worse . . . ? He might even have done better for he had an atom or two of genius in his composition while all one can discern in Merriam is cobwebs from an empty skull."

Despite the politics, the 1930s saw Mayer strive to bring the finest stars and the best "family" pictures to Hollywood. Helen Hayes won an Academy Award for *The Sin of Madeline Claudet*, an MGM film that had lured her from her successful New York stage career. Alfred Lunt and his wife, Lynn Fontanne, the biggest names on Broadway, were brought out for the film *The Guardsman*. However, this proved an embarrassment because Lynn Fontanne believed in throwing herself into a role as realistically as possible. When a scene called for her to be in a bathtub, she stripped naked and entered the bathtub. All other actresses wore clothing that would rise to a level just below what the camera would take in, but the Lunts said that they had to "feel what they were doing," a fact that shocked the crew.

Mayer was making family pictures. He was outraged by the Lunts and by any actor who violated his standards. Although Peter did not know any of this, his independent streak would eventually bring him into conflict with Mayer.

By the time Peter arrived at MGM, Hollywood observers felt that all the major stars of Hollywood were MGM stars—Lionel Barrymore, Jean Harlow, John Barrymore, Wallace Beery, Marie Dressler, Clark Gable, Joan Crawford. On and on went the list of stars. Then there were the writers and the directors, people such as Richard Rodgers and Lorenz Hart, Herman Mankiewicz, George Cukor, David Selznick . . .

Even the children brought to the lot became legend. Mickey Rooney, Judy Garland, Jackie Cooper, Freddie Bartholomew, and in the 1940s, a young girl named Elizabeth Taylor all began or found their greatest success at MGM.

By the time Peter moved to California, Mayer presided not just over a studio but over a family. In his mind, all the people with whom he worked were like brothers, sisters, cousins, and children. And Mayer was their supporter, confidant, provider, mentor, caretaker, and teacher. The only scandal on the lot, the drug use encouraged for young actors who had trouble getting to sleep or awakening with adequate energy to perform effectively, was innocent in its original intention. Only later, after Judy Garland's death and Elizabeth Taylor's admitted addiction, was there an awareness of how horrible that policy had been.

But in the 1940s, the dispensing of drugs was intended as a helpful act by the paternalistic studio. Alcoholism was something different, and children were not allowed to handle anything so dangerous. Known drug addicts were using such things as heroin, but these addicts were not actors. These were life's losers, the ghetto poor who were perceived as having neither brains nor a future.

There was stress on the lot each day. A child might be learning to sing, dance, and act; studying school lessons; and appearing in a picture. The day was long and intense, a situation that would make sleeping difficult. Thus, it made perfect sense for the loving parent, Louis B. Mayer, to see that his medical staff provided "his children" with pills to help them go to sleep. Of course, many of them became so relaxed from the drugs that they had trouble arising in the morning, a fact easily overcome by giving them stimulants to keep them going. Thus, they fell into a cycle of pills to sleep, pills to awaken, good food, good training, and salaries that exceeded those of the average adult. What more could a loving father offer?

Later this life style would be seen as exploitive. Later it would be known that taking such medication regularly could be addicting and deadly. But when the studios were involved with such programs for their people, their actions were in keeping with what were considered loving and ethical actions by a studio head who truly cared for the people who worked for him. It was also good business.

Mayer may have been a moralist and a bit of a prude, but he understood the human failings of his stars and did not hesitate to address them. Lana Turner, who played a brief, tempestuous role in Peter's life, ran with a group of young stars that included Mickey Rooney, Linda Darnell, Jackie Cooper, Betty Grable, and others. They would party together, go dancing, cruise the drive-ins, roller skate on Sunset Boulevard, and have seemingly endless series of romances that received a degree of media attention.

In her book *Lana*, Lana Turner commented: ". . . my nights on the town were getting more press than MGM's publicity people were churning out. Though I'd been shy as a young girl, once I came out of my shell I wanted to live it up. But now every time I dated someone, it made headlines as a 'hot new romance.'

"Eventually Louis B. Mayer himself took notice. He summoned me to his office, along with my mother. In an emotional, disappointed tone he told me that keeping late hours and making the papers were risking my wonderful future. He actually had tears in his eyes at one point, so I started crying too. Then he jumped up and shouted, 'The only thing you're interested in is . . .' and he pointed to his crotch.

"Outraged, my mother rose from her seat. 'How dare you, Mr. Mayer! In front of my daughter!'

"Then, grabbing me by the arm, she marched me out of his office. After that I did try to slow down for a while."

Sam Marx, story editor and producer for MGM, told me of the attitude at the studio when Peter was first hired: "When Peter showed up in 1941 or thereabouts, MGM was still riding the tremendous heights that Irving Thalberg had taken them to. When Irving died in 1936, Mayer had only hopes of keeping up those triumphant years and he wasn't always successful. However, with the help of producers like Arthur Freed making some marvelous musicals, and with the help of some of the producers like Hunt Stromberg, Harry Rapf, a few others, Mayer was bringing in people, always hoping to find another Thalberg. But in the early 1940s MGM still had its eyes on the best because that's what Mayer and Thalberg were after, being hailed as the top production company in the world. The pictures were still considered the best.

"We would go to previews where the audience didn't know what picture they were going to see, and the minute the lion trademark came on ahead of the title, they would burst into cheers. That's how head and shoulders we were above everybody else.

"And don't forget that, even during the years of depression that preceded the war, going to the movies was the greatest entertainment anyone could have. There was no television. We owned the theaters where we played our first runs and there was no doubt that the pictures could make money.

"I did a film with Wally Beery in which I was told in advance that if you keep it within this budget, we know we'll make a profit. So it was almost to the dollar the Beery pictures brought back money as if every fan went to see everything he did, but nobody else went."

Marx's statement about the movies was important. There was no television. Radio was extremely popular, but radio was not visual. Vaudeville and legitimate theater were somewhat limited in the places they could be viewed, but the movies had become the universal form of entertainment by the time Peter reached Hollywood. Rich or poor, small town or large city, the movies had become a common bond across America. And movie stars had become the nation's idols, the royalty of a democratic nation. They were the subjects of keen interest for politicians, the rich, and the powerful. Joe Kennedy was fascinated by the industry, as was his entire family. People wanted to share the aura of a star, even when their own wealth might be such that they could buy and sell the studios a dozen times over. It was the golden age for a man like Peter who could break into the industry in a starring role.

Peter was nineteen when he arrived in Los Angeles, a young man ready for fun and looking for work. He had traveled the world and been sexually experienced for half his young life.

Louis B. Mayer saw in Peter a youth who could be a star at a time when the male stars would soon be leaving for the army. But Peter had to be molded in the MGM pattern. Thus, he was moving into a world where direct conflict with one of the most important men in the entertainment industry was inevitable.

I don't think that Peter realized the importance of Hollywood's war effort and its ultimate impact on the nation. His life and career were shaped by the war and by what took place in the industry, and the effect the propaganda had on the men who made it ultimately was a factor in presidential politics almost forty years later.

The reality of World War II was that the Americans were unprepared. The Japanese avoided flying to the mainland of the United States after Pearl Harbor because they were convinced that our coastal defenses were too strong. The fact that they consisted of one antitank gun in California was not known.

Then, as Americans joined the war effort, almost every battle was lost. The soldiers were undertrained, underarmed, and dying both in combat and in training, a national scandal that was not publicly discussed. The miracle of the war years was that we were able to hold out long enough to develop a strong fighting machine that, in conjunction with our allies, eventually led to the defeat of both Germany and Japan.

In Hollywood, things were quite different. Americans had more money and leisure time than ever before. The Depression had ended with the almost full employment brought about by the war industries. Movies were the most popular form of entertainment, and Hollywood was anxious to provide for this demand. The film industry also recognized the importance of boosting morale through films that reinforced a positive attitude toward the war.

The result of this social consciousness came in many forms. *Mrs. Miniver* was the first of many films that told the story of the war years from the viewpoint of the British civilians. Other movies focused on American women waiting for soldiers who might never return, battles against the Germans and Japanese, and comedies ridiculing all our enemies. The Three Stooges took on Hitler and secret Nazi spies in America. Bugs Bunny singlehandedly disrupted the leaders in Tokyo. And an actor who was reaching the high point of a very limited entertainment career was being forever changed by this effort. Ronald Reagan became a victim of the propaganda he was helping to create, a condition the nation would not fully understand until he took the office of president of the United States many years later.

If Peter knew Ronald Reagan during this period, it was only by sight or reputation. They did not work together, nor did Peter pal around with Robert Walker and Walker's girlfriend Nancy Davis, until the latter came to Hollywood after the war years. Yet Reagan best personifies the blending of myth and reality that surrounded Peter during the war years.

Interviews with men and women who were a part of MGM's operations during World War II show the intensity of feeling that existed within the industry. Peter Lawford was made a star by the MGM publicity mill, yet he was also viewed with suspicion by those who were unaware of his handicap. They knew he was British and that he "claimed" to be the son of a general, so why hadn't he returned to his native land? Was he making movies to avoid his responsibilities? He did not talk about his damaged hand and arm. He learned to hide the deformity in such a way that almost no one knew he was handicapped, a fact that convinced people he was not in uniform only because he was a coward.

In one instance, a retired MGM producer had been angry with Peter on this score for more than forty years; he did not learn of the handicap until he was interviewed for this book. Yet even when he understood what had happened, the residual bias could be heard in his voice when he said, "But I've always thought that he would have tried to avoid the war even if he had been able to fight."

Other actors who somehow avoided the war threw themselves into the propaganda machine to such a degree that the fantasy of

Hollywood became their reality. Consider, for example, Ronald Reagan.

With such a mind-set, it was no wonder that Ronald Reagan would eventually rule the nation with stories that came from Hollywood, not history. For example, one of Reagan's favorite stories about heroism was an incident he claimed occurred during World War II. It is a story that was told frequently over the years as he moved from acting to politics, a story he seems to believe is true.

The story is that of a heroic B-17 pilot during World War II. The pilot, desperate to save his men, ordered the crew to bail out. This they did with the exception of a wounded belly gunner who could not move. The youth began crying when the crew left the ship, and the pilot was about to leave him alone. Moved to compassion, the pilot said, "Never mind, son, we'll ride it down together."

Often the story would leave Reagan near tears, his voice choked as he remembered the dramatic scene. The only problem was that the story came from a movie he had seen, not real life. Had Reagan used logic when thinking about what he was saying, he would have realized that had the incident actually occurred, the only witnesses would have died in the crash of the B-17. The incident might have happened, but it would have been impossible for anyone to know it.

Reagan's military career was typical of the way Hollywood created its own war and war history. Bad eyesight kept Reagan from active duty. In fact, the only time he flew in a plane during this period was when he went from Los Angeles to nearby Catalina Island on a small plane. The experience was so unpleasant that, though he was officially in the air force, he never again flew while in the service.

The Reagan war effort was the making of movies such as *International Squadron, Secret Service of the Air, Desperate Journey, Murder in the Air, This is the Army, Rear Gunner*, and *Mr. Gardenia Jones*, as well as various training films. He had been in the cavalry reserve and was placed in the cavalry when inducted into the army on April 14, 1942. From there he went to Fort Dixon in San Francisco, then transferred to the Army Air Corps, where he was assigned to work at the Hal Roach Studio in Culver City. The studio had been taken over for the making of training films and was ten miles from Warner Brothers, the studio where Reagan did most of his early work. He was thus able to live at home, a fact that was kept from the fans.

The Hal Roach Studio was where many actors and technicians

fought the war, a fact that led it to be dubbed Fort Wacky. It was used to produce training films and documentaries. The location also trained combat camera units.

An interesting sidelight of Fort Wacky that involved all the studios was its genuine assistance to one part of the war effort. In order to train combat photographers, it was necessary to recreate the sights the gunners would see when they attacked Japan. The film experts took old stock footage of Japan, then edited it until it looked as though it was being viewed through a gunsight. This enabled the men who were going into combat to better recognize the terrain they needed to spot when flying a mission over Japan. In addition, much of this faked footage, looking as though it was actually taken from a bomber, was used as "newsreels" to show the American public our soldiers' heroism in the Far East.

There was an unusual precedent for such an effort. During World War I, a number of major artists were hired to produce lifelike murals of the French countryside for artillery practice. These murals, created by some of the nation's finest artists, were then destroyed after being used for target practice by artillery units that were to be assigned abroad.

Jane Wyman and Ronald Reagan were not big stars in Hollywood in 1940 when they first began making a comfortable living there ($500 per week each versus just ten percent of that figure for the average couple). However, by the time Reagan entered the military, he was financially one of the more successful actors, his latest contract giving him $3,000 per week. Thus, the publicity departments wanted to turn Reagan into a war hero, gaining respect for him even while he "fought" the "enemy" in nearby Culver City. Stories were released that were as fanciful as his memories.

Some of the stories released to fan magazines such as *Modern Screen* and *Photoplay* gave Reagan motivation for "going to war." In July 1942 *Modern Screen* ran an article that told of Jane Wyman, who had worked for the Red Cross, having been awakened by antiaircraft fire (Jane did go on fund-raising tours, leaving California for the war effort, something her husband never did). The article said: "She'd seen Ronnie's sick face bent over a picture of the small swollen bodies of children starved to death in Poland. 'This,' said the war-hating Reagan between set lips, 'would make it a pleasure to kill.' "

The magazines discussed Jane Wyman's loneliness. She would look for her man and he was not there. She was left with her baby, another woman sacrificing her happiness for the war effort.

The fact that Reagan slept at home each night was ignored.

There would be frequent appearances relating to the movies, those appearances always described in a way that made it seem possible that the actor was returning from abroad. On January 4, 1944, for example, the *Los Angeles Examiner* reported that "Captain Ronald Reagan, former movie star and now serving with the Army Air Force First Motion Picture Unit, today will light the new victory torch of Southern California's women at war. He will report for duty at the Examiner Recruiting Headquarters, 424 West Sixth Street, to welcome the first contingent of women to apply for enlistment."

There would be references of Reagan being "on leave" to explain why he was appearing in a particular place at a particular time. In reality, his war work might take him to the Disney studio to narrate an animated film on the war or to Fort Wacky for his regular work.

The fantasies of Reagan and other men and women who were part of the war effort in Hollywood were supported by the studio public relations arm. Everything possible was done to boost the image of the stars, regardless of veracity.

For example, when Reagan's second wife, Nancy Davis, arrived in Hollywood after the war, her career was carefully orchestrated. She was not considered a particularly skilled actress, though Dore Schary, the producer of the film *The Next Voice You Hear*, in which she was introduced, had great hopes for her future. She had come to Hollywood from New York, where she had had supporting roles on the stage. Her goal was to be an actress; her avocation was to have a good time. She was rather wild, the delight of a number of men and the lover of the alcoholic actor Robert Walker, who died tragically in his early thirties.

"I remember when three or four of us walked into Bob Walker's house and saw a naked Nancy Davis standing there, looking shocked at being caught like that. She grabbed a towel and ran into the bathroom," said a longtime friend of Peter's, recalling an incident that remained in his mind after Nancy became the first lady. She was single at the time and there was nothing wrong with the affair except for the embarrassment at its memory after her life changed radically. He explained that his son became friends with Ron Reagan, Jr., and he always had the feeling that Nancy was afraid he would reveal the incident.

I can remember when Peter was watching the news right after Reagan was elected. He went over to the set, laughing and calling Mrs. Reagan a vulgar name. I was shocked and wanted to know what was bothering him. He laughed again and said that when she was single, Nancy Davis was known for giving the best head in Hollywood.

Then Peter told of driving to the Phoenix area with Nancy and Bob Walker. Nancy would visit her parents, Dr. and Mrs. Loyal Davis, while Peter and Walker picked up girls at Arizona State University in Tempe, a Phoenix suburb. He claimed that she entertained them orally on those trips, apparently playing with whichever man was not driving at the moment.

I have no idea if Peter was telling the truth, though I have to assume that he was because Peter was not one to gossip. When it came to both the good and bad qualities of the people he had known over the years, he was always brutally frank and honest. Both Peter and Bob Walker are dead now, but in researching for this book, the business with Walker was repeatedly mentioned by oldtime Hollywood friends of them both.

Checking the fan magazines and publicity releases, Nancy Davis was known to have been dating men such as Walker. However, by the time she was engaged, the studios had even restored her virginity. An effort was made to give the impression that she had been working so hard on her career that she had had no time for men until Ronald Reagan came along. Care was also taken to avoid mentioning his divorce from Jane Wyman.

The deeply loving relationship between Ronald Reagan and Nancy Davis Reagan has never been questioned. But the Hollywood version of their lives before they fell in love differed greatly from the truth.

And all of this stemmed from the fantasy machine of Hollywood during the war years, a Hollywood where Peter became a star.

Peter had no interest in the war or in pseudosoldiers like Reagan. He had the same desires as he had when I first met him. He wanted to surf, play volleyball, and chase women. In fact, Peter helped create the surfing craze that swept the nation in the late 1940s and gave the fun-in-the-sun image to parts of southern California. He was not the first person to ride a surfboard, nor was he anywhere near the most skilled. However, he was the first actor to be photographed enjoying the activity as part of MGM's publicity campaign. The pictures of his handsome, powerful body out in the water influenced the youth of the nation. It was because of that publicity that thousands tried the sport, liked it, and began refining it to its present level of popularity.

Peter also pursued the interests aroused by his nanny. He met Lana Turner when they were both trying to break into movies, though she became successful before he did. This was the period when he was still working as an usher at the Village Theater in Westwood.

Lana was seemingly as wild as Peter, and the two of them hit it off almost immediately. At first their dates were taken wherever possible. There was the night that Peter had Lana in the back of the balcony of the Village Theater in Westwood when he was working as an usher. The film was beginning, the house lights were down, and Peter was able to escape long enough to try to have sex with Lana while they were both standing. Suddenly Sir Sydney and Lady May Lawford came in, spotting Peter and Lana. Horrified, Peter desperately pulled up the zipper on his pants and tried to regain his composure, though it was obvious to his parents what was taking place. As Peter recalled the incident, his father looked at him with a mixture of pride and fondness, the old man admiring his son's good taste in women. Lady May Lawford reacted quite differently, declaring Lana to be a slut and choosing to ignore her son's role in the sordid incident.

Peter became a star within a year of his going to MGM. When he first arrived in Hollywood, a visit to the MGM commissary had him in awe as he glimpsed people such as Clark Gable, Katharine Hepburn, Spencer Tracy, and numerous others. By the time he was a star in his own right, the famous women were still making pictures but younger stars such as himself had replaced the "names" of the past who had entered the armed forces.

Peter never made a film with Lana Turner, though their affair was so intense that they became engaged to be married. This situation made his mother furious. With Peter's upbringing, he needed to be involved with women of position and breeding such as Princess Margaret and Sharman Douglas, the daughter of an American ambassador. Unfortunately for his mother, Peter felt that the princess was unattractive and he complained that Sharman both had dandruff and tended to cover a lack of personal hygiene with too-liberal doses of Shalimar perfume. Whether or not his statements were true, what was certain was that he enjoyed the company of the young actresses he was meeting in Hollywood.

Sir Sydney also enjoyed Peter's new friends, especially Lana. The actress owned a Lincoln Continental and would drive to pick up Peter for their dates. Although Peter had begun making money in films, he felt that he should use his early good fortune to buy his parents a house on Sunset Boulevard in Brentwood. The house was extremely inexpensive because the area was not a popular community in which to live. However, had the family retained the property, which is still standing, they would have benefited from changes in living patterns, which have resulted in its now being worth approximately $2.5 million.

Sir Sydney immediately put in a garden, a hobby he had until his death. This required regular watering of the plants, something he timed so that he would be outside when Lana drove by. Sometimes Lana would pick up Peter late when she got out of the studio, ten or eleven o'clock at night not being uncommon for some of their dates. But no matter what time it might be, there was his father, out watering the garden so that he could see the beautiful blonde in her blue Lincoln convertible driving up to the house.

Peter felt himself in heaven with Lana for many reasons. He told me that one of the things he liked best was the fact that she had a Japanese housegirl who was her personal servant and maid. The woman was apparently young and quite attractive, and Peter said that the three of them had a ménage à trois relationship that he called "fantastic." I never learned if the three of them had actually been to bed together, much like what he had enjoyed with his nanny and her friend, or if he had enjoyed their favors separately. I never had the nerve to ask him for details.

Peter had to meet Lana at the railroad station one afternoon, a romantic scene that seemed to be part of some movie. They would be marrying shortly and he was expecting her to rush into his arms. Instead, she not only did not show, she sent word that she had run off with the new love of her life, an Arab actor named Terhan Bey.

Peter was furious. He found some publicity still photographs from a movie titled *Lost in a Harem*, which starred comedians Bud Abbott and Lou Costello, as well as his friend Marilyn Maxwell and actor John Conte. They showed men in Arab costumes, so he carefully took a crayon and recaptioned them in order to ridicule Lana's new love. He called the man "Turban" Bey and titled one photo of Bud Abbott in costume "Turban Bey's father, Oi Bey." Another, showing Lou Costello in costume, was captioned "Turban Bey's mother, Elly Bey." The other images depicted what he claimed were scenes in "Turban" Bey's life.

The action was typical Peter. He was deeply hurt but he took out his anger through humor.

Despite Peter's actions, I suspect that he missed the sex that included the maid as much or more than he missed the relationship with Lana. He was seeing other women the entire time that he was engaged, a fact that upset her and may have caused her to dump him.

The primary extra relationship during the time Peter was engaged to Lana was with his close friend Judy Garland. It was an affair that caused great strife between the two women. Judy was jealous of Lana's appearance and Lana was jealous of Judy's abilities as an entertainer.

The dates with Judy Garland were humorous considering the reputation for wildness that Peter had at the time. They were "pals" more than lovers, though sex together was a common way for them to end the evening. The sex was not serious, just fun that they both enjoyed.

Peter told me that every date with Judy Garland was about the same. They would have carry-out Chinese food, which they would eat from the carton. Then they would go bowling, a sport they both enjoyed yet one that neither could do well.

Judy and Peter owned their own bowling balls, bags, and shoes, but could not consistently use any one bowling alley because they would regularly get thrown out.

Judy was worse than Peter because she never learned how to correctly throw the ball. She would lob it into the air with an underhand toss that might be aimed anywhere. Frequently her ball went two or three lanes over, rolling into someone else's pins or smashing the protective barrier that was lowered while the pin boys reset the pins. She thought that you scored when the ball went down your own lane and that you had a gutter ball only if it went down someone else's lane.

Peter had a little more sense but he could not bowl effectively with his left hand, the only one that functioned normally. Instead he would wedge the fingers of his deformed right hand into the holes, make a proper approach, then hope the fingers functioned well enough to release the ball. Usually they didn't, the ball either shooting out with a sudden "pop" like a cork fired from a child's toy gun, or pulling Peter down the lane when his hand failed to open. Only after he fell to the floor would the ball roll free, a fact that greatly upset the bowling alley owners.

Both Peter and Judy were readily recognized stars, but that was not enough to keep the bowling alley owners happy. The twosome would periodically be banned from such facilities.

Eventually Judy married Sid Luft, to whom Peter introduced her. As was usual for them, they insisted that Sid accompany them to the various bowling alleys, an experience he tried not to repeat after he married Judy.

Lady May Lawford had no illusions about what was happening in her son's sexual life. Her husband was a philanderer. She had been indiscreet. And now her son was involved with Lana Turner, a woman she could not stand, while her husband encouraged the affair. May wanted to hurt her son, even if it meant jeopardizing his relationship with Louis B. Mayer and his success as an actor.

Acting on the sly, Lady May Lawford made an appointment to see Mayer. Her performance in Mayer's office was a tour de force. She acted the part of someone who was embarrassed, worried, and seeking help from a man who would understand all and be able to solve all.

As near as the conversation could be reconstructed in later years, Lady May told the studio head that she wanted him to keep a private matter secret. When he assured her that he would, she explained that Peter preferred men in bed.

Mayer was neither angered nor shocked by the revelation. He explained that he would handle the matter and told May not to worry. Then he summoned Peter to his office.

Peter held Mayer in disdain. He did not like the idea of a man being molded in the MGM image. He refused to conform to the MGM dress code, thereby drawing Mayer's ire on more than one occasion. For example, if Peter had to be in formal attire for a particular scene but knew that none of the camera angles would take in his feet, he would remove the fancy leather shoes designed to be worn with the formal clothing he had on and switch into velvet slippers. The slippers were considered quite proper throughout Europe, where Peter had been raised. Wealthy and distinguished European men, when attending fairly formal functions in their native lands, routinely wore such slippers. It was what Peter had seen when allowed to attend gatherings hosted by his parents. It was a comfortable action and he saw no reason not to do it on the set so long as the shoes weren't shown. It was a rebellious act, Peter acting like Peter. And Mayer was bothered.

Peggy Lynch, a Metro featured player interviewed by author Kitty Kelley for the book *Elizabeth Taylor: The Last Star*, explained the system best. She said: "Publicity people formed us in those days. They really shaped our persona, our psyche, our selves. They chose the image they felt would be best for us; they would fine us and take the money from our paychecks if we did not live up to that studio image. I was supposed to be the girl-next-door type and act as a wedge against June Allyson not to let her get out of line, the same way Kim Novak was later supposed to keep Rita Hayworth in check. If I went to the store in a man's shirt hanging out of a pair of jeans, like we did in those days, I'd be fined. That was considered detrimental to the star system. As a pretty princess type, Elizabeth was never once fined by Publicity because her mother kept her dressed perfectly at all times."

After May's visit there was serious reason to talk with Peter.

Mayer invited the youth to his office, then sat looking down on him. The office was designed so that the desk was raised, Mayer always sitting so that height added to the illusion of power. He explained to Peter that he understood about his problem. He said that there were other men on the lot with the same sexual preference as Peter. He would provide Peter shots of male hormone to help him. He was surprised when Peter not only refused but was also irate.

Peter told me that he said, "Mr. Mayer, I don't know where this rumor's come from but it's completely false. How would I be with Lana Turner if I preferred men?"

According to Peter, Mayer replied, "I can't tell you where it came from, Peter, but I am insisting that you get these injections. We have several people who are doing it."

Peter said, "Do you want to tell me who they are?"

"No," Mayer reportedly said, "I'm not at liberty to tell that to you."

"Then who is the person behind this so I can straighten it out with them?"

"I cannot tell you."

"Fine. Then I'm walking out of this office now and I'm never doing another picture on this lot if that's what you want. I'll get a contract with Paramount or Warner Brothers. I don't care about your studio and this is the last time I'll ever see your office, Mr. Mayer."

The way in which Peter spoke to Mayer apparently had the right tone of both indignity and respect, despite his anger. Peter was not fired. However, a year later Peter learned that it had been his mother who was the source of the information about Peter's supposed sex preferences. From then on, Peter hated the woman. He also tried to get his father to move out of the house so the two of them could share bachelor's quarters somewhere. Sir Sydney did no go along with the idea, either because he truly loved his wife or because he was comfortably set in his ways.

Some of Peter's later troubles did start during those early years at MGM. When Peter was dying of a cross-addiction to alcohol and other drugs, he wrote: "I began on a small level around the age of twenty-one. In those days drugs were not 'in' with that age group; though I had heard that Sherlock Holmes was into them, it did not impress or make me curious enough to investigate them—thank God!

"The progression with booze seemed quite natural, except for some horrendous hangovers there were no real problems caused by alcohol until about four years ago, when my sweet liver turned on me. [This was written approximately six years before his death on Christmas Eve 1984.]

"I was never a 'problem drinker' as such. Only to myself and eventually to my health. I was never one of those unfortunate people who had a history of auto crashes, police problems, staying away from home or family for days at a time, bar fights, you name it! I was very lucky and, at the risk of sounding like a snob (which I am not), I learned to drink like a gentleman."

The nature of the drinking Peter did while under contract with MGM was in the line of active partying. Peter liked good times, yet never missed work or was a problem for his directors.

Peter's first film with the young Elizabeth Taylor was the movie *The White Cliffs of Dover*, filmed in 1944, in which she starred with Roddy McDowall. Elizabeth, born in 1932, was considerably younger than Peter, but they eventually became close friends. The fact that she was born in England, though the daughter of Americans Francis and Sara Taylor, gave her a dual citizenship and a minor link to his own origins.

Elizabeth Taylor joined MGM in 1943 for the film *Lassie Come Home*, which was part of the studio's B movie production unit headed by Samuel Marx. These were low-budget films that did not receive the same publicity, nor were they expected to make the same profits, as the A movies. However, many of them inadvertently became such great hits that eventually the featured players were given A movie treatment. The Andy Hardy series, which launched Mickey Rooney and Judy Garland, became typical of this type of successful film.

The Lassie films used the dog as the equivalent of a human star in emotional cliff-hangers. The story of *Lassie Come Home* involved Lassie's forced separation from her owners, a separation that finds her taken in by a "kindly Scottish couple." Eventually they release her because they sense that she belongs elsewhere and wants to return to her owners. The dog must walk for days, and travel through mountain storms; she gets attacked by sheepdogs, shot by sheepherders, nursed by people who help her, and then makes her way home.

Most of the actors and actresses in the film had British accents. People such as Dame May Whitty, Nigel Bruce, and Elsa Lanchester were among the adult stars, though Roddy McDowall was cast as the young owner of the dog. Because he was short, a short female child was needed to co-star with him. Elizabeth, who grew to just over five feet as an adult, won the part. She was ten years old and had enough important scenes to be remembered by the critics.

The movie was so successful that sequels were planned, including *Son of Lassie* (1945), which starred Peter Lawford as the grown Roddy McDowall. "I cringe when I tell you of the title," said Sam Marx, the producer. "It was the way we called pictures in those days. We didn't think to call it *Lassie II, III, IV, V*. We just called it *Son of Lassie*. 'Son of' became a general term. You had *Son of Dracula*, and I once had the suggestion to call one movie *Son of a Bitch*, which I think they should have considered."

Peter worked with Elizabeth for the first time in the film *White Cliffs of Dover*, where she was again teamed with McDowall. This was another of the wartime pictures meant to encourage Anglo-American unity. It is a dramatic story starring Irene Dunne as an American who marries a prominent British man just before World War I. They have a son, but her husband is killed in the war and she chooses to stay in England, a country she loves. Then, at the end of the picture, Roddy McDowall, who plays that son, is killed in World War II. Elizabeth Taylor's role was minor, that of a neighbor child who has a crush on McDowall. There is a brief moment at the end of the picture where Roddy and Elizabeth go up a hill and are transformed into adults—Peter Lawford and June Lockhart.

As Elizabeth reached puberty, she recognized what all the girls had seen in Peter and developed an intense crush on him. This concerned Sara Taylor, who had no illusions about her daughter's emotions and about Peter's reputation with young women. She went to Peter, told him that she was aware of Elizabeth's feelings, and ordered him to take it easy on her daughter. Eventually Elizabeth and Peter became lifelong friends; she was one of the few women with whom he never went to bed.

Despite the warning of Sara Taylor, there may have been another reason that Peter was never linked romantically with Elizabeth during those early years. Peter was extremely superficial in his decision making as to which women he would pursue and which he wouldn't. He made instant judgments about what was arousing and what was not, an attitude made possible by the adoring female fans who were his for the asking. Elizabeth had beautiful eyes, but Peter focused on what he decided were "fat thighs," making the instant decision to have nothing sexual to do with her.

Interestingly, Elizabeth was later sexually linked with Peter's son, Christopher, who looks exactly as his father did when Peter was the same age. Although there were supposed witnesses to this liaison, a relationship reported in at least one of the many books written about Elizabeth, her longtime friend and former lover

Henry Wynberg claims that the story is completely false. She never discussed such a relationship with him, and he also stresses that Elizabeth has always dated men approximately her age or older. The idea that she would get involved with a boy young enough to be her own son, even one who is as handsome as Peter, is completely out of character, according to Wynberg. Yet I was around at the time and saw how close Elizabeth and Christopher had become. I had no reason to doubt Peter's version, but I was never in the bedroom with them and have no idea how they conducted their private relationship.

Peter's life style during the late forties period was typical of the rest of his life. He was a movie star because of the opportunities the war years had brought him in Hollywood. His family position was such that he had socialized with royalty. He was comfortable with heads of state and leaders of major corporations, yet he was equally comfortable with "nobodys," people who did not have "names" or titles or power positions.

One of Peter's closest friends, beginning in 1947, was Joe Naar, a man somewhat younger than Peter who was a football player for UCLA. He met Peter through a mutual nonindustry friend, Charlie Dunne, and Charlie's fiancée, Molly Anne French. Charlie and Joe were good friends, Charlie also became a friend of Peter.

The four friends began going to the beach every day. When Joe graduated from college and admitted he had no real direction in his life, Peter took him on one of the MGM tours.

Touring the country on behalf of the studio, the war effort, and/or the film industry was a common experience during the 1940s. Films might have been the major form of entertainment for most Americans, but the MGM publicity department did not take the audiences for granted. They had such stars as June Allyson, Janet Leigh, Peter Lawford, and numerous others travel to major cities to appear before the premier showing of a film. The stars would talk to the audience and perform, often doing a song-and-dance number, then leave the stage so the film could be run. The public felt closer to the stars and were more enthusiastic about supporting the film.

During the war years the stars made appearances in order to convince the public to buy war bonds. After the war, there were tours involving groups of six stars whose job it was to encourage the moviegoing habit. These tours were put on during times when the movie exhibitors were experiencing a slump in sales, the tour designed to bolster business in general. "Those tours were purely and simply put together, not to exploit a single movie, but to exploit movies," explained Sam Marx, who went on one such tour to upper New York State. "I have a son who I heard when I came home used to tell his classmates, 'My father's out begging people to go to the movies.' "

Joe Naar talked to me about the first tour on which he accompanied Peter, a tour set up for Peter and Janet Leigh to help sell their movie *the Red Danube*. It was to be a multi-city tour in the East.

"Peter was dating Janet Leigh at the time," said Naar. "I was still in college and it was all new to me and I didn't know anything about anything. I was from the wrong side of the tracks, probably. Then I started playing football at UCLA, went to Westwood and met Peter. We started going around together. He took me home. I stayed at his house often because we just were there together a lot.

"Before I graduated at UCLA—I'd say this was 1949 now, before I graduated—he took me and Peter Sabistan with him on a tour for *The Red Danube* starring Janet Leigh. Before the movie opened, they would get up on stage and they would have Peter Sabistan planted in the audience and they'd throw a joke at him so Peter could look good on stage. Peter then, with Janet, would do some sort of a show. He was a song-and-dance man. He would entertain the people for fifteen minutes and say hello. He would sing a song or dance and answer questions. Janet would do something.

"But my job was to set up parties. I'd get the pretty girls and have some fun. I was supposed to be 'learning the business' because after I graduated I was going to get into the business, some way, somehow." In reality, Joe simply made certain that they all had a good time playing on the road.

Mayer had had no illusions about how little Naar was doing on the road. However, he felt that Naar was the ultimate vindication of Peter's manhood and liked the idea of having a football player traveling with him. In fact, at one point he had the MGM publicity department arrange for an article to appear in one of the movie fan magazines. The article, which carried Joe Naar's byline, told of the relationship between the UCLA football player and the actor. It was an extremely positive story, excellent for Peter's image, yet Naar knew nothing about it until it appeared. He was never told it was being written. He was never interviewed for the piece. He only learned of it after the fact.

"There was word out that Peter might have been homosexual because he knew Van Johnson and he knew Keenan Wynne," said Naar. "I have no idea if they were or not, though Van Johnson might have been. Peter couldn't have been more heterosexual. All we did was chase ladies in those days."

Mayer was naive about homosexuality, assuming that a gay man was one who was not athletic or involved in contact sports. But this was also a period when same-sex preference was little understood, greatly feared, and a reason for shunning a man in all aspects of his life. Believing the myths, Mayer was certain that football players were neither gay nor capable of associating with men who were.

Peter also acted as a mentor for Naar during those early years. He taught him how to dress, how to talk, and how to deal with the stars of the day. "Peter, in those days, would take me and tell me [what] to say to Mr. Berle, if I met him. 'Don't call him Milton. Call him Mr. Berle until he gives you approval to, say, call him Milt. You call him Mr. Berle. Anybody older than you, you show them respect.'

"He would tell me what fork to use when we had dinner with people who were important, and they always were. He would tell me what clothes to wear. He would tell me anything and everything that made me and my life more important. Anything good that's happened to me I owe to Peter Lawford."

Joe Naar felt out of place being friends with Peter Lawford. Peter was a star. His friends were stars, and Joe was really a stranger to the business. Ironically, it would prove to be a feeling similar to the one Peter experienced when he became active with the Clan in the early 1960s. Comedian Joey Bishop once commented that Peter seemed to be a little out of place when working on stage with Joey, Frank Sinatra, Sammy Davis, Jr., and Dean Martin. All but Peter were entertainers with extensive experience on the stage. Peter was a film actor and lacked the time in front of an audience that the others had had. Yet Naar was completely liked and accepted by Peter, just as Peter would be by the Clan.

Peter's career was going well during that period, though Naar was naive about Peter's success. "I had no idea how people looked at him and thought of him when I met him. They looked at him the way they looked at Richard Burton. They followed him. He was handsome. He attracted people everywhere.

"His hero was Fred Astaire. Everything Peter wore, Fred Astaire wore. I didn't particularly like Fred Astaire, but Peter liked his style. Peter was the first to wear sandals without socks. He was the first to wear a tie instead of a belt around his waist. He claims he got it from Fred Astaire. I found out later that everybody else gives Peter credit for most of the style."

There was a tragedy during this period, a personal drama that could not be anticipated. Charlie Dunne was a handsome man who eventually was separated from his wife, a woman he loved but to whom he was not always faithful. There were a number of versions of the story concerning Charlie's actions before the separation, but afterward the group still hung around together. However, Peter seemed to intensify his friendship with Molly, who had been hurt by her husband's affairs.

Whether or not there was intimacy between Peter and Molly, Charlie told friends that he believed the two were seeing each other more than they should. He still loved his wife despite their problems, and he had trouble handling the idea of Peter and Molly being close. When the Korean War came about, Charlie told a mutual friend that he was going to reenlist in the marines, go to Korea, and get killed. Then he proceeded to do just that, being declared a hero for single handedly attacking an enemy machine gun nest, commiting suicide in a way that would save others.

Peter probably never knew that Charlie deliberately sought to die during the war. Certainly there was no reason for him to feel responsible for the apparent suicide. Yet, in a sense this event would foreshadow the tragic end of Peter's involvement with Marilyn Monroe.

The other important aspect of those MGM years was that Peter met Frank Sinatra. Because this story is so intimately connected with Peter's relationship with John Kennedy, it appears in the next chapter. But it is important to understand the background that preceded that meeting.

There was nothing about the very young Frank Sinatra that should have made him a major entertainer. Even his friends saw little more to him than a skinny kid with big ears who came from Hoboken, New Jersey. His speech was atrocious, the street slang of the uneducated hustler. Yet the approach to singing that he developed after gaining big band experience was flawless, the words clearly enunciated. Even before he had fully mastered his voice, he had developed a style that gave the impression to each woman in the audience that he was singing specifically to her.

The high point in Sinatra's early career came in May of 1941. He was twenty-five years old and had been named the top band vocalist by *Billboard* magazine. He went on in that same year to receive the honor of being *Downbeat* magazine's most popular male vocalist. This was an honor that had been held for the previous six years by Bing Crosby; the rivalry between the two singers would resurface more than twenty years later, bringing President Kennedy and Peter into the middle. In this early period, the differences between Sinatra and Crosby were important to gossip columnists.

Typical of the way the two men were discussed in print was a poem written by Larry Siegel, later a comedy writer, which was published by "saloon columnist" Earl Wilson, for years one of the most respected Broadway and Hollywood columnists in America. The poem read:

Oh Dear, What Can Sinatra Be?
A hanging curl, two dreamy eyes,
Looks that swirl to distant skies,
The unconscious girl sits and sighs.

A quivering lip
Blaring lovesick rhyme,
Her insides flip in double time.

A slender frame with sagging knees
Yet garnering fame with uncanny ease
The stricken dame pants the breeze.

Eyes of blue, two hands alike
Stretching forth true
Lovingly to strike
Close to you? No, his mike.

Although this lank's
The latest thing
He'll never outrank the "groaning" king
You take Frank, I'll talk Bing.

In 1942 Sinatra decided to move beyond the work he had been doing. He had been singing with the Tommy Dorsey band, had been involved with two minor movies, and had made over eighty recordings. Yet the money was limited compared with what he could make on his own. He also was unable to establish his own identity.

Sinatra was obsessed with reaching for the greatest success he could achieve. He worked hard on his performing and he worked hard on generating publicity. He worked to appear in important columns such as the one written by Walter Winchell. He made certain his records were sent to important shows such as the Lucky Strike–sponsored "Hit Parade." He took radio disc jockeys out to eat, knowing that air play was vital for his future. He courted reporters and anyone else who could do him some good.

The approach Sinatra used seems normal today. We have seen

such efforts become routine for anyone seeking publicity. However, in the 1940s such a concentrated effort was unknown. Disc
jockeys and radio stations were ignored. Columnists frequently
had to rely on their imaginations or the creative powers of "reli-
able sources."

The timing for Sinatra to go on his own was as good as Peter's
arrival in Hollywood. America was at war in 1942; factories
employed men and women working two and three shifts. People
had money to spend and a desire to spend it. As a result, movie
theaters in some parts of the country stayed open all night. Many
theaters held "swing shift matinees" that ran from midnight to
four A.M. While vaudeville no longer preceded motion picture
"chasers," as had occurred when Louis B. Mayer began in the
business, movie theaters still had acts playing with the films. Most
of these were big bands and famous singers, such as Jimmy
Dorsey, Helen O'Connell, Glenn Miller, Benny Goodman, and
Peggy Lee. It was an opportune time for the young Sinatra.

Sinatra also had the added help of George Evans, a press agent
whose client list included many of the most famous entertainers in
the business. Evans created the Sinatra image that helped make
him so successful.

Evans paid girls to mob Sinatra, shouting "Oh, Frankie! Oh,
Frankie!" They would swoon at key moments, yell, squeal, and
talk to him at critical points in songs. They were supplemented by
high school girls thrilled to receive free tickets for performances
where it was important that the press view Sinatra as a sellout.
The fact that Sinatra was a skilled singer who worked hard at his
trade, constantly developing himself as a musician, was important
to his long-term success. But for the period when he was first
going out on his own and needed to rapidly establish a unique
identity, George Evans's antics were critical.

Evans's work went beyond arranging for audience reaction.
There were "special events" such as Frank Sinatra Day, and
contests such as "Why I Like Frank Sinatra" and "I Swoon for
Sinatra." The work went so well that the girls hired to swoon and
carry on were eventually overshadowed by unpaid fans, who
seemed to want to top the "professionals." They would carry his
picture to contests, kissing it, hugging it, squealing and yelling.
They wanted to touch him, to have a piece of his wardrobe, to be
a part of his life.

The success was understood by *Billboard* magazine, though.
The editors recognized the quality in Sinatra's voice and performance style. They also respected George Evans, presenting him with a

scroll in 1943 that attested to his achievements. The scroll was for "Most Effective Promotion of a Single Personality."

Sinatra, like Peter Lawford, was 4-F (physically unfit for military service), though his avoidance of the army was more controversial. Sinatra claimed that he wanted to enter the marines, though the truth is that he probably was not interested in the military. He had quit the Dorsey band, gone on his own, and was facing greater success and more money than he had ever seen before. His popularity was at an all-time high, and the military meant potential obscurity. The fact that major celebrities, such as baseball greats Joe DiMaggio and Hank Greenberg, felt that their careers were not so important as military service created some criticism of Sinatra. Yet the 4-F was apparently legitimate, the result of a punctured eardrum caused by a series of mastoid operations he had had as a child.

Later Sinatra's classification would be changed to 2-A (eligible to be drafted into the armed forces but not eligible for combat). This questionable change stated, in effect, that while Sinatra was probably still 4-F for military service, he was in a profession that was "necessary to the national health, safety, and interest." Thus, by early 1944 he knew that he would not have to serve, a fact that made him of even greater interest to the film community.

George Evans might have been brilliant at manipulating events when Sinatra sang, but when the singer went to Hollywood to begin making moves such as *Anchors Aweigh*, his first important film, he discovered a very different world. In Hollywood the columnists could make or break you. They also would do anything for a story, a fact that their "spies" knew and utilized.

Typical was the way in which columnists could anticipate marriages. They would arrange to pay waiters to see which female stars were regularly going out with which men. As bizarre as it seems, they would tip the women in the dressing rooms, the powder rooms, and other locations where intimate personal acts of hygiene were performed. As soon as the rest room attendants and dressing room personnel could see that a single movie star, dating one man regularly, was missing two periods, the gossip columnist would immediately announce a sudden engagement, probable elopement, or some other euphemism that would tell the public that the woman was pregnant. Some of the readers understood the code and delighted in the titillation of such insider knowledge. Other fans had no conception of the hidden messages, delighting instead in the sudden intensity of the romantic life of their favorite stars.

Sinatra became friendly with New York and Hollywood "saloon" celebrities such as Toots Shor and Mike "'Prince" Romanoff. This led to his first exposure to political power and influence.

Toots Shor, friendly with Robert Hannegan, the Democratic National Committee chairman, arranged to be a guest at the White House for a tea with President Franklin Roosevelt. Shor also arranged to have comic Rags Ragland and Sinatra accompany him there.

Roosevelt was intrigued with Sinatra because he knew the younger man's reputation. However, he was not impressed, commenting to Marvin McIntyre, his secretary, "Mac, imagine this guy making them swoon. He would never have made them swoon in our day, right?"

The celebrities were extremely impressed 'with meeting Roosevelt, Toots Shor later explaining to Earl Wilson: "I was nervous. I kept thinking, 'A bum can go in and see the president. A crooner, a restaurant guy, and a burlesque comic can go call on the prez!' I kept eating cake to keep myself busy. It was damned good cake. I wish I could get the recipe for my joint [Shor owned a restaurant]. Sinatra did a Sinatra. He fainted."

Sinatra did not faint, but he did decide to become active in Democratic politics. New York governor Thomas E. Dewey was campaigning for president in 1948, four years after Sinatra had been to the White House to meet Roosevelt. Roosevelt had since died, and Harry Truman was then president. Since Sinatra supported Truman against Dewey, he deliberately went to the entrance of the Waldorf-Astoria Hotel in Manhattan when Dewey was scheduled to be there. The crowd that had arrived to see Dewey was much more interested in Sinatra's glamour. They immediately moved to Frank, embarrassing the governor.

Sinatra's support of Truman did not save Truman from some of the same embarrassment that Dewey experienced. The president was eating at Toots Shor's at the same time that Sinatra was dining there. A crowd had gathered outside and, when Truman left the restaurant first, the crowd surged forward. Then, recognizing that it was "only" the president, they moved back, disgustedly commenting, "We wanted Frankie."

Two other important events were taking part in Sinatra's life in Hollywood. One was his growing friendship with Marilyn Maxwell during a period when his first marriage, to wife Nancy, was breaking up; at around the same time he signed a $1.5-million contract with MGM. The other was his becoming involved with Phil Silvers, playing out a contract at the Copacabana after their mutual friend Rags Ragland died. Sinatra agreed to be Silvers's stooge.

The Silvers act began with Sinatra sitting in the audience as though he were just one of the fans. Phil told the electrician to turn up the house lights after the show started. "If there's anybody here famous, I'll introduce them." Then he studied the crowd, decided that no one of importance was there, and had the lights turned down. At the same time he touched his tie, the signal for Sinatra to stroll onto the floor and walk onstage.

This was followed by Silvers, who had a voice that sounded a little like a man who gargled with sandpaper, giving Sinatra a singing lesson. Sinatra could never seem to learn to do it "correctly," the disgusted Silvers finally slapping Sinatra for his stupidity before sending him back to his seat. Sinatra did not take a bow, having been thoroughly chastised for his "inability" to learn. When the show was over and the two men took their bows, the crowd went wild. Sinatra had also learned an important lesson in adding comedy to a nightclub act, a lesson he would use when he eventually performed with Peter, Sammy Davis, Dean Martin, and Joey Bishop—the infamous Clan.

3
The Post-War Years

"Everybody kisses everybody else in this crummy business all the time. It's the kissiest business in the world. You *have* to keep kissing people when you're penned up and working together the way we are. If people making a movie didn't keep kissing, they'd be at each other's throats."

—Ava Gardner

"In a novel a hero can lay ten girls and marry a virgin for a finish. In a movie, this is not allowed. The hero, as well as the heroine, has to be a virgin. The villain can lay anybody he wants, have as much fun as he wants cheating and stealing, getting rich and whipping the servants. But you have to shoot him in the end. When he falls with a bullet in his forehead, it is advisable that he clutch at the Gobelin tapestry on the library wall and bring it down over his head like a symbolic shroud. Also, covered by such a tapestry, the actor does not have to hold his breath while he is being photographed as a dead man."

—Herman Mankiewicz

"A sex symbol becomes a thing. I hate being a thing."

—Marilyn Monroe

THE YEARS BETWEEN THE END OF WORLD WAR II AND THE TIME when Peter became involved with the Kennedys reflected a period of play for Peter. Older male stars were returning to the industry, but Peter was still in demand. He had money, he had friends, and he wanted to have fun. Joe Naar, his closest friend during this period, described what he was like:

"The beach was a huge part of our lives. Peter was glued to the beach every second he wasn't working. He was a super volleyball player. He taught me to play volleyball. He was a board surfer and tried to teach me how to board surf. Everybody in our crowd did everything he did. He was the star of state beach.

"And always there were parties, a lot of parties at his house, at people's homes. I went to Arthur Loew's house one night and Gene Kelly was there with Dean Martin and Jerry Lewis. Elizabeth Taylor was about fourteen or fifteen and they were trying to get her to say the word *fuck*, and they couldn't.

"Arthur had a strange sense of humor. He'd go to her and say, 'Say *intercourse*.' So she'd say 'Intercourse.' Say this. Say that. Now say *fuck*.

"That was when she was fourteen or fifteen years old with those purple eyes that were so gorgeous. She had a crush on Peter. In those days you'd see Elizabeth Taylor on the beach. She'd be waiting for Peter, looking for Peter."

This was the crush Peter never took advantage of.

"I'd picked up Ava Gardner to take her to the beach because Peter couldn't pick her up. . . . We all sat in the same place and Peter would join us.

"Ava Gardner, for Christ's sake! I was still in college. I would walk down to my friends in college and say, 'That's Ava Gardner.'

They'd look at me and say, 'Sure it is.' They didn't believe it. *I* didn't believe it.

"They did believe it was Elizabeth Taylor because Elizabeth Taylor didn't look that good. Except for this fantastic face, she had big thighs, while Ava, in a bathing suit, was still smoky and smoldery.

"Elizabeth Taylor, if you had seen her in a bathing suit, you'd have said, 'Gee, I'm a little bit disappointed.' "

Peter became friendly with Marilyn Monroe during this period. She was an aspiring actress, emotionally fragile, extremely attractive, and willing to do anything to succeed in films.

Marilyn was a woman whose life Peter could understand. She had been abused as a child to a degree that troubled her throughout her life. She was not particularly well educated, yet, like Peter, she had a good mind.

Marilyn was desperate for male approval, her numerous lovers and husbands, her several abortions all attesting to this fact. She wanted attention any way she could get it and told a story of her childhood to one interviewer: "The wish for attention had something to do, I think, with my trouble in church on Sundays. No sooner was I in the pew with the organ playing and everybody singing a hymn than the impulse would come to me to take off all my clothes. I wanted desperately to stand up naked for God and everyone else to see. I had to clench my teeth and sit on my hands to keep myself from undressing. . . . I even had dreams about it. In the dreams I entered the church wearing a hoop skirt with nothing under it. The people would be lying on their backs in the church aisle, and I would step over them, and they would look up at me."

There was at least one same-sex partner, though Marilyn was neither lesbian nor considered to be a lesbian. The relationship was between Marilyn and Natasha Lytess, the head drama coach at Columbia Pictures, and it took place in 1948. Marilyn always had the attitude that no sex was wrong if there was love involved. She also understood that other women felt things that she did not. Sometimes she questioned whether or not she was frigid.

Marilyn also knew how to create a personal history that would enable her to get away with what, for the time, were outrageous actions. She willingly posed naked for a photographer, an act considered shocking in its day. Then, when the photograph was purchased by Hugh Hefner in 1953 for a calendar that would be part of his new magazine, *Playboy*, she took a newspaper reporter, Aline Mosby, into her confidence to tell her that she was the subject. Marilyn claimed that she had been without food or work for so long that she decided to pose for the photograph in order to get enough to eat. It was a good story, a touching story, and Marilyn had certainly known hard times in the manner of so many aspiring actresses. Yet her decision appeared to be as calculated and voluntary as her "letting her hair down" with Mosby, a nationally syndicated writer who would spread the touching story and bring her greater attention.

There were other tricks as well. Marilyn was known for her walk, a movement that made her back end almost as famous as her face and bustline. It seems that Marilyn would cut a quarter of an inch off the heel of one of the high-heeled shoes she wore. It was not enough of a change to be noticed by a passerby. It was just enough so that it was impossible to walk completely evenly. There would be a little dip that would cause her rear end to wiggle.

Marilyn also believed in physical fitness. She ran for her health and her looks long before that was popular. She followed a fitness regimen that brought her into contact with the athletic Peter. He was intrigued by her, sensitive to the pain she often hid, and asked her for a date. Although they remained friends throughout her life, the dating aspect did not even last the first evening. Peter told me that when he arrived at her house, she told him she needed additional time to get ready. Lateness, he was to learn, was a classic Monroe trait, and that evening's delay lasted an hour. However, it was not the lateness that bothered Peter.

Marilyn had a dog that was not housebroken, yet was kept in the house. Everywhere Peter looked in the living room, small piles, some fresh and some at least a day or two old, were in evidence. Marilyn had not only not trained the dog, she apparently was oblivious to his fouling of her home. Peter spent that hour using paper towels and cleaning supplies he found in the kitchen to remove the animal waste. Although they liked each other enormously, he never considered dating her again. The idea of going to bed with Marilyn disgusted him. He felt that her personal hygiene was probably as bad as her housekeeping, something he could not tolerate when he thought of physical intimacy. In fact, he could not finish the evening with her, though he was comfortable having her in his home for card games and dinner over the years.

Peter and Joe Naar double-dated that night; Joe's date was a woman named Barbara Darrow. Peter had been so upset by Marilyn's acceptance of the dog waste that, as Joe tells it: "He said to me, 'Will you take Marilyn home?' And I said 'Sure.' He said, 'I'll take Barbara, you take Marilyn,' and I took Marilyn home.

"After that I would see Peter at home. His mother would say things to me like 'So you're getting into television?'

"Then she'd look at me and say, 'Will you look at my television set?' And Peter would say, 'Would you shut up, Mother? He's trying to get into television as an agent.' She wanted me to fix her set."

Naar was delighted with the general, though. His family was also from England, so he brought his father to meet Peter's father. They got along extremely well, but Lady May thought Joe's father a social inferior, making that fact clear to everyone.

"I must say that Peter handled his mother's attitudes extremely well, though," says Naar. "He'd walk out and be close to tears because of what she would say. But he'd just put it out of his head. He never apologized for her. He gave everyone the credit of knowing that he wasn't that way. Of course, his father was a very, very genuine, very classy man and that's who he loved dearly.

"His father was so old, I would guess at that time that he was eighty-two or eighty-four and she was in her sixties. There was a major age difference. I don't remember his father being out of a wheelchair by then."

Joe Naar began working at the William Morris Agency. He was a junior agent who was assigned to take care of Peter.

Naar's skills as an agent were based on his experiences as a street fighter and football player. He was not accustomed to verbal finesse, no matter what Peter taught him. When Peter got into an argument with a producer over a script change that Peter felt was necessary, Naar decided that he had to protect Peter from the producer's verbal abuse. He walked over to the man and punched him in the jaw.

As much of a playboy as Peter was during this period, he was also gaining a reputation as a consummate professional. This was most obvious in the way he became involved with actor Jack Lemmon.

"Peter was a terrific guy at an important time for me," Lemmon explained. "And I think out of his good nature, period, not because he felt 'Oh, I'll help this kid because he's getting his feet wet and he doesn't know.' I think it was just his nature. He was just basically a hell of a nice guy."

Lemmon's early career was in New York, not Hollywood. He had acted in live television, then primarily headquartered in New York, and on stage on Broadway. "I was doing a Broadway play which was a flop. It was a revival of *Room Service*, and we shut that theater up in about three weeks or something because the play just didn't hold up. But the actors got very good notices and I did, too, thank God, and they [the Hollywood producers] were looking for someone to play the lead opposite Judy [Holliday]. They were looking for two of them [leads] and Peter [already] had one.

"So they [the producers of the film *It Should Happen to You*] tested me for it and I got the part. I was not only fresh from Broadway, the only time I had seen a camera, I had done one little army short years before. That was it.

"And I did live television. I did a hell of a lot of that, but that really is closer to theater. And on that little box, your eyes aren't three feet wide as they are on a theater screen. So as a result, I think my acting was good. Judy was also from the theater but she had had more film experience.

"We'd get carried away and I'd be going up and down and Cukor [director George Cukor] kept telling me at the end of every take, he'd say, 'Oh, that's wonderful. That's wonderful. But let's do just one more. Less, Jack, less.'

"Finally, after about two weeks of stomach aches because of this, I screamed at him, which is uncharacteristic—I didn't really realize what I was saying—I said, 'Are you trying to tell me not to act at *all*?'

"And he said, 'Oh, yes. God, yes.' And crossed himself.

"I was playing to a theater. What he was really trying to say . . . was bring it down. Just feel it and think it, but you don't have to be as big [of voice].

"Peter was on the set when he said that and I laughed, and so did everyone else. Peter was very sweet. He came over and he squeezed my elbow—I remember this very vividly—and he whispered to me, 'You don't have to.' "

Lemmon continued: "The experience was so terrific, working with them, that a year later I moved out [to California]. I bought a little house and I moved out permanently and I've stayed here ever since. I don't think that would have happened if Peter and Judy hadn't been so wonderful to work with.

"Another thing that I will always remember was when my former wife and I tried to drive out here with our little dog, Duffy. It was impossible.

"We got out here finally, almost absolute wrecks from trying to make it. The car broke down. The dog ate up all the seats. We were sitting on newspapers. It was just a terrible, terrible cross-country trip for about five or six days. And we got here to . . . no movers. The house was totally empty. We couldn't even stay there.

"It was not late afternoon and we didn't know what to do. But I remembered from when I was first out here that there was a nice little restaurant right on Sepulveda, a little country-type of restaurant . . . which was only minutes away. And I said, 'Well, let's get something to eat.' We had to eat. We had to do something. I thought we could go to a motel . . . and I was trying to look to see if I had enough money to spend the night in a motel before I could get into Columbia the next day and try to get an advance.

"We walked into the restaurant and it was as if I saw Jesus. There was Peter. So we sat with Peter—he was alone, just grabbing a quick bite—and we told him the story.

"He just smiled and said, 'Finish your dinner.' So we finished the dinner and he said, 'Follow me.' He brought us back to his house and he went in . . .

"The guy went in. He got sheets. He got a mattress. He got blankets. He brought a couple of lights from his house. He brought things we would have to have. He was even starting to put food into boxes for us until I stopped him and said, 'Oh, we can get to a market.'

"Then he drove back with us, helped us set up a mattress on the floor . . . It was something that was terribly important to me at the time, that guy's kindness was just wonderful. I always appreciated his kindness.

"I remember the very first day when we were reading the script a few days before we started shooting. We were sort of reading, rehearsing, etc. with George on the sound stage. We were at the old Columbia Studios on Gower Street and Peter said, 'Do you want to have lunch?'

"We went to Naples, which was a restaurant on the corner of Gower and Sunset, and on the way, we had just read the script a couple of times. I said 'God, that's a marvelous script, isn't it?'

" 'Yea, it is,' said Peter.

" 'The parts are so good.' And Peter just smiled and said, 'Yours sure is.' But he said it with a smile, because it was a better part than Peter's. It was the lead, so to speak, although there were two leading men. It was the better of the two parts and there was more of it. It had a little more depth than Peter's part. But he said it with a smile, then proceeded to take me to lunch and we had a ball.

"There was a certain limitation—because of the accent and everything else—on the parts that Peter could play. If he had an American accent, he might have had, God knows what other parts in his career.

"That first picture worked wonders for me, but I had Judy and

I had Peter. If I hadn't had them, if either one of them had not been terrific, the picture would not have worked. If the picture had not worked, I'd not have gotten the recognition just on my performance and I know it. No question."

The impact of the interview with Jack Lemmon meant even more to me considering when it occurred—approximately five days after the prestigious American Film Institute had given him its Lifetime Achievement Award, one of the highest honors an actor can receive.

"That experience [with Peter] was very important to my early career," Lemmon added. "If that had been an unpleasant experience or . . . had it not been as exciting . . . I doubt very much that I would have concentrated that much on film."

Lemmon discussed Peter's professionalism on the set: "Peter was very much like Judy. If anything was bothering him personally, you damn well never knew it. And that's a difficult thing to do. . . . Professionally, Peter was tops, and that I admired immensely because I've always prided myself on being professional, and if there's something bothering you, God damn it, put the blinders on, leave it at home, do your work! Try to keep everything else out no matter how tough it is.

"I know I personally, and this is not unique, all the time we were doing *Day of Wine and Roses*, my dad was dying. I'd leave the set and go to the hospital. . . . You have to be able to cope with that. And for the moment that you're doing your scenes, you've got to get that out of your mind or you're not going to be able to do it.

"And the other thing that I love is that Peter . . . well, Peter always had a great sense of humor and he was marvelous in comedy. He had a sense of comedy. . . . That's different. That's an appreciation of humor. He was always laughing, giggling, saying things or doing things. . . . What it does is keep a bubble on the set. That was one happy set with Judy and Peter, and I love to work that way. We had fun.

"There was still something in the business that's lacking now, in the change to independent production and no more studio slates. The fun has gone out of the business to a great extent.

"I don't care if it's Virginia Woolf or Tolstoy's *Power of Darkness*, you've got to have that bubble of energy, fun, and joy in your work going. Peter had that. Peter was a total pro but he had a ton of experience by the time I worked with him."

Off the set, Peter stayed with the cast, Lemmon explained, sometimes playing word games with Judy Holliday ("She was anything but the dumb blonde she played so often and so well"), sometimes running through a scene if that seemed necessary. "That's another reason I was attracted to him, because he was bright. You can't be a great actor unless you are bright. You can be a screwed-up emotional mess, but you have to be bright."

There were other experiences during the years between the MGM career and the switch to television. Joe Naar recalls that he and Peter were constantly around such friends of Peter as Gene Kelly and Ava Gardner: "We were at Ava's house and Nat Cole played the party. He was new in the business, hustling whatever jobs were available, his genius not yet discovered. That's why he was working . . . at Ava's birthday party.

"We would go to elaborate parties. There would be Ava Gardner, and Gene Kelly, and Gary and Rocky Cooper. . . . I don't remember if these were for something special, like New Year's, or what anymore. [The parties were held in the late 1940s and early 1950s.] I do remember that we all had to get up and sing or act, do little skits. We were given scripts and everything.

"I remember that Gary Cooper was seeing a lot of ladies, though he was doing it as quietly as anyone, and I remember he went after this bimbo whom all of us turned down because she wasn't attractive enough. And Cooper, who was . . . our hero in those days, was chasing this lady who I thought was beneath him.

"We were at a party at Roger Eden's [producer/songwriter for MGM] . . . Judy Garland was there and there were about eight of us or ten of us. Anyway, Judy would get up there and sing because there wan't anything else to do and Roger was at the piano.

"The reaction, and I'll never forget it, was 'Is she going to sing again? Jesus Christ, isn't she ever going to shut up?' She got up to sing and she wouldn't get down. And I remember looking around the room and saying 'Isn't this incredible? One day I'll be able to tell this story and say they couldn't wait for Judy to sit down because she was always on.' "

4

The Kennedy Years

"My dear Jack,

"Just a line to let you know how things are going here. A lot of the same that you left behind—bureaucracy bullshit and a president who can taste that second term in office so badly that he has created this false economy in which we are existing—and the poor people are believing it! I can't wait for the deficit to start falling in on him and his 'kitchen' group! And that's where they belong.

"Enough of that dreary stuff. I have managed to drink myself into the B.F.C. My liver drove me down and here we are—it's a very pretty Stalag 17 which is supposed to help one back to the world of sobriety. I must say they do their best and I'm sure it's helped me. You, my friend would hate it—not a pretty girl within miles and, everytime you turn around, you trip over someone's ego or someone expressing an authoritarian spasm (here they call it therapy). . . .

". . . I know you're having a good time. You always do. Are you pres. of anything? A garden club or bowling team perhaps! You must be running something, knowing you. Jackie is terrific—spent a lot of time with her at Sydney's wedding.

"How are Marilyn, Bobby, [unreadable]? Give them my love. If you should run into Steve McQueen or Vic Morrow, give them my best.

"Well that's about it for now. Believe me, you are sorely missed here and around the world if I may say so.

"All the kids send their love. Let us hear from you soon.

"Take care of you—

"Love, Peter."

(Partial letter from Peter Lawford to his late brother-in-law, John F. Kennedy, written while undergoing treatment in 1984 for alcohol and drug addiction at the Betty Ford Center in Rancho Mirage, California.)

IT WAS A PERIOD AFFECTIONATELY KNOWN AS CAMELOT, A TIME when the young "king" Kennedy was in the White House and all was right with the land. John Kennedy was tall, handsome, virile, the kind of man you could invite to your home for a touch football game and a can of beer. Yet there was also a sense of inner toughness, giving the impression that if someone backed you to the wall, he was a man you would want fighting by your side.

That old general and former president, Dwight Eisenhower, had served his purpose. Commander-in-chief of the Allied forces, Eisenhower had helped coordinate the destruction of Hitler's Germany. He presided over an era when World War II vets wanted nothing more than to use the GI Bill to get on with their education, to marry, and to move into the new tract houses in the planned communities being built throughout the country. The world of Eisenhower was supposed to be one that was safe, where the father worked and the mother stayed home with the children. Prosperity meant having a television set, a station wagon, and enough money to go bowling or to the movies every week. It meant knowing your place in society, a position determined by the color of your skin, your sex, your religion, and the amount of money you had in the bank.

Yet the Eisenhower era was not the safe period portrayed in the newspapers and on such television shows as "Father Knows Best," "Leave It to Beaver," and "I Love Lucy." The reality was that it was a period rife with fear, a time of uneasy peace during which there was the constant belief that the world might be destroyed at any moment.

Perhaps the greatest fear was the "Communist menace." The Russians had developed the atomic bomb, and the American media implied that they just might use it at any moment. School

84

children had bomb drills in which they were taught to "duck and cover." It was a simple exercise that would save millions of lives, an exercise the foolish Reds did not understand. When the warning sounds were heard, schoolchildren knew to hurry into the hall in an orderly manner, kneel down against the solid walls, duck their heads, then cover their necks with their arms. If circumstances did not allow for this ultimate protection, an almost equal degree of safety would come by ducking under their desks, then assuming the protective position. There would be a flash of light, higher than normal heat, but no loss of life because the children knew to "duck and cover."

Bomb shelters were also a popular item. Companies were created to dig holes in yards and stock them with food, water, books, a portable radio, generator lights, and maybe a rifle and ammunition to hunt for animals if the grocery stores did not reopen immediately upon the sounding of the all-clear sirens. The idea was that when an air raid came, everyone would go into their shelters, close their wooden doors, and live an adventure that would last from a couple of days to a couple of weeks. We could read, play games, have sing-alongs, and wait for the radiation to clear from the air. Then we would emerge victorious, the Russian bombs proving almost impotent because our civil defense effort had enabled us to be prepared.

The paranoia of the era was being fed by Senator Joseph McCarthy, who had discovered that libel and slander were the best ways to achieve political fame. He decided to capitalize on America's fear of the Communist menace by showing that the government, the entertainment industry, and numerous other areas of society had been infiltrated by Communists and their "sympathizers." Through his congressional hearings, hundreds of lives were ruined. Writers were blacklisted and not allowed to be involved with movies, television, and other creative areas, despite the innocence of their work and the clear-cut violation of their Constitutional rights. By the time McCarthy had been revealed as the lying, vicious fraud he was, the United States was a nation in fear.

There were other concerns as well. The Russians launched the world's first orbiting satellite, Sputnik, in 1957, causing a reevaluation of our scientific and technological capability. Schoolchildren were found to be undereducated and physically unfit. Parents who had been raised during the Depression, who had fought in World War II, wanted a world in which their sons and daughters could live an easier life. As a result, the nation was perceived as having evolved into one where laziness, poor training, and a lack of common goals could cause a once triumphant people to be defeated from within.

There were other forces at work in the United States. Blue-collar workers had never had so much money before. It was possible for a man to hold a laborer's job and be able to afford a home for his family, two cars, adequate food, and a college education for his children. Wives frequently did not have to work in order to ensure that the bills would be paid. There was a complacency about a life style that involved going to work, coming home, watching television, and feeling secure about life.

Children being raised in this environment often found it stultifying. The life style that their parents embraced with relief after the nightmare years of the Depression and the turmoil of World War II seemed self-centered, complacent, lacking in purpose. They had material possessions but they wanted something more.

In a sense, the children who were about to become rebels were revolting against a social structure that worked. They did not have to work their way through school. They had the time to be students. They could seek leadership and direction because they believed that since the present was better than the past, the future could be better still. All they needed was someone to spark that desire within them.

John Kennedy spoke of selflessness and purpose. He implied that this would be a generation that united for peace as previous generations had come together for war. It was a message whose time was right and it made Kennedy a folk hero in the minds of many who supported him. And Peter Lawford, the actor, husband of Kennedy's sister, Pat, was thrust into national attention in a very different way than in the past.

John Kennedy was typical of most of the publicly active children of Joseph P. and Rose Kennedy when they first entered the political arena. He was aggressive in pursuit of his goals, yet he had more style than substance.

Jack Kennedy, the Massachusetts senator with a glamorous wife, was little more than an adolescent in his personal life. Unable to emotionally commit to any woman, his marriage was in name only. He spent much of his leisure time in pursuit of the pleasures of the flesh. He was rumored to have said that he was not done with a woman until he had had her three different ways. Regardless of the truth of that remark, interviews with former Secret Service agents, White House staff members, and friends reveal that he had sex with as many as two different women a day.

By contrast, the next oldest Kennedy male, Bobby, was an odd combination of moralist, pragmatist, and extremely aggressive politician. He had worked for Senator Joseph McCarthy during the period when that senator was destroying reputations through slander and defamation of character. Oddly, during the period when Joe McCarthy was still respected, Bobby was doing the one area of research into Communist influence that seemed valid as it related to national security. He had found that at least 355 ships owned by companies headquartered in Allied nations were shipping cargo to the Red Chinese during the Korean War. Americans fighting in Korea were being killed with equipment transported by our allies. It was a situation that was so potentially explosive for the Republican party that the Eisenhower White House asked Republican Joe McCarthy not to disclose it. The information was just too valuable to the Democrats.

Bobby was irate when his work was censored. It was the one incident where McCarthy acted responsibly, yet Bobby had been right to be frustrated. Bobby was often accused of being opinionated, militantly aggressive, and abrasive, and was generally disliked by those around him. Later Bobby became a supporter of many of the people and groups he had previously ignored. He had been neutral at best on the issue of civil rights until, as U.S. Attorney General, he realized that his future would be assured, in part, if he was perceived as a strong advocate for minorities. He was also the only one of the Kennedy males who believed in monogamy, interpreting his Catholic training literally.

Although there would be rumors of Bobby Kennedy's infidelity, Peter frequently told me that they were not true. He stated, often with some surprise, that the only time Bobby was ever involved with a woman other than his wife was during a brief, rather intense affair with Claudine Longet. She was then the wife of entertainer Andy Williams, a close friend of Ethel Kennedy. The accuracy of Peter's remarks was later confirmed by William Sullivan, the man who was third in command of the Federal Bureau of Investigation (FBI) under J. Edgar Hoover.

In his book *The Bureau: My Thirty Years in Hoover's FBI*, Sullivan stated: "Although Hoover was desperately trying to catch Bobby Kennedy red-handed at anything, he never did. Kennedy was almost a Puritan. We used to watch him at parties, where he would order one glass of Scotch and still be sipping from the same glass two hours later. The stories about Bobby Kennedy and Marilyn Monroe were just stories. The original story was invented by a so-called journalist, a right-wing zealot who had a history of spinning wild yarns. It spread like wildfire, of course, and J. Edgar Hoover was right there, gleefully fanning the flames."

Peter said that in most instances where Bobby was linked to
some woman, it was because of Jack. The woman was having an
affair that had become blatant enough that Bobby felt it might
compromise the White House. He was taking upon himself the
role of convincing the woman that it was time to leave his brother
alone.

Peter never discussed the reasons that Jack and Ted Kennedy
were so determined to have sex without commitment, perhaps
because this was a life style he also enjoyed. In Peter's case, much
of the blame may go to the way he was raised. With the Kennedys, the brothers probably were influenced by the life style of
their father, a man whose actions gave the family both their
fortune and their early notoriety.

The Kennedy family rose to regional prominence under P. J.
Kennedy, Joe's father, who was a Boston politician. The political
connections he forged made the family extremely influential in
both their community and their state. However, Joe felt that
many of the people who sought favors from his father, and there
were dozens coming to the house every month, were opportunists.
They saw P.J. as a soft touch, while he viewed them as honorable
individuals temporarily in trouble.

Joe Kennedy decided to make his living in the business world,
initially in banking, then later in such diverse fields as shipping,
the stock market, liquor distribution, show business, and other
profitable areas. While attending Harvard University, he and a
friend, Joe Donovan, purchased a tour bus and took groups of
people on guided visits to historic locations in the area. The men
cleared a profit of $10,000, a tremendous sum back in 1912.

Kennedy put those early earnings into real estate, then came to
realize that no matter what business he was involved in, bankers
were always in the middle of it. He determined that becoming a
banker would not only give him a vehicle for amassing personal
wealth, it would also give him access to other people's money. By
1914, the same year he married his childhood sweetheart, Rose
Fitzgerald, he had maneuvered his way into the position of the
presidency of the Columbia Trust Company.

Joe Kennedy was eager to learn. He began to master both the
stock market and the ways in which it was possible to take control
of companies through the manipulation of their stock. He was
becoming a man of worldly affairs, a power broker who was not
yet thirty years of age when World War I ended.

The business acumen revealed in Joe Kennedy's life is shown at
its best when Prohibition came around. There have been frequent
rumors that Joe was a major bootlegger, and there is evidence that

he was involved with the illegal importation of alcohol. However, he was probably never a bootlegger on the scale that some of his detractors believe. In fact, part of his reputation came from his understanding of how to take advantage of a negative situation about to happen.

Kennedy had both the money and the storage facility to buy up thousands of bottles of whiskey and other beverages and stockpile them in anticipation of Prohibition. He also was able to work through pharmacies, which had licenses to dispense alcohol by prescription. Since doctors throughout the country wrote prescriptions fairly freely, his legitimately purchased alcoholic beverages had a ready market. In many instances, bottles were allegedly sold "from the back room" as well as by prescription, though the prescriptions were just a legal way to circumvent the law. Physicians during Prohibition were no more likely to consider liquor "medicinal" than they are today. But it was this stockpile that put Joe Kennedy ahead of the game, guaranteeing himself large profits because he had both the foresight and the ability to store the bottles.

Joe's young bride, Rose, would prove to be both Joe's greatest advocate and his most difficult emotional attachment. She was torn between the desire for independence sought by many highly intelligent women of her day and the strict Irish Catholic upbringing the Fitzgeralds had provided. Rose Fitzgerald first revealed her intellectual prowess while in high school. She was only in her junior year when she accomplished the almost unheard of achievement of gaining acceptance to Wellesley College. Wellesley was a school dedicated to providing women with the same high academic standards as were available to men, a rarity among higher education programs for women. At the same time, she had been raised to think that marriage was the high point of life, the ultimate achievement possible for a woman.

Rose was also taught that sex, no matter how enjoyable, was meant for procreation. The teachings of the Church never spoke against sex as pleasure, nor did most of the male Church leaders feel that sex should not be frequently enjoyed between married couples. However, many nuns taught young girls in their care that sex was for the purpose of having babies. To continue sex during pregnancy, or after there was no longer a desire to have children, was sinful. It was a concept that did not reflect the true teachings of the Catholic Church, yet one that was perpetuated by many teaching nuns in parochial schools as late as the 1950s. Thus, Rose would eventually be torn between the strict teachings of the nuns and her spirit that demanded knowledge, excellence, and the sharing of all life's adventures with her husband.

Tragically, in the end, the strictness of her upbringing would dominate, Rose settling for the traditional role of housewife while her husband traveled the nation and the world. Absent from home, his sex life limited by his wife's beliefs, Joe Kennedy eventually would stray, having a series of affairs that became common knowledge to his children.

The more I learned about the Kennedys, the more tragic their story seemed to be. People were willing to look on them as gods, not mere mortals. Their wealth and power gave them almost a mythic reputation. They were seen as people who could have no problems, who would experience none of the traumas of life known all too well by the rest of society. Even worse, they chose to accept this image, insulating themselves, avoiding the counseling that might have helped their marriages, their family relationships, their personal lives. They frequently lived with unhappy and/or errant spouses, irresponsible children, drug dependency, and fawning sycophants instead of friends. They were like people in a wagon train, pulling themselves into a circle, drawing weapons and isolating themselves from the outside world in order to ensure their survival.

Oddly, the Kennedy women seem to have been conditioned to womanizing husbands. Rose's father was a man known for his affairs. Jacqueline Bouvier, who became the wife of Jack Kennedy, had a father who was both an alcoholic and a womanizer. In fact, Black Jack Bouvier, as her father was known, had an affair with another woman during his honeymoon with Jackie's mother. Such women were deeply hurt by their husbands' infidelity, yet they had seen from their own fathers that such a situation was "normal" and one to be tolerated.

Perhaps the most interesting comparison between Joe Kennedy and his son Jack was their delight in bedding the most famous movie stars of their day. Long before Peter helped his brother-in-law secretly meet and bed Marilyn Monroe, Joe Kennedy had an affair with actress Gloria Swanson. At that time, Joe Kennedy was active in the film industry and Gloria was making a break from the studio-controlled star system. She turned down a million-dollar contract, only the third or fourth such contract ever offered in the fledgling film industry, in order to gain more control over her own pictures. She wanted to have the creative control that producing her own work would allow, a fact that fascinated the businessman side of Joe Kennedy almost as much as her beauty triggered his lust.

The difference between Kennedy father and son was in the way they handled the moral dilemma of marriage and affairs. Jack Kennedy never gave any indication that he was in the least bothered by his actions. Joe Kennedy, on the other hand, was extremely troubled. During his liaison with Gloria Swanson, for example, he arranged for Boston's William Cardinal O'Connell to visit Gloria toward the end of 1929 to try to convince her to end the affair.

According to Swanson's autobiography, *Swanson on Swanson*, Cardinal O'Connell explained that each time she saw Joe Kennedy, she became an occasion of sin for him: "He told me that Joe had spoken about our relationship with some of the highest representatives of the Catholic Church. Since there was no possibility of dissolving his marriage under Church law, he had sought official permission to live apart from his wife and maintain a second household with me. That was impossible, the cardinal explained. Furthermore, he went on, as one of the most prominent Catholic laymen in America, Mr. Kennedy was exposing himself to scandal every time he so much as appeared in public with me." Swanson told the cardinal that she felt that if her relationship with Joe Kennedy was a problem for Kennedy, then it was up to him to do something about it, not her.

Despite this apparent public guilt, Joe Kennedy was known to flaunt his sexual activities in front of his wife and children. He regularly called the girls that Jack dated, often taking them to dinner and questioning them about their personal lives. He also told them about Gloria Swanson, a liaison other men might have kept more discreet.

Rose Kennedy, in her memoirs, *Times to Remember*, spoke of Gloria Swanson, giving insight not only into her acceptance of the situation but also the influence the affair might have had on Pat Kennedy, one of the couple's daughters. Pat Kennedy would become Peter's first wife, tolerating not only his periodic womanizing but also the fact that her brother regularly had sex with other women under the roof of the Lawfords' California home. I have no idea if Peter wanted his earlier wives to engage in ménage à trois or whether that was something he decided to try when his sex drive was waning from all the drugs and alcohol. But the infidelity of both Jack and Peter was blatant enough that it was hard for me to understand its being tolerated until I read Rose's comments. Although they seem innocent enough, remember that this was written about a period in her life when the Kennedy/Swanson affair was common gossip in Hollywood and other parts of the country. They were photographed together and regularly mentioned as an obvious "item."

Rose commented: "Gloria Swanson was our houseguest for a couple of days in Bronxville and brought along her small daughter, who was about the age of our Pat, who was about ten. The two got along well together, and Pat took her down to show her the Bronxville public school and meet her classmates and perhaps show off a little, as she did by introducing her as 'Gloria Swanson's daughter.' Nobody believed her. They all just grinned, thinking it was a joke. After all, Gloria Swanson was, to them, practically a supernatural being, so she wouldn't be in Bronxville and wouldn't have a daughter, and Pat was just doing some silly spoofing. I can't recall the exact details but I do remember how completely indignant Pat was when she and Gloria's little girl came home and told us."

Rose Kennedy also talked of trips abroad, including one to Paris when Gloria Swanson's marriage was falling apart. There was a closeness that most women would not have tolerated, yet that Rose accepted. Her only comment was about the "competition" in general, not any specific affairs. She said: "During Joe's years in the movie industry he was surrounded daily by some of the most beautiful women in the world, dressed in beautiful clothes. Obviously, I couldn't compete in natural beauty, but I could make the most of what I had by keeping my figure trim, my complexion good, my grooming perfect, and by always wearing clothes that were interesting and becoming. And so, with Joe's endorsement, I began spending more time and more money on clothes. Eventually, I began landing on some lists of 'Best Dressed Women.' "

There were also stories of the way Joe Kennedy reacted to his daughters' friends. Female friends of his daughters who were staying at the family compound on Cape Cod found that Joe liked to kiss them goodnight. His actions were those more in keeping with a teenager on the make than with a father and respected business leader.

By the time Peter met Joe Kennedy's daughter Patricia, Jack Kennedy was different from his father only in that there was no guilt for his actions and his affairs, which were far more numerous than the old man's.

Jack Kennedy's attitudes toward life seemed to match those of his favorite fictional hero, James Bond. If Ronald Reagan's presidency was colored by the war films he made during the 1940s, Kennedy's was influenced by the image of the casual sex, machinelike brutality, and cold sophistication of Bond. His intensity with his work, his casual affairs, his fascination with elite military units (which led him to create the Green Berets despite the existence of special units that could have handled the same demands), indicate that influence.

There was no emotional involvement with women for Kennedy. His marriage seemed to be a matter of convenience; being single was seen as a political liability. There was a chance he would be called homosexual, and there were rumors, apparently without foundation, that he was meeting both men and women at one hotel in the Washington, D.C., area during his days as a senator. The idea of a man who was such a rampant womanizer being homosexual seems ridiculous, but during that period in history a man in his thirties who was not married could not gain the respect of the nation. He had to either marry or recognize that his bachelor status would keep him from being a serious candidate for higher political office.

Kennedy may have been a swinger, but the women who were willing to talk about his prowess in bed never considered him much of a lover. Actress Marilyn Monroe, who at one time expected to marry Jack Kennedy, laughingly explained to columnist Jim Bacon that there was never any foreplay. He would enter, satisfy himself, and return to work. The woman adapted or remained unsatisfied.

Judith Campbell, a lover who was also involved with alleged Mafia leader Sam Giancana and singer Frank Sinatra, commented: "I understood about the position he had to assume in lovemaking when his back was troubling him, but slowly he began excluding all other positions, until finally our lovemaking was reduced to this one position. It is impossible for me to pinpoint when I first realized it, because it was such a gradual process, but slowly I began to feel that he expected me to come into bed and just perform. There would be a moment of stillness when I came into bed and it was almost like he expected me to roll over and put my arms around him and make love to him. . . . I was there to service him."

Peter first met Jack Kennedy at Gary Cooper's house, a meeting that sparked no friendship but that greatly impressed Peter. Kennedy had just been released from the military, a war hero who gained fame because the PT boat he commanded had been shot out from under him. The sinking of the ship had almost cost Kennedy his life and left him with severe back problems that made him extremely uncomfortable whenever he sat in a normal chair. Not only was the sinking of the ship an incident that would eventually be used to help him get elected president, it would not have happened had it not been for J. Edgar Hoover.

William Sullivan, the ex-FBI man, related that, in 1942, wiretaps were being made in order to track a beautiful Scandinavian woman believed to be spying for Nazi Germany. Then Lieutenant John F. Kennedy was a White House liaison who might have been able to sit out the war on the home front. However, he had had an affair with the Scandinavian woman, Inga Arvad, who was apparently innocent of the suspicions levied against her.

Jack Kennedy was in a position to have access to intelligence information, a fact that made the relationship a danger. His father knew what was happening and was irate with his son for doing something that could affect his military career. At the same time, Joe Kennedy recognized how attractive the woman happened to be. Since he was not in a position of handling intelligence information, he tried to get her interested in an affair with him, or so she later would tell her son. Whatever the case, the matter was so serious for the future president that Joe Kennedy had to use his influence to keep his son on active duty. The affair had been reported to President Roosevelt along with the suggestion that Jack Kennedy be transferred to prevent a breach of national security. The young lieutenant found himself going from intimate liaisons to fighting the Japanese in the Pacific.

Kennedy was still undergoing rehabilitation therapy for his back injury when Peter met him. Kennedy weighed only 130 pounds at the time, had none of the vigor of his later years, yet Peter liked him instantly. "My immediate reaction was that there was no bullshit with him. He was very straightforward and had a marvelous sense of humor. I knew there was a force in the room when I shook his hand. I felt that he was a rather extraordinary fellow."

The seriousness of Kennedy's back injury was kept from public awareness even more carefully than was Franklin Roosevelt's inability to walk when the latter first ran for president. Peter told me that a medical technician followed Jack everywhere carrying a syringe filled with what, I believe, was a cortisone-type drug. It was meant to be injected immediately if the president's back went out. The partial disability he had was so severe that he could suddenly find himself unable to move. The attacks could be both intense and without warning. The only way he could continue would be with an immediate injection of the drug. Peter said that it was not unusual to see the technician jab the needle right through Kennedy's suit in order to inject him as quickly as possible.

Perhaps Kennedy's ways of handling his disability were rather immature. But Peter admired the way the man did not let himself live the life of a cripple despite being in almost constant pain. No matter what else might be said of him, when it came to facing personal adversity, he showed remarkable courage.

Kennedy was also impressed with Peter, if only because Peter was an actor. "He had an affinity for Hollywood and its personalities that I think came from his father. He would read weekly *Variety* voraciously. After he was president, he would sometimes ring up and tell me what the grosses were on new films. He was that kind of fellow."

Peter met Eunice Kennedy (now Shriver) in 1949, when he was on a promotional tour in Washington, D.C., for the movie *The Red Danube*. It was an MGM film and, typical of the time, it had an anti-Soviet theme.

Whether through a sense of humor or because she had not seen the picture, Eunice took Peter to a cocktail party at the Russian embassy. A couple of the Russians had seen the film and began making rather nasty remarks about it. Peter, rather frightened, quietly told Eunice that they had better make their escape.

Peter saw Eunice occasionally after that, but it was when she was attending the 1952 Republican convention that he met Pat Kennedy, the woman who would became his first wife. Peter had become friends with a number of wealthy, influential eastern business leaders, including Henry Ford, a delegate to the convention. Peter joined Ford as an observer, having the same curiosity about the event that was shared by the Kennedy sisters when they decided to attend.

Peter and Pat began talking, each intrigued by the other. Then, later that year, Peter's father died while Pat was on a world tour. She took the trouble to send him a note of sympathy, a gesture that deeply moved Peter.

"One night we were having dinner in L.A. and we started talking about love and marriage. I told [her] I thought I was falling in love with [her] and that maybe she might consider making it permanent. She said, 'How's April for you?' Obviously we shared dreams of a marvelous, happy life together."

Joe Kennedy was not happy about his daughter's decision. He said to Peter: "I don't like the British. I don't like actors. And I don't like men who wear red socks." I asked Peter what he did about Kennedy's statement, and he merely smiled and said, "I stopped wearing red socks."

There was no sex before the marriage. Peter respected Pat Kennedy and did not force the issue. Whether or not he cheated during the engagement went unmentioned. However, Peter did not remain faithful after the marriage, eventually having an affair with actress Lee Remick that was so serious that there was a chance Peter would leave Pat. At one point he talked with his brother-in-law, Jack Kennedy, about the fact that the marriage had fallen apart. It was 1962 and Peter knew that a divorce within the Kennedy family would result in bad press that could affect the reelection. He alerted Jack to both the family problems and the fact that he had no intention of doing anything that could create a scandal, at least not until after the reelection.

The bride's father, ex-Ambassador to the Court of St. James Joseph P. Kennedy, the bride-to-be Patricia Kennedy, her mother and her sister Jean, who was to serve as maid of honor, were waiting at the back of the church, beside the baptismal font—when there was a sudden great roar from the street.

Joe Kennedy grinned down at his lovely daughter.

"He's here, Pat."

The bridegroom, handsome Hollywood actor Peter Lawford, son of an honored British soldier and knight, had arrived at the Church of St. Thomas More in E. 89th St., where he was to claim yesterday as his bride one of the seven (living) children of the fabulous Kennedy clan of Boston, London, New York, Chicago, and Palm Beach, Fla.

In a few minutes the vows were made and the multimillionaire's daughter and her actor-bridegroom who had heard the Rev. John J. Cavanaugh, former president of Notre Dame University, say that they must . . . "have faith in each other" and learn to "surrender individuality," were coming down the aisle together radiant and, as you could see, touchingly proud to belong to each other.

For all its simplicity, there was magnificence in the dress the bride wore. It was made by Hattie Carnegie of pearl-white satin in the new style of fullness drawn to the back and falling into a long train. With it, she wore a voluminous tulle veil attached to a cap of satin, and carried a bouquet of white orchids. Her only attendant, her sister Jean, wore a Dior creation of taffeta in a pink and blue hydrangea print, with a large blue hat. She carried an old-fashioned bouquet.

Waiting outside in 89th St. the crowd of 3,000 persons broke through police barriers and surrounded Peter and Patricia when they emerged at 4:15 P.M. from the church. Even after the couple managed to enter their automobile at the curb, the vehicle was unable to move for five minutes. Finally 23 policemen cleared a path.

Patricia is the third of the Kennedys to marry in less than a year. Eunice was married to Robert Sargent Shriver of New

York last May, and in September, Senator John Kennedy was married in Newport, R.I., to Jacqueline Bouvier.

Although yesterday's ceremony and reception did not attempt to rival in size or splendor the other two Kennedy nuptial events, it was strikingly beautiful. Pink snapdragons with white lilies decorated the church and pink flowers and candles glowed at the reception in the Plaza's grand ballroom.

There the elegance of the bride's attire was observed again when she rose from her table for the first dance with her dashing bridegroom. For that memorable whirl, Emil Coleman played "No Other Loves Have I."

Tall, slender, chestnut-haired, the former Patricia Kennedy is the second beautiful daughter of ex-Ambassador Kennedy and Mrs. Kennedy to wed into the glamorous atmosphere of the British peerage. Her sister Kathleen was wed during World War II to the Marquess of Hartington, heir to the dukedom of Devonshire, who was killed in action. Kathleen died later, in a plane crash.

Patricia's bridegroom is the son of the late Lt. Gen. Sir Sydney Lawford, a captain in the Boer War and a general in World War I. His mother, Lady Lawford, who lives in Hollywood, was present at yesterday's festivities.

The bride was given in marriage by her father with three of her brothers serving among the ushers: Senator Kennedy and Robert Kennedy, both of Washington, D.C., and Edward M. Kennedy of Boston.

It'll be a honeymoon in Hawaii.—*New York Sunday News*, April 25, 1954

The guests were the rich and famous from around the world. They ranged from actresses such as Greer Garson and Marion Davies to Prince Christian of Hanover, the brother of the queen of Greece.

Peter told me that the first few years of his marriage to Pat were relatively happy despite Peter's philandering. However, Patricia was not one of the stronger of the Kennedy women. She and Peter used to drink fairly heavily and use sleeping pills to compensate for the long hours they frequently maintained. After enduring the shocks of having both Jack and Bobby assassinated, then her father's death in 1969, she developed serious problems, according to what the Lawford children later related. At her worst, Pat Kennedy Lawford took sleeping pills to excess. But such behavior was far in the future when Peter and she got married. She had conquered a handsome British movie star with whom she was deeply in love, and Peter had gained not only a wife but a family, the one thing he had always lacked.

Pat Lawford was fascinated with Hollywood and anxious to meet some of the celebrities with whom Peter was friends. Among the first was Frank Sinatra, a name Peter would rather she had not mentioned. He had not spoken with Sinatra in years, the result of a misunderstanding on Sinatra's part that had never been resolved and certainly did not permit him to call the singer so he could introduce Pat.

The Sinatra relationship went back to the early years at MGM. Sinatra had just been signed by the studio after extremely successful performances at the Paramount Theater and the nightclub La Bomba in New York. Both men were friends of Marilyn Maxwell, then an aspiring actress, and she introduced them during an extremely boring dinner.

The dinner was a command performance for the MGM actors under studio contract. Any time Louis B. Mayer wanted to honor a friend, he would invite many of the contract players as a way of impressing the individual. In this instance, the party was for Henry Ford II, the same man Peter would later accompany to the 1952 Republican convention.

Marilyn Maxwell knew about the problems of Hollywood. She had been a band singer who was considered both beautiful and one of the nicest actresses to try to succeed in Hollywood. She never had the vicious aggressiveness that characterized so many of the actresses trying to rise to the top. She had been married to John Conte, an actor from whom she was getting a divorce. Sinatra had been dating her, despite his marriage to then wife Nancy. Although Nancy refused to consider a divorce, Frank flaunted the relationship with Marilyn, something he continued to do until the making of the movie *It Happened in Brooklyn*, in which he would star with Peter Lawford, Jimmy Durante, and Kathryn Grayson.

Peter was intrigued by Sinatra. He later commented, "I would be lying through my teeth if I said I was not more than a little curious and interested to meet this somewhat frail and gaunt young man who obviously had the power in his God-given lungs, and a built-in, smoldering, quiet mystique to cause continents of women of all shapes and sizes to have to change their pants [they wore them in those days] more than once a day, listening to his woeful, sensual, and doubtless scratchy seventy-eights."

Peter thought that Sinatra had a delightful sense of humor and no sense of self-importance. Only later would he find that Sinatra was extremely volatile, quick to anger if he felt he was slighted.

Peter later commented, "I will always think of him as the lovable land mine—something no sturdy American household should be without."

Later, in his notes, Peter facetiously commented, "You may get the impression that the gentleman in question was a total ogre. Far from it. I mean, just because he punched a few defenseless girls, broke a few cameras belonging to new photographers in the line of duty, instigated the roughing-up of a couple of parking lot boys who were guilty of that unpardonable faux pas in the world of status, that his car was not prominently first in line outside the old Romanoff's Restaurant, or probably the most infamous of all, by having one of his illiterate, but blindly loyal, goons bury a six-inch cut glass ashtray into the head of a man sitting in the booth next to him . . . in the Polo Lounge of the Beverly Hills Hotel, who he happened to overhear, make a mildly derogatory remark about him. I gather that, to this day, the unfortunate gentleman is still not himself, due to some form of brain damage. So you can plainly see, he's not all bad."

Yet for all the facetious remarks, for all the bitterness that would afflict Peter in later years, he genuinely liked Sinatra. The times that they parted company were painful ones for Peter. Even sadder was the fact that, toward the end of his life, the drug-induced paranoia he experienced caused him to misread Sinatra's impact on his life. When he could no longer face his own failings, he blamed Sinatra for hurting his career, a charge totally unfounded.

But this was still the 1940s, the friendship was young, and Peter was taken with the brash, skinny singer from Hoboken. They attended parties together, Peter meeting the elite among songwriters, playwrights, and conductors. He came to know Sammy Cahn, Jimmy Van Heusen, Julie Stein, Axel Stordahl, and numerous others. Each man opened new avenues of the entertainment world to the other.

In 1947 Peter, Frank, Jimmy Durante, and Kathryn Grayson made *It Happened in Brooklyn*. It was one of Sinatra's early films, and he was still rather nervous. He had known great success as a nightclub and big band singer, but he was not yet at home on the movie set. The result was the side of Sinatra that Peter respected to his death. "He took direction beautifully, listened, contributed, and was generally extremely professional about the whole operation. In other words, he was a joy to work with, which surprised everyone from the prop man to L. B. Mayer, because of his reputation, which preceded him, of his being difficult to get along with."

Oddly, Kitty Kelley, in her biography of Sinatra, *His Way*, quotes MGM production memos from this period that indicated that Sinatra was frequently late for work or off the set without permission. There is no reason to question the authenticity of those memos. However, considering how much Peter felt hurt by Sinatra in later years, if Sinatra's actions had ever caused a problem on the set, Peter would undoubtedly have mentioned that fact. Since he did not do so, I can only assume that Sinatra's relationships during the filming were much like Peter's. People such as Sam Marx attacked Peter's actions during the filming of such shows as the "Thin Man" television series. Yet the directors and actors who worked with Peter and agreed to be interviewed for this book considered him cooperative, highly professional, and a delight to be around on the set. It must be assumed that Sinatra was the same way—a delight for his immediate co-workers and a pain in the butt of the top brass.

This was not to say that Frank's "other side" would not be present when he and Peter worked together. Peter explained: "As the years went by, and he mastered his craft in a myriad of movies and several very good performances, this, unfortunately, was all to change. By the time we did *Ocean's 11*, a property I found many years later, he had reached the point where he would tear handfuls of pages out of the script and allow the director only one take of a scene, unless there was a technical difficulty of some kind. I remember once the sound man kept complaining about an unusual number of low-flying airplanes, which he was picking up through his earphones, and which were consequently being heard on the track. Well, after about the fourth take, which was unheard of for Frank, he said, 'Aw, fuck it! Everyone knows they're airplanes.' Indeed! But flying through a bathroom? Which was where the sequence was being shot."

The relationship with Sinatra was a close one until an incident with Ava Gardner, Sinatra's ex-wife, was blown out of proportion by gossip columnist Louella Parsons. That incident followed an earlier, humiliating experience for Sinatra at the hands of Miss Gardner while they were still married.

Sinatra and Ava had been in the Plaza Hotel, having an argument in their suite. She ignored his advances and he announced that he was going to commit suicide. He took a gun he carried, locked himself in the bathroom, and fired a round.

Ava was not fooled by Sinatra's dramatics. She knew that whatever he had done, it would not be shooting himself. She assumed that he expected her to come rushing to his side, pounding on the door, begging for a second chance with him. He would then throw open the lock and she would sob gratefully at the sight of his being alive. The incident would probably end in bed, Sinatra getting his way. The only problem with the scenario was that Frank had not reckoned with the type of woman Ava Gardner happened to be.

Instead of rushing to Frank's side, Mrs. Sinatra calmly left the suite, took the elevator to the lobby, and walked up to the front desk. "Mr. Sinatra has shot himself," she said, casually. "You'd better call an ambulance." When the police and ambulance crew arrived, they found an irate, thoroughly embarrassed Sinatra pacing back and forth in his suite.

The Sinatra/Ava Gardner marriage was over when Peter met her for a drink in Frascati's, a bar and restaurant that was located on Wilshire Boulevard across from the Beverly Wilshire Hotel. Ava was with her business manager, a fact the Parsons column happened to omit.

As Peter later explained: "Ava and I embraced and, as it is with so many true friends, we simply resumed our conversation where we'd left off two years before, but with one exception: no mention was made of Frank. She knew we were friends and we all knew the marriage ended badly. No point in causing pain. Ava had to conduct business with her manager over dinner, and so I promised to grab a bite at another table and then join her for an after dinner drink.

"There was a small patio outside the restaurant, and that's where we went for our drink. We chatted and laughed, recalling some of the antics of the Metro years, and then we said goodnight. Ava went home one way, and I went home another. And that should have been that.

"It would have been, too, except that Louella Parsons, whose spies were everywhere and were generally inaccurate, announced, in a nice big headline, AVA'S FIRST DATE BACK IN THE U.S. IS PETER LAWFORD, the day after we were together. The day after that, at about three A.M., the phone rang.

" 'Peter?'

"I recognized the voice instantly, even though I was still half asleep.

" 'What the fuck are you doing going out with Ava? You want both of your legs broken?'

"It was a threat I'd heard before. I immediately launched into an explanation, figuring the truth would set me free. I never got past the word *but*, but I did manage to utter it about three times during Frank's tirade.

" 'I don't want to hear that shit,' he shouted every time I tried to speak. Then he hung up.

"Much later that morning I began calling around, trying to find him. I finally tracked him down in New York where he was staying with Jimmy Van Heusen.

"Jimmy got on the phone and said Frank wasn't around just then.

" 'You know what happened?' I asked Jimmy.

" 'Oh, don't worry, Peter. You've been around long enough to know he'll get over it.'

" 'But nothing happened,' I insisted.

" 'Just let him calm down. It'll blow over.'

"It finally did blow over—seven years later. When it happened, Frank was at the nadir of his career. He hadn't yet made *From Here to Eternity*, and the crooning was not going well. His recovery, of course, was spectacular and, by the time we became friends again, he was back on top and I was married to Patricia Kennedy."

But that friendship had not been restored when Peter was a newlywed and his bride, Pat Kennedy, wanted to meet Sinatra. He explained the situation to Pat, then thought nothing more about it for the next four years. Then they were invited to dinner at Rocky and Gary Cooper's home and the situation was about to change in ways Peter could not have anticipated.

Peter was working on the Jimmy Durante show but expected to get home in time to pick up Pat and take her to the dinner party. However, an accident on the set delayed him enough so that he called Pat and told her to go alone. He would follow as soon as he could, having Pat explain what was happening and telling the Coopers to go ahead with the meal without him.

The accident, a minor though painful one, came about because Durante was putting together an elaborate skit for the show. Part of the skit involved an ashtray in which there was to be a small fire. However, whoever was setting up the prop made too big a fire and Peter's hand was burned. By the time he was finished being treated at the infirmary and could get to the Cooper home, the dinner was over. The women were going into the drawing room and the men were having brandy in a different area of the house.

Peter went to the drawing room without stopping to see Cooper. He was concerned that Pat might be worried about the accident and he wanted to show her the bandaged hand so she could see he was not badly hurt.

"Guess what?" she said to him. "I've got bigger news than you've got."

When he asked her what her news might be, she said, "I just had dinner with Frank Sinatra. He's very charming."

Peter and Frank began talking as though there had never been an argument. They avoided the past, talking about a film they might make, *Ocean's 11*. The property had been purchased by Peter for $10,000, and it would be filmed in Las Vegas. The story involved a theft from a Las Vegas casino. Frank wanted to include Dean Martin and Sammy Davis, Jr. Peter felt that Lewis Milestone should direct, and both men agreed to begin putting all the elements in place.

Not long after this meeting, Frank decided to join Pat and Peter on a trip to Rome. Ava Gardner was living there, and Sinatra thought he might be able to see her, something she did not allow. However, despite Sinatra's personal frustration, the friendship between Peter and Frank blossomed. As Peter later explained: "In those days I was still drinking, so we stayed up all night and I'll never forget the next morning. It was very early and the sun was shining, really beautiful. Frank looked at me, bleary-eyed, and said, 'Charlie, I'm sorry.' All I said to him was, 'I am, too.' It was such a waste of time, but it was so hard for Frank Sinatra to say he was sorry."

Despite the reconciliation, the "dark side" of Sinatra reared its head on New Year's Eve, 1958. The Lawfords had become so friendly with Frank that Sinatra kept a room in his Palm Springs home for them, a room where Peter and Pat stored some of their clothing. Thus, it seemed as though it would be a good idea for the Lawfords, Sinatra, and two other friends, Robert Wagner and his wife, Natalie Wood, to drive to Sinatra's home for the holiday.

Sinatra and the two couples were in Beverly Hills for New Year's, attending a private party being held by restaurateur Mike Romanoff. They were all in formal clothing without topcoats, when the weather turned unusually cold. The temperature dropped into the forties, the wind came up, and Pat and Natalie became extremely uncomfortable. The Lawfords and the Wagners decided that what they really wanted to do after the party was to go to bed as quickly as possible. They would drive to Frank's home in the desert the following morning.

As Peter told it: "I was a close enough friend to know that Frank, once he's got his mind made up and his plans made, didn't like to deviate from his chosen course. (Somewhat reminiscent of a dynamite truck traveling down the road. Fine until it hit a pothole.) It was a character trait we shared, and so I approached our suggestion [to wait until morning] carefully, making sure it made sense and was understood as a majority opinion, one that I hoped would appeal to his chivalrous nature. After all, the girls were cold and worried.

"Frank froze, glared from one of us to the next. 'Okay. Well, I'm going [to drive to the desert].' And with that he turned and walked out of Romanoff's. The rest of us went home to our warm beds.

" 'He'll get over it,' I said to Natalie, Pat, and RJ. 'I'll call him in the morning before we all leave.' "

What happened next formed an odd pattern that Sinatra repeated occasionally whenever he was angry with Peter and Pat. When Peter called the house the next morning to alert Sinatra that all of them were still coming, he talked with George Jacobs, Frank's butler. Jacobs explained that Sinatra arrived about 5 A.M. and went to bed just after 6. However, the butler's voice sounded odd and, when pushed by Peter, he said, "I guess Mr. Sinatra's really pissed off about something."

"How so, George?" Peter asked him.

"He came in and had a couple of drinks. Then he went into the room where you and Mrs. Lawford stay and took all of your clothes out of the closet."

"What'd he do with them, George?" Peter asked him.

"Tried to make a bonfire out of them out by the pool. When the first wouldn't get going, he threw everything into the pool."

Peter was shocked, then amused. He also realized that the gathering would not take place. "Don't worry, George," Peter said. "Everything will be all right. Just tell him when he gets up that we won't be coming down today."

"I fished the clothes out this morning," added George. "I'm afraid they're ruined."

Pat was amused by Sinatra's immaturity, but Peter was annoyed that he had lost a favorite pair of jeans. "We'll age another pair," she said. "Just make sure you don't take them down to Frank's."

Peter related other incidents of a similar nature. Apparently, no matter how close the men grew to one another, upsetting Sinatra meant losing whatever clothing was being stored at the entertainer's home.

During this period, Peter was working in television. He had a short-lived series called "Dear Phoebe," which was the story of a male journalist hired to act as Phoebe, the female writer of an advice-to-the-lovelorn column. In a sense, that series foreshadowed present reality, since the Ann Landers column was eventually taken over, in part, by a male writer.

The second series was "The Thin Man," which evolved from

the book by Dashiell Hammett that had been adapted for a half dozen MGM movies starring William Powell and Myrna Loy. Peter was paired with Phyllis Kirk, an attractive brunette who, because of her current position with CBS, refused to be interviewed for this book. Others on the set at the time said that she apparently was the subject of a number of hostile remarks and practical jokes.

Peter intensely disliked Phyllis Kirk, though others who worked with her found her a total professional and an extremely friendly woman. She was handicapped, a degenerative illness having affected her muscles so that her walk was slightly awkward. She never spoke of this fact, and she had learned to hide her problem, though her walk was just odd enough so it seemed stylized. She did not want sympathy or special working conditions, a fact that caused those few who truly knew her to be impressed with her courage. John Newland, one of the show's directors, said that Peter hated her so much that his contract actually stated that he would not have to touch her.

The hostility was a problem because of the nature of the characters. Peter and Phyllis played Nick and Nora Charles, a couple who were wealthy New York sophisticates as a result of her inheritance. As Sam Marx explained about the series: "I was executive producer of MGM Television during its very first years, and we had decided to do 'The Thin Man.' I was seeking a good kind of replica of William Powell because he had made such a smash hit in the part of Nick. I was pretty close to a couple of other actors who we were going to give the nod to when I got a call from Eddie Mannix, who was the tough, rough, Irish studio manager, who said, 'We've got your Nick for "The Thin Man": Peter Lawford.' . . . At that time, Peter was the brother-in-law of President Kennedy. And I have no doubt that Joe Kennedy, who had pulled many strings and was a friend of Mannix, had simply got Peter the job.

"I had no voice in it. I won't say that I would have been against it because getting into it was fine. He was young, good-looking still . . . and we were going to have Phyllis Kirk play Nora. And I would say that they were going to make a good team.

"It turned out that Peter may have disliked Asta, the dog, but he sure as hell disliked Phyllis more. He had the gall, really, to come to me one time in his typical abrasive way and say, 'Why am I tied to the hip with this dame? Get rid of her. Kill her off and I'll hold the show.'

Marx's comments about what happened have been partially confirmed and partially disputed by others. "The Thin Man" ran from September of 1957 through June of 1959 before entering syndication. Senator John F. Kennedy was elected president in November of 1960. He was a powerful figure in the Democratic party, he was quite open about his aspirations for the presidency, and his father, Joe, was an influential man in the film business, but he was not yet president. The fact that Marx kept referring to Peter as the brother-in-law of the president during this period raises the question of whether he was wrong on other counts or simply not remembering the historical context. But Joe Kennedy might very well have helped his son-in-law, regardless of his son's position.

Director John Newland, one of several directors for the series, recalled the hatred Peter had toward Phyllis Kirk: "He was never bad to her. He was never rude to her. It was just a few times that we had some sharp words about physical contact with her and he'd remind me of his contract.

"They [the Nick and Nora Charles characters] were intimately related and there were many times when they should have been shown in bed together. He never really touched her. And I never knew why he hated her. He could never tell me why he hated her, because she was good, she was never unprofessional. I never understood it.

"Peter was one of the most enjoyable men that I have ever known. He was droll, witty, charming, gracious, very intelligent, very well read, and a very good actor.

"Everybody who worked with him loved him. Except Phyllis Kirk, and she did her best. She was embarrassed that he did not like her. She did not dislike him.

"She had made a couple of pictures. The one with Vincent Price, *The Wax Museum*, was her big claim to fame. I'd used her a lot on live television on the Robert Montgomery show, and then she came out here and did that. And she was beautiful.

"But she always had this physical incapacity that made her walk in a strange fashion. People thought she walked affectedly but she wasn't. You couldn't shout through the streets that Phyllis Kirk has an infirmity.

"It was some sort of muscular deterioration so far as I know. But I know she handled it very, very well.

"I never, ever knew why he didn't like her. Particularly because of this imposition of no physical contact in 'The Thin Man,' there were moments that were very tricky to get around. And his adroitness at getting away from her physically was really something to see. Like Fred Astaire, dancing. He'd find things to do that went around her, over her, it was like manic almost. It had no sense to it at all. Everybody knew it, including Phyllis.

"I don't know why it wasn't totally mortifying. I guess because she handled it so well.

"At first, when I was exposed to it, I was dumbfounded as to how to handle it because he said, 'Johnny, I'm never going to lay a hand on her, on that girl.'

"I said, 'Why?'

"And he said, 'I'm not going to do it. It's right here in my contract.' And he sent one of his toadies to get the contract. Sure enough, there's a codicil saying that at no time should Mr. Lawford be required to make love or do anything physical with Phyllis Kirk.

"It was such a curious neurotic game that I became inventive of how they should not have to touch each other. But it was strange."

Despite the problems, Newland said, "He was never late. He was never drunk. . . . I encountered nothing about him except the utmost professional attitude."

I tried to learn what bothered Peter about Phyllis Kirk. It was possible that her handicap reminded him so much of his own that he became uncomfortable with her. Or it might have just been one of those peculiarities in life where someone takes an instinctive dislike for another person for no obvious reason, even to himself. Whatever the problem was, he never revealed it to me.

Peter also hated the three terriers that played Asta. The dogs were high-strung, and Peter complained to me that they would wet on him without warning and, seemingly, without reason. There were many instances during the filming when Peter handled both the dog problem and his hostility toward Phyllis by simply placing Asta in her arms. That way he would not have to hold either one of them.

Sam Marx, who disliked Peter, commented: "Peter under no circumstances would follow in the path of William Powell, who played it the way Hammett wrote it, an impeccable, smooth, charming, and a very witty kind of man. And the relationship between Nick and Nora in the original 'Thin Man' we used to do through character touches without even hanging on them. You know, of course, the marvelous scene where Nick is half loaded at a bar and Nora walks in and says to the bartender, 'How many has he had, Joe?' And Joe says, 'Six.' And she says, 'Set 'em up!'

"And there's a scene in which they're having a spat, or she says to him that they might get killed and he has to be on guard because he's going into a dangerous place. And he says, 'Well, you won't be a widow long. Not with your money.'

"Now that was the spirit of the original Nick and Nora. But

Peter went completely opposite. He was content to wear a soiled sweater. He had no particular feeling for character.

"One of my most disappointing moments [happened] when we were making that series, because I could see it beginning to go down the drain. It was going down the drain because he was so adamantly in charge himself.

"An example of that was when my office was maybe twenty-five yards away from him in a different building. And every week, when the scripts came in, he only read his part, I'm convinced. If he didn't think he had a big enough part, or if he didn't like what he was going to do, he didn't call me. I'm the executive producer. We had a producer named Ben Star who more or less knew what he was doing, but he was also a writer, and Peter would call . . . Joe Kennedy in Florida and say, 'Daddy-in-law, I don't like next week's script.'

"Daddy-in-law would call Joe Vogel, who was president of MGM in New York, and I assume that fathers of presidents only talk to presidents. So Joe Vogel, president of MGM, would then call Bud Berry, who was in charge of sales, distribution, and everything else, and was actually president of MGM TV in New York. And Joe Kennedy would say to Joe Vogel, 'Peter doesn't like next week's script.'

"Joe Vogel would call Bud Berry and Bud Berry would call me, twenty-five yards away from Peter Lawford, to say, 'Peter doesn't like next week's script.' And that went on all the time. That was one of the problems of making the Thin Man series."

Sam Marx explained other incidents of conflict he had with Peter during the filming. "Phyllis Kirk was well aware that there were deficiencies in the series, and we often talked about it. And then I made a suggestion. One of the most respected directors at the studio (MGM), a dear friend of mine, was curious about the workings of television and I knew it. So I went to see him in his office and I asked if he would mind coming down and talking with me, with Ben Star, the producer, with Peter, with Phyllis, and at that time we had a director named Don Weiss doing the show that was current, with the idea of discussing the characters of Nick and Nora Charles.

"It never occurred to me that anybody would not like George Cukor to come down. Peter flatly refused to allow it. And when I said he had no choice, he said, 'Yes, I do. The minute Mr. Cukor walks on this set, I walk off.' And he did. And he took Don Weiss with him. I never spoke to Don Weiss again, and that was the beginning of my ongoing hostility toward Peter Lawford. It was utterly insane, in my estimation, and Phyllis joins me in that, I'm sure, not to be willing to listen to a man of that caliber talking about only things that can be to your own benefit and best interest. He walked off the set."

Marx then added: "When you've got a recalcitrant leading man who stands back and says, 'My brother-in-law is president of the United States and you're not going to tell me what I'm going to do,' you're finished."

Speaking of the Thin Man television series, Marx said, "Phyllis was a very liberal-minded lady, and knew men like Mort Sahl, who was kind of a rebellious comic against the establishment, and some of the Negroes . . . blacks . . . who were prominent in those days, were friends of hers and would come on the set. And I used to get ridiculous kinds of phone calls in my office from some prop man on the picture. 'Miss Kirk has just taken a black man into her dressing room and you've got to come down and open up that door or there'll be trouble down there,' says some idiot. I did not go down, but I talked it over with Phyllis and she finally, somewhat unhappily, agreed that rather than provoke trouble on the set, she wouldn't do it again. But it was totally innocent. She was just a bit ahead of her time.

"I can't say that Peter shared that, though later on he hung around with the Rat Pack and became friends with Sammy Davis, so I won't even hint of any racism with him because I don't believe he had it.

"What I do think is that Peter sauntered through, at that time, feeling a sense of tremendous importance because of his marriage and letting everybody know it. He then owned, through Patricia Lawford, the house that Louis B. Mayer had owned on Santa Monica beach [The records I have from Peter indicated that he owned the house, paying the bills from his earnings, not the money inherited by his first wife—AUTHOR], another great sign of success."

John Newland countered some of Sam Marx's hostility by adding: "One of the sweet anecdotes I remember about him is, after we had finished 'The Thin Man' and 'One Step Beyond' [a series Newland helped create] was sold, he sent me a big case of champagne. We were making on the MGM lot, the back lot, number three on Culver City, one of the episodes. And an adjoining Metro shoot was right next door to our set, or the outdoor part of it was. And I recall Peter, who was working on this picture with Sinatra, a war picture of some sort, but their location was right next to ours on the Metro back lot.

"Peter appeared on the top of a knoll, and he said, 'Johnny.'

That was when we were doing our thing and had our crew. And he said, 'Johnny.' And I said, 'Hi, Peter.'

"He said, 'Frank wants me to tell you something. Could you be a little quieter over on this set?'

"I said, 'Tell Frank to go fuck himself, Peter.' Then I forgot all about it."

At the time this was taking place, the press was filled with stories about Sinatra's mob connections. The entertainer was friends with men who were identified as being involved with organized crime. However, the implication was that somehow Sinatra, himself, was capable of ordering the murders of anyone he wanted. It was an example of character assassination by some of the writers who discussed Sinatra, yet it was believed by many of the workers on the set. Thus, Newland's comment, when overheard by some of the crew, was taken as foolhardy, though they knew it was a joke on the director's part.

Half an hour went by, Newland directing, when suddenly he noticed that the set had become quiet. It was as though an angry, violent presence had come into their midst, a presence that might lash out at anyone on the set with a force that would be terrifying to behold. Newland turned in the direction the crew was looking and saw Peter standing with Sinatra, the two of them looking down like avenging angels. Sinatra, his voice ominous, said, "John, I got your message."

And then Newland and the crew realized that there was a smile on Sinatra's face and a twinkle in his eyes. He found both Newland's comment and the reaction of everyone around quite funny. As Newland explained, "It was just a total delivery of charm and humor."

Later, unrelated to either the television series or the incident with Newland, Sinatra was to provide an important link in the show business connection that helped Jack Kennedy succeed in his campaign for president. Unlike Peter, whose interest in politics was not particularly intense before he married into the Kennedy family, Sinatra had been involved ever since the period when he met Franklin Roosevelt with Toots Shor.

Roosevelt had been criticized for spending any time at all with Sinatra. Republicans accused Roosevelt of ignoring the death and danger in Germany by entertaining so controversial a figure. Yet the few minutes that were spent with the singer hardly represented either a national crisis or a dereliction of duty. Still, Sinatra was undoubtedly annoyed with the reaction and pleased with the president. He donated $5,000 to the Roosevelt reelection campaign and made recordings on behalf of the Democratic National Committee.

"I'd just like to tell you what a great guy Roosevelt is," he was quoted as saying. "I was a little stunned when I stood alongside him. I thought, 'Here's the greatest guy alive today and here's a little guy from Hoboken shaking his hand.' He knows about everything—even my racket."

Sinatra was a dedicated Democrat, so it was natural for him to support Senator John Kennedy when Kennedy decided to run against Richard Nixon for president. The fact that he was friendly with the Lawfords added to the appeal, but Sinatra had a strong interest in politics of many years' duration.

Sinatra's backing was all the more memorable because he mobilized show business personnel for a type of support that had never been seen before. In addition, around the time that Peter, Sinatra, Sammy Davis, Joey Bishop, and Dean Martin were making *Ocean's 11*, they also formed one of the most publicized groups of entertainers of their day, a group called the Clan and misnamed the Rat Pack. They would later work together on other projects, especially *Soldiers Four*, a remake of the movie *Gunga Din*.

The "real" Rat Pack, as longtime Hollywood personalities state with great vehemence, was the Holmby Hills Rat Pack formed by Humphrey Bogart and Lauren Bacall. Frank, who lived in the area, was a part of this group. They also had Judy Garland during the period when she was married to Sid Luft, Nathaniel Benchley, agent Irving "Swifty" Lazar, actor David Niven, restaurant owner Mike Romanoff, and a couple of others. Bogart once commented that the group was created "for the relief of boredom and the perpetuation of independence. We admire ourselves and don't care for anyone else." They also found the Rat Pack a delightful way to justify drinking, bad jokes, and late nights.

Oddly, the Holmby Hills Rat Pack was severely criticized by other entertainers. Many of them resented its members' liberal attitudes, which made them supporters of the Democrats (and also suspect because of the McCarthy hearings investigating Communists and Communist sympathizers). The fact that the Rat Pack came to an end in 1956 after Bogart's throat cancer was diagnosed was of no concern to the public. The Holmby Hills Rat Pack was dead; long live the Clan, who became the new Rat Pack.

There were other differences between the two groups. The Rat Pack had been a private group, and the antics of its members had been personal. Typical of Sinatra's humor was arranging to have a plasterer go to Lazar's apartment when the agent was at work. The plasterer put up a drywall over the entrance to Lazar's closet so that when Swifty returned home he would be unable to get to his clothing.

The Clan's practical jokes were usually played out for an audience, even if that audience consisted of the members of the cast and crew of a film in production. It was also less creative, including setting off firecrackers on the set of *Ocean's 11* in order to be disruptive in play.

Ocean's 11 was the story of a group of World War II vets who decide to simultaneously rob several Las Vegas casinos. They cut off the electricity and successfully take the money. The script was so good and the idea so workable at that time that Jack Warner joked that he didn't want to make the movie, he wanted to pull the job.

The movie was filmed in Las Vegas, a situation that enabled several of its stars to obtain jobs performing at the Sands Hotel each night. The experience was described by Joey Bishop, the writer who created the comedy that was far funnier and more sophisticated than the practical jokes. He was discussing the nightclub act, a medium where Peter, despite a love for performing and some experience onstage, was not at home. His world was film, and this created a minor problem.

"Originally we were supposed to draw straws. The one with the shorter straw was supposed to perform that night [while working on the film set during the day]. I drew it, prearranged, the first night, but the guys jumped up onstage and that's when we started to have so much fun. But the people were under the impression that there was going to only be one [of us] each night.

"The joke around was, the loser . . . at the crap tables says, 'With my luck, I'll go see the show and Peter Lawford will be the headliner.'

"Peter was a little ill at ease in it [the Las Vegas shows]. Working with Durante, you're playing straight. But here you're onstage with three guys, two who could sing very well. The third guy sings great, does impressions, and dances, and I did comedy. There was no identification with Peter Lawford.

"I remember he did a number with Sammy—'Shall we dance? Shall we lay down some leather, shall we dance?'—which I always thought was unfair. And I realized how unfair it was later when I did *Sugar Babies* and I had to dance with Ann Miller.

"I imagine Peter knew how to dance because he was in all those movie musicals. But it was the kind of number in which, if he made mistakes, it was all right.

"I always thought that Peter felt uncomfortable in that. Everybody had an attitude in it [the nightclub act] except Peter.

"I remember I told Dean one night, 'Pick up Sammy Davis in your arms and say, "I want to thank the B'nai B'rith for this trophy." That was the attitude. Sammy was black and Jewish, so he had an attitude.

"I had an attitude that was one of not belonging. I remember one time . . . I don't know where I had the nerve . . . I told Frank, 'Stop singing and tell people about the good work the Mafia does.'

"I remember years ago there was a guy, Richard Gehman, wrote a book called *The Rat Pack*. And in chapter four, the first line that he wrote was 'The only guy who can tell Sinatra off and get away with it is Joey Bishop.' He neglected to say 'humorously.'

"Those were the kinds of things I did. I was the underdog who had nothing to lose. I was the guy who never fought more than a four-rounder that decides he's going to fight for a title. And then he uses all of the false bravado to get him into the ring. That's more the feeling I had.

"As a matter of fact, it worked so well, we did a number called 'The Birth of the Blues' and I did the bridge: 'From the whipporwill'—I have no voice at all. I explained that only Jewish dogs can hear me—'From the whipporwill, high on the hill . . .' and that's as far as I got and they chased me off. The audience actually stamped their feet, saying 'We want Joey back.' And I'd come out as though I didn't care to come back on that stage.

"My attitude was that the only reason I was in the show was that they needed a big name and I promised them I would help them. But I don't want to be with them forever. And I said, 'As a matter of fact, to show you how gracious I was, outside, on the marquee, I put my name on the bottom.'

"I looked like I didn't belong, but was aware of the fact that I didn't belong and tried to act like I belonged. And it worked great. It was a great, great attitude.

"What was great about Peter Lawford or Frank or Sammy or Dean, was that whatever line I thought of at the spur of the moment, they never questioned it.

"One time when Dean was singing—we were always wearing tuxedos—I said to the others,' I think it would be very funny if we all three took off our pants, folded them neatly over our arms, and walked across stage behind Dean while he's singing and pretend we're discussing business. It was one of the biggest laughs!

"Peter was very gracious to me. I remember that I was the master of ceremonies for the inaugural. Even though I was the least known of the group, I was treated as an equal and that always felt good to me.

"I remember one time in Miami Beach, we were going down to the Fontainbleu for Elvis Presley's first show out of the army. And the accommodations were, everybody had a suite on the fifteenth floor, and they gave me a room on the seventh floor. But Frank didn't know it, so he said to Peter, assuming I was also on the fifteenth floor, 'Run down the hall and get Joey. I want to rehearse something.'

"So Peter said, 'Joey's not on the fifteenth floor. He's on the seventh floor.'

"Frank said, 'What's he doing on the seventh floor?'

"Peter said, 'They gave him a room [there].'

"So Frank called up and said, 'If Joey Bishop is not in a suite on the fifteenth floor within five minutes, there'll be no show tonight.'

"I don't know this. I'm in my room, writing some material. Six bellhops came running in. They didn't take out my clothes. They took out the drawers in it with the hangers and everything. I thought the place was on fire. And I found out where I was going.

"I remember one time when I got a call from Peter Lawford. He said, 'I want you to come down to Malibu.' He had a home down there. He said, 'I just signed with the best manager and I want you to sign with him, too.'

"So I said, 'I do have a manager.'

"He said, 'Joey, this is your chance of a lifetime. Listen to me and do like I'm telling you.'

"So I said, 'Okay.' And I went down there.

"The manager was John F. Kennedy. He wanted me to come by the house. He was there with Pat. John Kennedy was in the ocean. . . . He said, 'He's in the water now.' I didn't know it was John Kennedy. I thought it was a manager. So I was kind of flattered. It was exciting for me."

Joey was asked if Kennedy could handle his career, but Joey facetiously commented, "No, I needed a bigger person. Someone I could take care of. Managers are good if you can provide for them, not if they can provide for you."

Kennedy's involvement with the Clan meant more at the time than people understand today. Sammy Davis was a black man who was daring to live in a white man's world. Racial hatred was intense, and top black entertainers were relegated to ghetto theaters such as the Apollo in Harlem. Many major black stars of the 1960s were actually in their decline, having not been allowed to perform before mixed audiences during the many years they were at the peak of their talent. They had been deprived of an audience and the whites had been deprived of the chance to see brilliance in a person who happened to be black.

Peter was disgusted as he explained to me that racial prejudice was so great that when he and the others went gambling, Peter had to take Sammy's money and play for him as Sammy directed. It was a combination of bigoted paternalism and irrational fear, yet whatever the cause, the result was great pain and daily humiliation. Men with lesser inner strength than Sammy were often broken in spirit. The first time they tried to break the meaningless color barrier, they were so emotionally hurt that they gave up show business entirely.

Peter had come to accept the existence of racial prejudice, hating it and not fully comprehending how it had evolved. He simply accepted Sammy as he would anyone, disregarding so superficial a matter as the color of his skin, yet playing along with the charade of gambling for him. It was the only way they could function while in Las Vegas.

For Jack Kennedy to be seen with the Clan meant risking hostility in the South. He was not an advocate of civil rights. He was not a man who had ever had to confront the racial issue in his home state. If anything, he was for the status quo at that time. Yet the act of being seen with Sammy and the other members of the group could have cost him critical votes in the South and he did not seem to care. It was a circumstance that spoke well for his character at a time when other men might have just avoided the entire issue.

Jack Kennedy became a part of the show business world after Peter's marriage to his sister. Jack had long enjoyed women in Hollywood, including actresses such as Gene Tierney. However, in 1954, after Peter's marriage to Pat Kennedy, Peter bought Louis B. Mayer's house in Santa Monica. The purchase was ironic because it was the ultimate thumbing of the nose at Mayer. Even more ironic is the fact that it became the playground for Jack Kennedy, who had many affairs in the bedroom next to that of his sister and brother-in-law. Because of his injured back, Kennedy also enjoyed having women in the large bathtub that was a feature of the bathroom he used to use.

Kennedy liked Sinatra; the two men and Peter frequently enjoying the same women. Both Sinatra and Peter fixed up Kennedy with showgirls; Justice Department files indicated that Kennedy's suite in the Sands Hotel had almost a swinging door for the beautiful women who worked in the area.

Frank Sinatra, Peter, members of the Clan, and other show business people became quite active in the Kennedy presidential campaign. Sinatra proved especially important in New Jersey, his home state and an important one for the election. The late 1950s was a time when the industrial Northeast still dominated the nation's population. Anyone who could help deliver the votes in such an area was important to the campaign.

There were many reasons for the intense show business support. One was Kennedy's love of show business. He took great pleasure in the entertainment world and was that best of all individuals for a performer—a good audience.

During the filming of *Ocean's 11* Kennedy once stopped by the Sands to catch the Clan's nightclub act. There were numerous jokes at Kennedy's expense. Sammy Davis was to become ambassador to Israel, a joke based on his having converted to Judaism. Sinatra was to become ambassador to Italy, and Joey Bishop's request was more modest: he just didn't want to be drafted by the army again.

His interest in show business showed another remarkable facet of John Kennedy, one that Peter and I often remarked about. It was impossible to imagine President Eisenhower acting like the average man, having a beer and delighting in watching a comedian perform. Kennedy was seemingly active, vital, a handsome, sophisticated presence in American politics. Yet he was also a little like the guy next door or the man who worked alongside you in the shop. He liked to relax, to have a good time, to be "one of the boys." Again, the image aided his career in ways seldom seen in presidential politics.

Other entertainers became involved with the election for a variety of reasons. During the interviews for this book, many female friends of Peter, all of them television and/or motion picture stars, were found to have photographs of themselves with the late president. In several instances they were known to have shared the intimacy of his hotel rooms as well as the platform at political rallies. Yet these were all women who became involved because they believed in him as a presidential candidate. The sexual relationship was a "bonus," not the reason they were campaigning. They also did not brag about it, considering the relationship personal, private, and, surprisingly, in some instances unique. By contrast, women openly discussed having had a date or a sexual fling with Peter, often creating fantasy parties that did not check out. The latter wanted to brag about having had sex with a handsome movie star. But Kennedy's women often seemed to feel that their relationship had been "special," even though they were coldly referred to by his friends as "another of Jack's fucks."

John Kennedy embraced Hollywood, but behind-the-scene rumors indicated that something quite different was taking place. One story had it that Kennedy actually disliked Sinatra, consider-

ing the singer a friend of Peter and Pat's, not of his. Another story
said that Jack thought Sammy Davis was an embarrassment because the entertainer was planning to marry a woman who happened to be white. There were even stories that Joe Kennedy was
trying to end the entertainment world relationships his son had
developed to ensure that the election would be won. Yet "according to Peter" none of the rumors were true.

What was not discussed, and it was to be an important aspect in
Peter's life, was the attitude of Bobby Kennedy during this period. Bobby was the ruthless brother, the one driven by causes
and the desire for personal power. He was pragmatic, tackling the
Teamsters Union and its president, Jimmy Hoffa, only after
being shown by friends that a major cause would help him with
his career. He had worked with Senator Joseph McCarthy, a
potential blight on his record despite the fact that his work had
been sincere and his reports accurate. With the publication of his
book, *The Enemy Within*, he established himself as a foe of organized crime.

Bobby was also a moralist who worked hard to both slow his
brother's womanizing and keep it from becoming common knowledge. The stories of Bobby sharing women with his brother make
for compelling reading. They also are fabrications. Bobby was a
zealot in the areas that mattered to him, and there would be a
price Peter would have to pay.

Many people gave Frank Sinatra some credit for the voter
turnout in the East. This led to comedy routines based around
that idea, such as Don Rickles's comment: "Kennedy's boss—that's
Frank Sinatra—said to Kennedy, 'Jack, Baby, you see? It turned
out just like I told you it would. Listen, Jack, Baby, now about
Italy.' "

Another problem was that Sinatra's world was primarily nightclubs. Peter performed, both with Jimmy Durante and with the
Clan, but club work was a minor part of his career. Thus, he was
considered relatively "untainted" by the people who ran such
establishments, many of whom had ties with organized crime.

Sinatra's friends were often accused of being either members of
the Mafia or involved with underworld activities. Even those who
were completely honorable, such as Jack Entratter, who ran the
Sands, had a brother who had been murdered during the period
just after Prohibition.

More important, no matter what else they might be, many of
Sinatra's friends were colorful characters whom Sinatra enjoyed.
So long as they were not convicted criminals, the charges against
them were unproven allegations. Yet their business activities were

well known in the Justice Department, and when Bobby Kennedy became attorney general he was determined to avoid having his brother's name linked with gangsters. If this meant stopping the Sinatra relationship, then that is what he would do.

Oddly, there were occasions when Bobby Kennedy was in Las Vegas, at least one of those times to meet Chicago mob boss Sam Giancana, who was using the name Mr. Match. Joe Naar was present with Peter and Bobby at one such meeting, though the reasons for it were unclear to Naar, who has no knowledge of what might have taken place behind the scenes. Most likely the subject of the meeting was Judith Campbell (later Judith Campbell Exner), a woman who was a girlfriend of Sinatra, Giancana, and Jack Kennedy during the late 1950s and early 1960s. She also allegedly served as a go-between when Kennedy was planning methods to either overthrow or murder Cuban leader Fidel Castro.

Campbell was used by Kennedy, yet she found him to be jealous as well. She later commented: "Jack knew all about Sam and me, and we used to discuss him. He was angry about my seeing him. He had all the normal reactions that would take place between two people that cared for each other. Yes, he was jealous."

But be that as it may. What mattered for Peter was the hostility between Bobby and Sinatra, a hostility that would later result in an incident that deeply hurt Peter.

All of this happened after the election, though. Prior to that Sinatra did whatever he was allowed to do. There were subtle uses of Sinatra, including having him sing a Sammy Cahn–rearranged version of the song "High Hopes." Through Cahn's efforts, the song had verses such as:

> K-E-double-N-E-D-Y,
> Jack's the nation's favorite guy.
> Everyone wants to back Jack
> Jack is on the right track.
> And he's got HIGH HOPES
> High apple-pie-in-the-sky hopes.

The record was installed in jukeboxes in West Virginia, of all places, then a Kennedy aide paid the tavern owners twenty dollars each to play the record as much as possible.

During this same period, another controversy surrounding Sinatra emerged. Sinatra was involved with the television production of "The Execution of Private Slovik." This was the story of the only American soldier in World War II to be executed for desertion. It was a controversial production, especially since the orders to execute Slovik had come directly from General Eisenhower. While Eisenhower was serving out his last few months in office, the movie pointed up what many felt was a blight on his career. The film could have been considered an attack against the administration, indirectly having a negative effect on the campaign of Richard Nixon, Kennedy's opponent and the then vice president.

To make things worse, Sinatra hired Albert Maltz, a member of the Hollywood Ten (writers who had been blacklisted as Communist sympathizers at the time that the House Un-American Activities Committee [HUAC] had investigated Hollywood). Maltz refused to answer any questions put to him by HUAC and was sent to jail for his actions.

Maltz had been blacklisted since 1948, and Sinatra thought that it was time to break the blacklist. The decision was controversial, but Sinatra did not care. He felt that Maltz should be hired and that the announcement should be made.

The reaction was much rougher than anyone anticipated. The *New York Post* declared Sinatra a hero for having the courage to stand up against secret blacklists and groups such as HUAC that had created terror in America. The *New York Mirror* decided that Sinatra had hired "an unrepentant enemy of the country." And the *Los Angeles Examiner* was horrified at prospects that the movie could become a vehicle for Communist propaganda.

Then came corporate pressure. General Motors threatened to cancel their advertising and other companies agreed. Leaders of the Catholic Church, strongly aware that Kennedy was the first Catholic politician to have a chance to become president, urged Joe Kennedy to disassociate the family from the singer.

Sinatra fought back. He took full-page advertisements stating that he believed in the Bill of Rights, which gave him the legal authority to hire anyone he wanted. He claimed that Maltz was the best possible writer for the script.

The controversy was a danger for Kennedy because Sinatra was such an active and visible fund-raiser. Peter was essentially apolitical, continuing with both his career and the work he was doing for his brother-in-law. He, like Jack Kennedy, was essentially an innocent bystander.

Peter never expressed concern, not did he feel any need to take a stand either for or against Sinatra. The situation was none of his business and, in theory, should have been minor. But all the other companies and people involved were intensely partisan, putting pressure against Maltz in a way that no other writer had experienced since the days of Joe McCarthy and the HUAC investigations. It was an obscene blight on Hollywood, the Writer's Guild, the Producers' Guild, the Director's Guild, and other organizations.

Finally, Sinatra could take no more. He agreed to pay Maltz the $75,000 fee agreed upon for the screenplay, then to replace him with another writer. While many commentators unfamiliar with the era or the intensity of the attack have used the incident to show Sinatra's "weakness," the truth is that it is doubtful that anyone else in Hollywood would have gone as far as he did.

Sinatra was sensitive to the potential impact of what he had done once he realized the intense emotions that surrounded his earlier announcement. As a result, he kept a low profile until the July Democratic National Convention in Los Angeles, where he worked to help stage a fund-raising dinner at the Beverly Hilton Hotel. He was able to bring out 2,800 people, including numerous stars, some of whom would later be romantically linked with Kennedy, and all of whom paid one hundred dollars a plate for the meal.

The problems Sinatra had did not estrange him from the Kennedy family, as some reports indicate. Joe and Rose Kennedy used to stay at the Beverly Hills home of Marian Davies. Sinatra was there frequently, occasionally acting as bartender for the politicians, advisers, and others who dropped by.

The only mistake that resulted from having entertainers as a major part of the nominating convention came in not recognizing that some might not censor their material. This was a problem with Mort Sahl, a man who delighted in making jokes at anyone's expense. His attitude was irreverent, but it was the wrong approach for the convention.

The members of the Clan had only heard Sahl's anti-Eisenhower jokes. They knew he talked of Eisenhower's riding to the White House on a white horse. His punchline was that, after four years, the horse was still there but the rider was gone.

But the humor Sahl brought to the convention spared no one. Among his comments: "We've finally got a choice, the choice between the lesser of two evils. Nixon wants to sell the country, and Kennedy wants to buy it."

But nonpartisan humor was not what the convention delegates wanted to hear. Sinatra was angry and Peter was embarrassed.

The Kennedys gathered at Bobby's home in Massachusetts for election night. Jack's cottage had been converted into the communications center, an area where fourteen operators were coordinating voting information in order to tabulate how the election was going. Nearby, in Hyannis, the National Guard was letting its armory be used as a press headquarters.

The voting was close; it was one of the closest elections in history. The electoral votes were decisive, 303 for Kennedy to 219 for Richard Nixon, but the popular vote was only 118,550 apart. Had Nixon taken Texas and Illinois, states that he barely lost (Kennedy's popular vote edge in Illinois was only 8,858), Kennedy would not have been president.

But the closeness did not matter. John Kennedy *was* president-elect, and Peter Lawford had gained both the status and the enmity that came from being his brother-in-law.

5

The Camelot Years

"I used to always cover JFK when he came west to Palm
Springs. We knew all about his girlfriends, but the press in
those days was a little different than they are now. Everything
changed after Watergate. We always looked upon Kennedy's
affairs with girls as a hobby, just like Eisenhower's golf. And
then when Nixon came and did to the country what Kennedy
was doing to the girls, it made it different."

—Jim Bacon, Hollywood
columnist and author

THERE HAD NEVER BEEN A PRESIDENT QUITE LIKE JOHN KEN-nedy. Young, aggressive, handsome, crippled beyond what the public knew, a drug addict, a womanizer, and fascinated by show business to such a degree that his hobbies seemed to interfere with his position as head of state.

As I mentioned earlier, Peter used to speak with awe and horror at the severity of Kennedy's injuries. He had Addison's disease and a severely injured back that affected his daily activities. Though seemingly recovered from his past problems, the man had diffi-culty sitting and walking at times.

The one addiction Kennedy experienced had nothing to do with his back. Determined to be strong and physically fit, Kennedy received what he thought were vitamin injections from Dr. Max Jacobson. This was a doctor whose clientele included many highly respected celebrities, including composer Alan Jay Lerner and singers Andy Williams and Eddie Fisher. Jacobson was given the nickname Dr. Feelgood because of his patients' reactions to his treatments, which everyone believed to be healthy. However, Kennedy and the others came to feel that it would be difficult for them to get through their hectic schedules without those vitamins. They were unusually dependent on them. But vitamins are not addictive, and there should be no withdrawal symptoms when you stop getting extra vitamins, whether by injection or by tablet. This caused some people to check out the doctor, the end result being the revelation that Jacobson was actually injecting Kennedy and the others with both vitamins and methamphetamine (the addict's highly coveted "speed"). Fortunately, the problem with the injections was eventually resolved, and the addiction did not damage Kennedy's mind, not did it affect his zest for life, includ-ing the film industry.

Kennedy's interest in and awareness of the entertainment industry after he became president amazed Joe Naar. He talked of being at lunch with the president and a wide range of guests, including such people as Frank Sinatra, producer Billy Wilder, actress Angie Dickinson, Peter, the agent Bullets Durgom, and others. Kennedy would go around the table, making conversation with each guest, always aware of what they had been doing.

"He knew you personally and liked you. He had that ability to make you feel important," said Naar.

Peter explained: "He was always ringing up, and I'm not trying to make myself a big man by saying the president was always ringing me up, because I'm sure he was always ringing up a lot of people." He said that the president wanted to know what was happening, "who was making it with whom, what pretty new girls were on the scene. His interest was everywhere. He'd ring up and say, 'What's going on? What about so-and-so? Is she really that pretty?' Imagine, even with all the things he had to worry about."

Nowhere was Kennedy's show business interest more obvious than at the Inaugural Gala held the night before the inauguration. Peter and Frank Sinatra were in charge of putting the event together. Their headquarters in New York would be the Conrad Hilton Suite of the Savoy Hilton Hotel.

Sinatra worked the telephone, using his influence to bring entertainers from all over the world. The actor Fredric March was given time off from his role in the film *The Young Doctors* to participate, after a call to the film's producer, Stuart Millar. Helen Traubel was being brought in to close the show. There would be Ella Fitzgerald, flying in from Australia for the event. Conductor/composer Leonard Bernstein would be on hand, along with singer/dancer/actor Gene Kelly, who was flying in from Switzerland. Eleanor Roosevelt, widow of the late president, comedian Joey Bishop, poet Carl Sandburg, singer Nat King Cole, entertainers Jimmy Durante, George Jessel . . . the list seemed to continue forever, a *Who's Who* in the fields of show business and the arts.

The gala was meant to raise money as well. There were seventy-two box seats being made available at $10,000 a box. Other seats, though cheaper, were designed to bring Kennedy into office without outstanding debts. By the time they were done, Peter reported that $1.9 million had been obtained.

A number of incidents have been reported concerning the gala, the most memorable being one that was widely known and another one that has been rumored. The latter is the more interesting, yet has not been proven.

According to a statement Peter made to me (and the same allegations were made by others to the co-writer of this book), an incident occurred in New York when Peter, Frank, and other entertainers were coordinating the gala. A famous performer, who obviously cannot be named here because there has been no criminal indictment made, was enjoying the favors of some women, one of whom was a prostitute. There were bodyguards and hangers-on present, as was always the case with so many of the famous, and they were not pleased to watch the prostitute begin drinking more than she should.

Eventually the prostitute became quite drunk. She began fawning over the performer in question, spilling her drink and carrying on in a disgusting manner. The performer, not realizing how his orders would be taken, told a member of his entourage to get rid of the drunk. The man did so, allegedly killing her, then arranging to have her body removed and dumped far enough away from the hotel so that there would be no connection with the performer or the Kennedy people.

A check with people connected with New York City law enforcement indicates several facts. A known prostitute was found dead during this period of time, though there was nothing to indicate she had in any way been connected with the incident described. Without a name and something specific about the way the prostitute in the story had been killed, there was no way to say, even circumstantially, that the deaths were connected.

Second, the hotel mentioned as the location for this incident did cater to the rich and the famous. There were several special exits from the hotel, exits designed to be used by guests who wanted to leave unnoticed.

Third, the person mentioned as being the one who did the alleged killing has a history of violence. A driver who worked for him at one time told of witnessing the man badly beating his date, a beautiful blonde, then ordering the car stopped and throwing her out. Peter was afraid of the man and was irate at such an incident, which could have greatly damaged Kennedy's image, even though the president-elect was hundreds of miles away at the time and never knew anything about it.

Yet the fact that more proof is not available, that no direct links have ever been made, and that the violent death of a New York City prostitute is not that uncommon makes the story questionable. So much connected with that period has been conjecture, misrepresentation, and rumor that I hesitate to give this reported incident too much credibility. Only the fact that Peter was there when the woman was drunk, heard the orders given, and was convinced that the murder later took place has caused me to mention it.

The other problem connected with the gala was a natural one—snow. At best, Washington, D.C., is not equipped to handle snow. A snowfall of two or three inches, no problem in the snowbelt regions of the country, could completely paralyze traffic for many hours. The night of the gala there was one of the worst storms Washington had ever encountered. By 6 P.M., most cab-drivers had gone home for the night. Rented limousines were stuck somewhere between their pick-up points and the armory where the show was being held. Buses were able to get through, though, and people were determined to come. However, the final guests, of six thousand in all, did not arrive until almost 10:40 P.M., when Leonard Bernstein led a seventy-piece orchestra in "Stars and Stripes Forever." Master of ceremonies Joey Bishop looked at the partially filled house (only a third of the people holding tickets arrived), mentioned the weather, then commented: "Those Republicans are sure sore losers."

The night was a memorable one for all those in attendance. Many of those—Marge Durante, Angie Dickinson, and others interviewed for this book—were somewhat vague about specific facts. They remembered the joke numbers, such as Helen Traubel's song dedicated to Jacqueline Kennedy, who had given birth to her son, John, Jr., immediately after the election:

> Everybody knows, Mrs. K, the baby is quite a hit
> But if you'd had him earlier, it might have helped a bit.

They also remembered the glamour of the night, the respect, the sense that show business and politics had blended in a way never before achieved. The Hollywood establishment had come of age, gaining the stature it had lacked ever since the first show people made the trip west to entertain miners in the boomtowns of the gold rush era.

The show ended three hours later. John Kennedy went on stage and said, "I'm proud to be a Democrat because, since the time of Thomas Jefferson, the Democratic party has been identified with the pursuit of excellence, and we saw excellence tonight. The happy relationship between the arts and politics which has characterized our long history I think reached culmination tonight.

"I know we're all indebted to a great friend—Frank Sinatra. Long before he could sing, he used to poll a Democratic precinct back in New Jersey. That precinct has grown to cover a country. But long after he has ceased to sing, he is going to be standing up and speaking for the Democratic party, and I thank him on behalf of all of you tonight. You cannot imagine the work he has done to make this show a success. Tonight there are two shows on Broadway that are closed down because the members of the cast are here. And I want him and my sister Pat's husband, Peter Lawford, to know that we're all indebted to them, and we're proud to have them with us."

It had begun. The best of times and the worst of times for Peter.

One of the first problem the new "first brother-in-law" faced seemed to come from the isolation he suddenly experienced from his own roots. The general, a man he deeply loved, was dead, and there was no chance for a relationship with his mother now that he was considered by the public and the press to be a part of the Kennedy family. She had been growing increasingly emotionally disturbed since the general's death; apparently his influence had served as a controlling factor. She was also without funds, living on Peter's generosity. The money the general had always claimed was "frozen" in England during the war was either nonexistent or had been lost to creditors. Whichever occurred, no one in the family chose to discuss the matter, letting it remain what, for them, was an embarrassing family secret.

Shortly before the election, May Lawford amazed Peter and delighted Los Angeles residents when she rented an elephant, had a sign painted to read VOTE FOR NIXON, then proceeded to ride down Wilshire Boulevard. Her bitterness toward the Kennedys continued. It was best explained when she became irate after the president's death, when she was invited to a film covering his brief life and career. Her refusal stated (emphasis and asides are as she wrote them), in part: "I am no longer going to ask for insults. Before Peter's wedding I was invited to lunch *alone* with Mr. Kennedy and later a dinner alone with Mrs. Kennedy [quite incorrect].

"I was not allowed my correct place at the pre-wedding dinner. I was put in the corner alone with a priest.

"My escort for the wedding was a strange man, a Police Inspector, not one of the ushers or the family [which is correct].

"During the campaign for Mr. Kennedy's $100.00 plate, etc., Mrs. Lawford offered me a ticket. She said, 'If you can find someone to let you sit at their table.'

"I invited the children to a small party in the house. Mrs. Lawford said: 'Much too far away. Besides they are flying to Florida in a day or so.'

"Peter has been in this house—once four years ago. Mrs. Lawford and the children never.

"I was invited to visit the children one hour about twice a month by the secretary. I asked the children: 'Do you know who I am?' and they said, 'Yes, your name is May.' I said, 'I am your grandmother.' Both the children said, 'Thank you so much, but we already have one.' I have not bothered them since.

"Old Mr. Kennedy had a stroke. I did the correct thing and telegraphed my condolences. Three months later I received an official reply from his New York office saying, 'Your telegram received.'"

Peter was having trouble adjusting to the Kennedy life style. The family was a closed one in which you either took an active part, as people such as Steve Smith and Sargent Shriver were able to do, or had people run over you. Peter hated the fact that the family's favorite joke was tossing a guest into the swimming pool with his or her clothing on. They found such slapstick funny, never thinking that not only might it not be appreciated, but also that in many instances the water damaged clothing and jewelry, especially watches, the owner could not afford to repair.

The family's life style was also a self-destructive one. Card games went until two or three in the morning, everyone drinking and smoking relatively heavily. Early on in the Lawford marriage, Joseph Kennedy made mention of this fact when writing to Pat. In a letter dated June 25, 1956, the elder Kennedy commented: "In the meantime take very good care of yourself, don't drink too much Scotch, nor smoke too many cigarettes and stay up so late at night. How do you stay so beautiful doing all these things is the eight wonders of the world."

By the time Kennedy was in office, Peter was a heavy user of sleeping pills and alcohol so that he could unwind. He also needed stimulants when working in order to maintain the pace.

Peter's involvement with nightclub entertainers did not help. Peter was an actor, not a nightclub entertainer, despite his appearances with both the Clan and with Jimmy Durante. Nightclub entertainers become accustomed to turning night into day, their bodies adjusting to the pace they have to maintain. Actors, on the other hand, keep hours that would surprise most of their fans. If a movie is being filmed at eight o'clock in the morning in order to take advantage of the early morning light, makeup and costume preparation might begin two, three, or four hours earlier. This means that the actor has to arise even earlier than that in order to prepare to go onto the set. Staying up past eight or nine o'clock at night can be exhausting with such a schedule. Peter, trying to live

One of Lady May's many odd notions was to dress her son up as a girl. He is seen here in 1928 coy and quizzical.

Peter on the left in a scene from the 1938 MGM film *Lord Jeff* with Freddie Bartholomew and Mickey Rooney. Peter later claimed that Rooney taught him how to play the horses at this early age and even had a bookmaker. Rooney is second from the right and Peter on the far left.

Peter often found his father parts in movies playing a General wearing his own attire. His mother was also given occasional roles to play, most notably in *Hong Kong* starring Ronald Reagan.

A scene from the 1947 MGM movie *It Happened in Brooklyn* with Jimmy Durante and Frank Sinatra.

Peter with Fred Astaire during a break in filming *Easter Parade*, the 1948 MGM movie.

Peter here gives Liz Taylor her first screen kiss in the 1949 MGM film *Little Women*.

Photo: Lukomski.

Peter and Frank with Grace Kelly at the Palace in Monaco in the early fifties.

Courtesy Special Collections,
Arizona State University Library

Peter with Phyllis Kirk and their mutual friend Asta. The trio starred in the famous *Thin Man* movies of the 50's.

Patricia Kennedy adds Lawford to her name at their wedding reception on April 24
1954 at the Plaza Hotel in New York City.

Jacqueline Kennedy Onassis took this snapshot of Peter and Jack at the Kennedy house in Palm Beach in 1955.

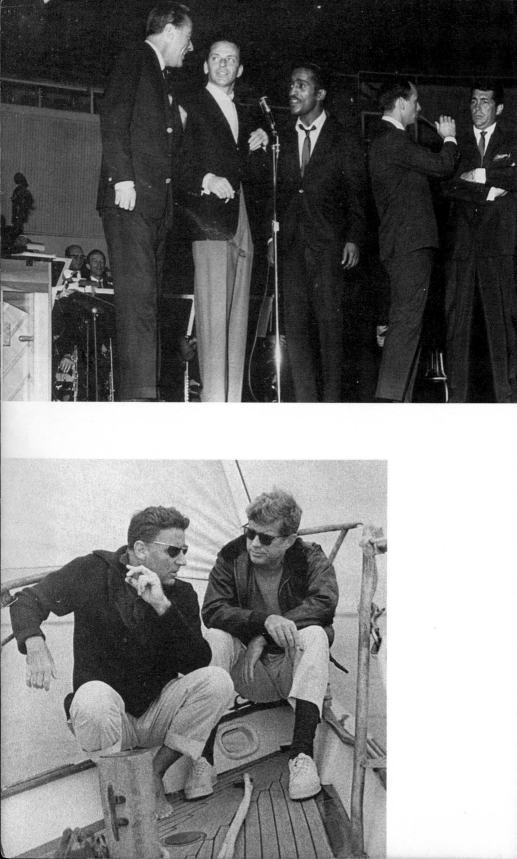

At Patricia Kennedy's wedding to Peter in 1954. From left to right: JFK, Jean Kennedy Smith and parents Joseph and Ross.

Facing page, top: Joey Bishop (second from the right) in a performance with Rat Pack members Lawford, Sinatra, Sammy Davis, Jr. and Dean Martin. Besides giving concerts they were also filming *Ocean's 11*.

Facing page, bottom: JFK listened intently to Peter while sailing off Boston Harbor in 1960.

Facing page, top: At the Old Romanoff's restaurant in Los Angeles in the late 50s. Patricia Kennedy Lawford has her back to the camera.

Facing page, bottom: This 1961 shot of Jack Kennedy talking with Frank Sinatra was taken by Peter at his beach house in Santa Monica, once owned by J. B. Mayer, the head of MGM.

Hyannisport 1961. All the children used to wait for Uncle Jack to take them for a ride on the golf cart which usually involved a stop at the local candy store. The children from left are: Christopher, Victoria and Sydney Lawford.

Peter and Marilyn Monroe at the Cal Neva Lodge one week before her death in August 1962.

Facing page, top: Peter arriving in Honolulu with Jackie Kennedy and children, from the top: John Kennedy Jr., Christopher Lawford, Caroline Kennedy and Sydney Lawford. He went there in the spring of 1966 after his divorce from Patricia Kennedy.

Facing page, bottom: Peter and Liz in the mid 70s at the Candy Store, a nightclub in Beverly Hills. These were the Henry Wynberg partying days.

Photo: Peter C. Borsari

Patricia Seaton Lawford with Peter in 1976 at Pepperdine University viewing a
sporting event. At the time, Peter was on crutches after an injury sustained on
the set at Fox studios.

Courtesy of Special Collections,
Arizona State University
Library.

Facing page, top: Christopher Lawford is on the right, age 27 at the wedding of
Sydney Lawford. His resemblance to his father at the same age is striking.

Peter Lawford Collection

Facing page, bottom: Sydney Lawford McKlevy's wedding in Hyannis in 1983.

Peter and Patricia at a friend's house in Beverly Hills in April 1984 ten months before he died.

between two worlds, was becoming increasingly punishing of his body.

Part of Peter's life style involved poker games at the house. There were several of these, the participants ranging from high-stakes players such as Milton Berle and Ernie Kovacs to casual players such as Pat Newcomb, Marilyn Monroe, and Judy Garland. Some of the people interviewed for this book say that Pat Kennedy Lawford did not participate, choosing to act as hostess, watching from the sidelines. Others remember her playing with them. Whatever the case, Peter was an active, though not very skilled player.

Dick Martin, a director who was then working as a comedian in partnership with the late Dan Rowan, the father of the woman who would become Peter's second wife, mentioned one time when he entered the wrong game. He was in a high-stakes session with Milton Berle and others, neither his skill nor his income matching what was taking place. At that time he and Dan Rowan were earning $1,500 per week for performing. Although a much higher than average income, their on-the-road expenses, the percentages they had to pay to the people who handled them, and the normal costs of living in southern California meant that he could not afford to lose. Suddenly he realized that he owed $800. He knew then that it was time to get out, feigning exhaustion rather than admitting to poverty. He left the game with a debt to Milton Berle, a debt he said he did not think he had ever repaid, even more than twenty-five years later.

The closeness of the Kennedy family was uncomfortable for Peter. Joe Kennedy had once commented that his children were so close to each other that he was surprised they had ever married. The relationship was not incestuous, yet it did not leave room for an outsider who could not adjust.

Peter once said that going up against the Kennedys was like going against a Panzer division. They could be brutal, even in fun.

Perhaps Peter's worst moment came during a visit to the family home in Cape Cod. A touch football game was held, something in which Peter participated reluctantly. Because of the way in which he had been raised, because of his infirmity, Peter was not comfortable playing team sports. His body might be lean and muscular, his skills at tennis and surfing might be on the professional level, but those were solo activities. Working as part of a team, being struck ("touch" was a misnomer the way the family, including the women, played the game) by the others, engaging in such sports in general were all foreign to Peter. Thus, he did not know what to expect when Steve Smith told the others to "get Peter."

Suddenly the "touch" part of the game became "tackle." Peter was struck several times; and the wind was knocked out of him. He was upset, feeling that they had brutalized him because he was an only child never knowing a family in the way they did. He felt that some of them, such as Steve Smith, wanted to put him down, to show him his place. He felt others just considered their actions an exuberant introduction to a "real" family. Either way, the Kennedy family way of doing things was always something he disliked.

Peter felt that in other ways the family seemed to like him and respect his profession. But Peter said that Steve Smith, who became powerful by virtue of his handling of the family foundation, which controls all of their wealth, acted like a school yard bully toward him.

One reason for Peter's hostility toward Steve Smith was Smith's alleged treatment of his wife. Pat Kennedy Lawford and her sister, Jean Kennedy Smith, were extremely close. They frequently shopped together and talked regularly about their more intimate problems. It was during one of these times together that Jean admitted that she wanted to leave her husband.

According to Peter, Jean met an Italian man with whom she fell in love. She told Pat that she was going to leave Steve because she was tired of the emotional abuse she felt she was receiving. Peter told me that Steve had been having affairs, a common situation with all the males in the family, and Jean had decided that she had had enough. She went to New York, packed all her things, and was preparing to fly away with her lover. They would divide their time between Rome and Paris, Jean not returning to the states to live.

According to Peter, Jean left a note on the mantel for Steve. The note essentially said that she had had enough. She was not going to be the martyr her mother had been when her father was having his affairs. She wanted to be happy, to have her own life. She said that she was filing for a divorce and that they would work out the arrangements later.

Jean reached Paris, only to find that the man she loved had decided not to get involved with her. The break was abrupt, and handled in a manner that could not have been colder or more hurtful. She felt that there was nothing she could do except return home, knowing that Steve had found the note. Ever since, according to Peter, they stayed together but Steve treated her miserably.

Peter told me that he would have understood a divorce, but not what amounted to the alleged ongoing psychological battering of a woman who almost broke the pattern of Kennedy wives.

Eunice Kennedy Shriver always disturbed Peter when they had to eat together. Peter said that she would eat off the plates of others. If he was sitting next to her and she became intrigued by something on his plate, she would reach over and taste whatever caught her fancy. It was an action that always frustrated and angered him.

There was more to the Kennedy scandals than titillating stories, though. The fact that the Kennedys were users and abusers of others, both within the family and without, reflects a deeper problem than the arrogance of power. It seems as though Joe Kennedy's children and the men and women they married had a history of emotional and/or physical abuse.

It is no secret that many members of the Kennedy family became serious drug abusers or cross-addicts, as did Peter, who desired a mixed variety of pills, shots, and alcohol. Drugs have killed or are killing a number of family members. Several of them became alcoholics, often breaking the habit only by leaving the Kennedys, as Ted Kennedy's wife, Joan, had to do. The women, no matter how strong and admirable in other ways, have frequently used drugs of one form or another to cope with a life difficult to tolerate. The men have a tendency to dominate others, often using women sexually, then discarding them, to mask their inability to feel, to commit, to deal with problems from their own upbringing.

On a personal level, I had a childhood that helped mold me into the perfect type of woman for such men. I was the accidental child, the child who is conceived when sex is the only neutral ground for a couple no longer in love and not yet courageous enough to divorce. My parents' relationship had failed. My father was involved with extremist activities involving both racial and political hatred. He was abusive to my mother and to others, yet my parents had not stopped having sex. One night they either failed to take precautions or their precautions were inadequate, because I was conceived.

From my perspective as an adult, I can understand what happened even though I can never entirely forgive the abusiveness I experienced when I was still a helpless child. Neither my mother nor my father ever enjoyed the riches that come from loving and nurturing a child. I was conceived in bed, a neutral corner, a simple "fuck" enjoyed only because it meant that they were not battering at each other with their words. I was not a love child. I was not planned. I was no one's joy and both parties' reminder that they had once shared a life, a dream, a hope for the future that proved to be a bitter delusion.

The situation was not my fault. Looking at it from the outside, I would tell some other child to not feel hurt. You can be lovable even though your parents fail to love you. You have worth even though those who conceived you do not wish to have you around. The foolish things adults do when they fall out of love have no bearing on who or what you are.

But the reality is that no one says that to a child and, even if they did, such understanding would not be a substitute for the loving attention needed for healthy growth. I became an append-age, something with which they were saddled whether they wanted me or not. My mother moved to California, and my father alter-nated between New York and Europe. They followed a joint custody arrangement such that I lived with one or the other of them at various times, eventually making California my primary residence. Yet no matter where I lived, I was an uncomfortable reminder of the past. This became even more difficult when they began dating others and when my mother remarried.

By the time I reached puberty my relationship with my parents became even more difficult. I felt that the men in my mother's life saw me as a memory of the "other man," a person to be conquered in whatever way that meant.

The women in my father's life saw me as the "other woman" since I undoubtedly was reaching an age and an appearance that were reminiscent of my mother when she first knew my father. And my father, in his sick mind, developed the need to both love me and hurt me, neither reaction coming from a natural father/daughter relationship.

By the time I met Peter I had been battered, raped, and subjected to incestuous molestation. I was experiencing the hor-rors of the damned, and no one who knew or should have known had the courage to take action. I finally decided that I would take no more, leaving home without graduating from high school (I later took my GED and attended UCLA), getting a job, and trying to turn my back on the sordid past that had almost de-stroyed me.

The problem was that I had almost no self-esteem. Like so many adult victims of child abuse, I felt worthless, unwanted, unneeded. I avoided talking about it, yet I later realized that women such as myself unconsciously project a certain vulnerabil-ity that some predatory men are able to sense. Some make de-meaning demands on us, knowing that we are so desperate for approval that we may go along with whatever they wish rather than risk rejection. Others play on our weaknesses, treating us with kindness until they get what they desire, then dropping us. I had been hurt in these ways so many times that if a man had said to me, "Get on your knees, zip down my pants, and suck, bitch!" I would have thought that he loved me. He would have been the first man in my life to tell me what would give him pleasure, not just take what he wanted, hurting me if I could not read his thoughts.

From what I since learned from Peter, this type of emotional destruction was not unusual among the women who married into the Kennedy family (with the exception of Ethel, Robert's wife) or, in many instances, who were involved with the Kennedy men. Some had been physically abused in the past. Others were emotionally battered, though they did not often realize it. Their fathers might have been domineering, alcoholic, emotionally abusive, distant and aloof, or almost anything else that was destructive because the children did not feel loved. But whatever the specific circumstances, we shared a common bond.

Peter, because of his own childhood, slipped nicely into a dual role of abuser and abused during this period. He allowed himself to be subjected to activities that he found demoralizing and humiliating. He accepted the role of an outsider, bearing his pain without letting Pat see the extent of his vulnerability. At the same time, he played out the role that Joe Kennedy had played. He sexually indulged himself, never commiting fully to the woman for whom he expressed love.

Peter's attitude toward Pat Kennedy probably saved her some of the emotionally shattering sexual requests Peter made of me. Her Catholic upbringing, her nightly prayers, and her other acts of devotion were unnerving for him. They had not had sex before their marriage, Pat probably being a virgin. He could not reveal to her that he liked to be restrained and abused. He could not show her that intercourse gave him less pleasure than sensual experiences involving less physical and emotional commitment. He could not tell her that he wanted to see two women fondling each other, then having oral sex with him. These were both the high points of his sexual pleasure and the dirty little secrets about which he felt uncomfortable. During the Kennedy years he had to seek their satisfaction outside the home, a fact that destroyed his marriage by the time Jack Kennedy was in his second year in office.

Peter found a kindred spirit in Jack Kennedy, a man who had no respect for a woman's emotions and who delighted in the idea of trying anything sexually. He liked oral sex because it freed him to do other things, allegedly including reading while the woman was "servicing him." This was also true of Jack's youngest brother, Ted, though he lacked the style and discretion necessary to hide the women from his wife, family, and the press.

I am bothered by the idea that Peter was, at times, the procurer of women for his brother-in-law, a true statement people do not wish to face. Kitty Kelley claimed in her book on Sinatra that Peter felt that Frank Sinatra was the pimp for Kennedy and he, Peter, was the procurer for Sinatra. I doubt that Peter felt this way and I doubt that such a scenario was true. Sinatra, unlike Kennedy, had no need to hide his women from the press. But Peter admitted to myself and others that he obtained women for Kennedy, a duty he felt someone had to fulfill.

Jack Kennedy was handsome, rich, and powerful, a combination that many women find the ultimate aphrodisiac. Yet he was president of the United States, a man constantly before the public eye. He was given privacy when he stayed with Peter and Pat, yet that was only inside the house. Hollywood columnist Jim Bacon, who covered Kennedy's visits to the West Coast, mentioned a time when he was able to meet Kennedy on the grounds of Peter Lawford's home. The president was going into the ocean for a swim and asked Bacon to hold his sweatshirt, which badly needed laundering. When he entered the water, a photographer went in after him, though the photographer was fully clothed. "There must have been a thousand people standing around, trying to get a glimpse of him," Bacon commented, a situation that was not conducive to privacy.

Peter was in a position to arrange for meetings where Kennedy could have privacy with a woman. If the woman was in show business, such as Marilyn Monroe, it was easy for Peter to travel with her or be seen with her. Two actors out together implied business, especially if there was no hint of an intimate relationship. Thus, Peter could obtain the women, help them enter either his own home or some other rendezvous location, then discreetly step aside when Kennedy arrived.

This is not to say that there weren't women in the White House, including aides, longer-term girlfriends such as Judith Campbell (Exner), and casual acquaintances. Memoirs by former White House employees and statements made by Secret Service agents who had been assigned to the capital all report numerous women. Usually these affairs occurred when Jackie was away, though that was not always the situation. At least once, Kennedy was caught quite literally with his pants down by his wife. But on the road, especially in the Los Angeles area, Kennedy needed someone to help, and Peter provided the favor.

It is not difficult to understand why Peter agreed to provide the women. One reason that Peter discussed was the fact that he genuinely loved Jack Kennedy as a brother. They were friends in a way Peter never shared with any other man except Joe Naar.

A second reason, which I always suspected, was that Peter might have done it to spite Bobby Kennedy. Peter hated Bobby, a pragmatic moralist who was constantly trying to shield Jack from exposure for what he was. Bobby was the one to stop affairs, to play the heavy with women even before Jack had had his "three different ways" with them. Bobby was the preserver of the image, the myth, that White House Jack was having too much fun to take entirely seriously. Constantly fulfilling Jack's desire for girls with whom to have sex might have been Peter's way of tweaking Bobby's nose, something that would have given him great pleasure.

A third possible reason was an emotional one. Peter sold his soul to the Kennedys. They seemed to break whatever spirit he had when it came to friends and lovers. It was as though, once he decided to gain their favor, he feared losing it. He could not say no to their desires.

Peter's divorce did not end his Kennedy connections. He had children: a son, Christopher, and daughters Sydney, Victoria Frances (these two girls named after his father and Francis "Frank" Sinatra), and Robin, by Pat Kennedy. Pat raised the children, whom Peter seldom saw, yet they were a bond that would exist until his death. However, by the time I was involved with Peter the children were in their teenage years or older and capable of independent action. They could live their own lives, deciding what involvement they wanted with each parent. A break with the Kennedys would not destroy whatever relationship Peter had with his children any more than yielding to Kennedy demands would enhance his position. Yet there would come a time, to be discussed later in this book, when Peter was willing to provide me to Senator Ted Kennedy simply because Teddy asked to have "the young one" come for an affair. Peter did not think that the request was out of line, not did he see anything wrong with my providing such a service for his ex-brother-in-law, a man he hated.

The casual attitude in the White House was typified by an incident that occurred immediately after Jack took office. This was a time when Jack was first discovering the true shape of the country, making the famous remark that the most shocking dis-covery he had made after taking office was realizing that the country was in as bad a shape as he had been saying it was in during the campaign. However, this sober-sided evaluation did not alter the fact that Kennedy had just won the White House, a historic site that was also about to become an infamous trysting place.

Peter, Jack, and several of Jack's friends from his days at Choate and Harvard took great delight at being in the White House. They visited the Lincoln bedroom, a room that would go relatively unused throughout the Kennedy term in office except when Jack wished to have a little fun. The men took out some money that Jack would hold and that would be paid to the first among them to have sex with a woman other than his wife in the Lincoln bedroom. Peter was determined to win the bet.

The opportunity to win seemed to arise for Peter when he was on a cross-country flight. He had business in New York but planned to first stop at the White House. Pat was staying at home with the family, and he would be able to play.

There was an extremely attractive stewardess on the flight to whom Peter was drawn at once. He was flying nonstop, first-class, the flight was long, and there was plenty of time to talk. By the time they were ready to land, the stewardess had agreed to go off with Peter, spending the day with him at the White House.

A limousine was waiting for Peter at the airport, his bags already taken care of for him, the service like a fantasy of the rich. They drove to the White House, where a guard stopped the car, glanced in the back, and said, "Oh, it's you, Mr. Lawford. Go right inside." Again the woman was impressed.

The limousine arrived in time for them to have breakfast with the president. The stewardess was suddenly in the middle of a world of fame, power, and money, a world Peter was certain would serve as an aphrodisiac.

After the breakfast was over, Kennedy told Peter that he had taken the liberty of having their luggage placed in Peter's "usual" suite, the Lincoln bedroom. The stage was set. Peter could almost count the money.

The couple adjourned to the Lincoln bedroom, where they talked and enjoyed each other's company. An hour passed, then two. Neither had made a move toward intimacy yet Peter knew the stewardess was enjoying herself. It was time to become more aggressive.

Peter kissed her. She responded, though not with the passion he had hoped. He touched her breasts, her body stiffening slightly though not rejecting him. Then he moved in. If they did not get their clothing off and climb into bed quickly, it would be lunchtime and too late for sex. It was at this moment that the woman pushed him roughly back, refusing to tolerate anything more.

"I'm sorry," she told Peter. "I like you and I'm having a wonderful time here, but please don't try to have sex with me. For the past five years I've been involved in a very loving, very meaningful relationship, and I simply cannot betray her."

Betray *her*? Of all the women Peter could have gone after, he made the mistake of choosing a lesbian. She wasn't just not interested in Peter; she wasn't interested in any man.

Thinking fast, Peter managed to calm her and keep her from thinking badly of him. They had genuinely enjoyed each other's company, and she agreed to play along at lunch, never indicating what had happened between them. She did not know about the bet, but she did realize that, had she liked men, they would have gone to bed together and she might have enjoyed it. There was no reason to further ruin Peter's day by being indignant, angry, or aloof at lunch.

Jack Kennedy watched the two of them as they ate. He watched the way Peter treated her as an intimate, making moves and gestures that seemed to imply that they were a lot closer than they had been at breakfast.

When the meal was over, Jack called Peter aside. He brought out the money he had been holding, gave it to Peter, and said, "You son of a bitch! I knew you'd be the one to win the bet."

Peter never told him the truth.

There were numerous other stories of those Kennedy years, good times and strange times, as a family that had achieved the ultimate public power available in the United States took full advantage of it in their private lives. And when it came to Jack, Peter was right beside him in many instances, a trusted intimate.

Fiddle and Faddle were an unlikely pair of Kennedy loyalists. Their real names have actually been forgotten by many people; "Fiddle" and "Faddle" were the code names assigned to the two women, who actively campaigned for Kennedy during his run for the presidency. They were anxious to meet him, and he had been told so much about them that he wanted to meet them as well. They turned out to be extremely attractive women who were quite willing to share sexual favors with the president. When he took office, he brought them in as secretaries, though their nicknames remained in use behind their backs.

The incident concerning them that remained foremost in Peter's mind occurred when he was carrying some vials of amyl nitrate, otherwise known as "poppers." The drug, which smells like ether, is extremely dangerous, yet used in small quantities it increases the sexual experience. People who like to play with such drugs will take the amyl nitrate just as they are achieving orgasm in order to heighten their pleasure. What they don't realize, often until it is too late, is that the drug affects the heart and respiratory system. (Peter Sellers was a classic example of a man who experimented with amyl nitrate once too often. He took several poppers at once, suffering a near-fatal heart attack. His health was so damaged after that that the drug probably was a major contributor to his death.) Even worse is the fact that no one knows just what his or her body can handle until the drug is tried, and a single dose can be fatal for some people.

Jack Kennedy wanted to try one of the poppers. Peter, shocked, refused to give it to him. He explained that Jack was the president of the United States and could not risk his health for a sexual experience. Instead, either Fiddle or Faddle, Peter never could remember which, was given the drug.

Her blood pressure changed, her body becoming severely flushed. She seemed to be hyperventilating, her eyes closed as she experienced the reaction. And Kennedy stood watching her in fascination, as though she were a laboratory animal being studied under clinical conditions. There was no sense of the possible danger to her. There was no thought of any consequences. Her experience was simply satisfying his curiosity.

The woman continued working for the president. She apparently just accepted his callous action, never thinking the less of him.

Peter enjoyed playing tricks on friends during the Camelot days. For example, there was the time that he, his manager, and Jack Kennedy were flying on Air Force One. Peter was accustomed to the plane and the service that was provided, having flown with Kennedy many times. His manager, on the other hand, was new to the experience.

The attitude on board Air Force One was one of great deference, respect, and discretion. The first time Peter flew on it, the plane did not have Tanqueray gin, the brand Peter enjoyed. The plane was only stocked with Beefeater's. However, they made note of his preference and, from that time forward, anytime Peter flew, his gin was in stock.

The Secret Service and the military personnel understood that the plane was a place for privacy. No matter what might occur, from sex to the use of illegal substances, no one was going to say anything unless the president's life was in danger. But Peter's manager, Milt Ebbins, did not know this.

Flights on Air Force One begin with a careful check of the entire plane. Every section is checked, including the disposal areas for the toilets, to be certain that nothing will go wrong. It is an impressive security display, and Peter said that Milt watched it with interest.

Finally the two men settled in an area with the Secret Service agents, Kennedy in a different section set aside as his private quarters. The plane also carried both the code book and the special box that would allow Kennedy to begin a nuclear war should that have been necessary. In addition, a single parachute was on board for the president, the only person who was considered important enough to have to be saved at any cost.

As the plane settled into the flight, Milt mentioned that he was tired because he had spent the night with a number of jazz musicians. One of them knew Peter and had given Milt a present for him—three extremely potent marijuana cigarettes.

Milt was not a boozer or drug abuser. Although he worked with people who used drugs, their life style was not his. He merely accepted their actions without judgment. Thus, he never thought about the possible implications of giving Peter the three joints.

"Not now, Milt," said Peter, pointing out that they were in plain sight of the Secret Service.

Ebbins, startled, accidentally dropped the marijuana.

Peter, seemingly annoyed, quickly covered the joints with his foot, mumbling "Very good, Milt" under his breath. Then he waved at the Secret Service agents as though to tell them that everything was fine, carefully bringing the joints back to the seat, where he could pick them up.

Peter looked at Milt and said, "What the fuck do you think you're doing here? You just dropped grass on Air Force One, you shit."

Peter said that Milt's hat was wilted and there was sweat pouring from his forehead.

"We got a problem," said Peter, well aware that the Secret Service had seen everything and did not care. There was no way they were going to arrest the "first brother-in-law" while flying on Air Force One. That went beyond any duties of their job. However, Peter delighted in practical jokes, had a love/hate relationship with his manager, and enjoyed watching the man sweat.

"What are we going to do? What are we going to do?" Milt said, frightened.

"You've got three choices," Peter said to Milt. "Your first choice is that you can flush it, but they inspect the shit when we get off the plane." That was completely untrue. But Milt was too scared to think rationally about what was happening. He also had seen the precautions taken before they boarded and had no idea just how far they would go after the flight.

"They do? They inspect the shit?" Milt asked.

"They inspect the shit, Milt!" Peter said, firmly.

"You can smoke it," said Peter, offering a different suggestion. Both knew that such an action was ridiculous under the circumstances, marijuana having a very distinctive odor that isn't even slightly similar to that of normal tobacco.

"Or you can eat them," Peter concluded.

Peter knew that there was no problem. Either man could have just pocketed the marijuana. Either man could have flushed it down the toilet. But Peter was annoyed that Milt had been unthinking enough to bring the joints on the plane. He wanted to upset him by lying about what was really possible. So he sat back and watched Milt put the three joints into his mouth, eating them, paper and all.

Forty-five minutes later Peter was watching an extremely high Milt Ebbins. Peter said that, to Milt, the world had become a wonderful place. When lunch was announced and the two men went back to join Kennedy to be served, Milt was wildly happy. All through the meal, Ebbins was interrupting Kennedy, often spouting nonsense. It was totally out of character, but since Peter hadn't told the president what had happened, a joke he would probably have enjoyed, Kennedy was annoyed with the man's seeming rudeness and strange behavior.

When they were almost finished with the meal, several military men came through with the parachute, code book, and other emergency items in order to stow them closer to the president. Milt asked what the large package was, and Kennedy said, "Why, Milt, that's my parachute."

"Where's mine?"

And Kennedy replied, according to Peter, "Milt, you don't have one."

"How come I don't have one?" Milt asked.

"Why, Milt, if we get into trouble and this plane goes down, they put me out with the code book and the box because I have to protect this country."

"What happens to me?"

Peter smiled wickedly. Milt, unable to think clearly, spent the rest of the flight nervously watching the wings and listening to the engines, concerned that any unexpected noise might mean that the plane was in danger of crashing.

Later, when both Ebbins and Kennedy knew what had happened, the president was delighted with the joke that Peter had played. Peter's manager, though, was rightfully hurt and embarrassed, and didn't speak to Peter for quite some time afterward.

Peter's relationship with Ebbins gradually became an extremely volatile one. When Peter eventually fired him, he wanted to make more of a statement than just changing managers. We were living in an apartment with a balcony that overlooked the area where Milt had parked his Jaguar. Peter went onto the balcony, pulled down the zipper of his pants, pulled out his penis, and proceeded to urinate over the side, sprinkling the car. It was a crude action, but it was typical Peter. In fact, there was a period when we had five television sets and Peter would walk over to whichever one was on and piss on it if whatever entertainment was on it at the time seemed offensive to him. I always knew that whenever Richard Nixon was being broadcast, I had better be ready with paper towels, Windex, and a disinfectant.

Peter enjoyed Jack Kennedy's human qualities. He told me about the first day that the red telephone rang while Jack was in the White House. It was the hotline and would only be used in dire national emergency such as an attack by Russia. Kennedy, realizing what was happening and recognizing that he really had no idea what to do, stared at the telephone, listened to it ring, and said, "I'm not going to answer it." He was terrified of what it might mean.

The problem proved to be much simpler than he expected. There was a wiring problem that the telephone company had to correct. The phone had rung by accident.

There was a time when both Peter and Winston Churchill were at the White House with Kennedy. Peter was in awe of Churchill, who had kept the British united during the dark days of the Battle of Britain.

Churchill stayed on the second floor and had a tendency to be rather casual about his personal habits. He was frequently seen wandering the floor wearing a towel and nothing else. Peter said that Churchill would get dressed while an aide held a newspaper for him to read, turning the pages as requested.

One morning, about 2:30 A.M., Kennedy knocked on the door of Peter's bedroom, awakening his brother-in-law. He wanted Peter to follow him, knowing Peter would not believe the sight that Kennedy wanted to show him.

Peter followed Kennedy down the hall as if they were two little boys having an adventure they knew was naughty. Then, before Peter could see what was going to happen, Kennedy got out a camera.

Suddenly Peter saw Churchill just as Kennedy began snapping

pictures. The former prime minister was stark naked, passed out on the back stairs, cradling a bottle of port wine in his arms.

"Didn't you cover him?" I later asked Peter.

"No. We wanted to see what happened when he awakened." But Peter never did find out because he became embarrassed and left. He greatly admired Churchill, and he realized that his actions had been childish and disrespectful. The fact that Churchill had gotten drunk was not adequate reason for such a prank. He felt shame for what had occurred.

There were additional games on the West Coast. Jack Kennedy delighted in upsetting the Secret Service, because they placed so many restrictions on his life. When he stayed with Peter and Pat, he would frequently find a way to sneak out the back and go into the ocean before the agents could find him. They were worried about his going onto the beach, both because there was public access and because, if he went swimming in the ocean, he could get in trouble and drown. Yet he felt the precautions were foolish and thought it was funny when he'd swim out, then see them rushing into the water, fully dressed, so they could protect him.

Peter and the president, along with the Secret Service guards, would go to a bar that Peter said was little more than a shack. It was called Sip-N-Surf and was the hangout for the surfing crowd. There they would both pick up girls, taking them back to the house for sex when Pat was away for a few hours. While Pat probably did not care about her brother's actions, both because of the way she had been raised and because she did not like Jackie, Peter's were unthinkingly cruel. She must have smelled another woman's perfume or recognized that the bed was not the way she had left it. But this was the period when divorce could not be considered because of the need to have a united family image for the second-term campaign. She might have said something to Peter and she might have suffered silently. Either way, his actions further destroyed what little was left of their marriage.

Yet despite playing Peck's bad boy throughout the Kennedy years, Peter was deeply moved by the White House. He became close friends with Jackie and learned, from her, the history of the building. She was the first person to actively pursue the renovation of the White House, restoring a building that had essentially gone into disrepair. She raised money, located antiques that had been buried in storage, and obtained long-term loans of items she considered important for the history of the place. She also talked with Peter about all of it, teaching him the unusual history it had.

I didn't realize how much Peter loved the place or how many memories it held for him until we attended a dinner there during the Carter White House years. Peter had become involved with a group called the National Organization to Reform the Marijuana Laws (NORML). I remember going to meetings in a building in Washington where the room was illuminated by blue lights, Ravi Shankar's sitar music was playing in the background, and everyone sat around smoking marijuana and saying things such as "We've got to change the laws." They seemed like a group of nuts, and I always wondered what we were doing there, but the involvement somehow resulted in our being invited to have dinner at the White House.

During the dinner Peter told me about the building, including stories of Dolly Madison hanging her wash to dry in the East Room of the White House. Then, as he looked around and remembered, he suddenly became very quiet. I could tell he was remembering Jack, the parties, the history, and the fun. Tears filled his eyes, his face reflecting a depth of emotion he seldom displayed. It had been a time that brought him great happiness.

6

The Monroe and Sinatra Years

"He's so self-centered, when he has sex, he shouts out his own name."

—Jackie Gayle

"Gravity has a way of catching up with everyone." —Marilyn Monroe, speaking about the realities of being known for a big bust line

"Ladies and gentlemen, the 'late' Marilyn Monroe."

—Peter Lawford, introducing Marilyn Monroe the night she sang "Happy Birthday" to John F. Kennedy during a party at Madison Square Garden just a few months before her death

THE TRAGEDY THAT WAS THE END OF CAMELOT COULD NOT have been predicted. Peter had no idea that before Jack Kennedy could run for a second term of office his marriage and his relationship with Frank Sinatra would be in ruins, Marilyn Monroe would be dead by her own hand, and his brother-in-law would be murdered by an assassin's bullet. Two of these incidents were out of Peter's control. The divorce was brought about, in part, by his self-indulgence; but Monroe's death would haunt him for the remainder of his life. Compounding the tragedy was the fact that it occurred just after his relationship with Frank Sinatra was shattered.

The situation that caused his break with Sinatra in March of 1962 seems, at first, to have been trivial. However, you have to consider the fragile egos of show business personalities who have maintained intense rivalries on their way to the top.

The problem began when John Kennedy decided to fly to Palm Springs and Sinatra offered to let him use his home. This would not have been the first time that Sinatra had had Kennedy as a houseguest. During the 1960 presidential campaign, Kennedy stayed with Sinatra, an incident that was so important to the singer that he had a plaque placed on the wall of the room reading: "John F. Kennedy Slept Here November 6th and 7th, 1960." (The dates listed are incorrect, though the visit did occur.)

There seemed no reason why Kennedy would not stay there again. The two men were friendly, Kennedy regularly talking with Sinatra in order to hear the latest show business gossip. Thus, Sinatra went to the expense of assuring that his home would be ready for the president. As his daughter Nancy stated in her book, *Frank Sinatra: My Father*: "With the president coming, FS [Frank Sinatra] added a pair of two-bedroom cottages out by the pool. In the main house he built a big dining room with a cathedral ceiling, made the tiny kitchen into a butler's pantry, and added an industrial-type kitchen. He turned the little guest room into a library but left the J.F.K. plaque on the door. He pushed the living room and bar walls out a few feet and brought in giant boulders and cactus plants to shield the pool area from the adjacent golf course. He redecorated everything except his own bedroom, which seemed small now compared to the rest of the house. He painted and papered and carpeted and draped. Some of this, much of this, he would have done anyhow, but with the understanding that he would be entertaining J.F.K. he had a cement landing pad for a helicopter constructed.

What Sinatra did not realize was that Bobby Kennedy hated him and wanted the relationship to end. This was a period when many activities were taking place that could be embarrassing to Kennedy if they ever were revealed.

For example, Bobby Kennedy was officially fighting against organized crime. He had taken on the Teamsters and he was looking into various underworld figures, including Sam Giancana, a friend of Sinatra.

As early as 1960, Bobby Kennedy was concerned with Sinatra's relationship with the alleged Chicago Mafia leader. He had had special agents look into the question of whether Sinatra had gotten Phyllis McGuire a part in the movie *Come Blow Your Horn* because he liked her acting or because she was Giancana's girlfriend. Bobby had also been irate to learn that Judith Campbell Exner, a former girlfriend of Sinatra, was having sex with both John Kennedy and Giancana.

Peter later wrote about Judith Campbell and the assassination of John Kennedy, locking away the papers. He did this after she had written a book detailing a portion of her affair. But Peter talked with me as though he knew more about what had taken place and felt the desire to record that information on paper, hiding it away because he feared its release while some of the people involved were still alive. All he would discuss about the assassination was the fact that it was Mafia orchestrated in conjunction with a wealthy Texas family who felt that their mutual oil investment interests were threatened by Kennedy. Lyndon Johnson was either perceived as more controllable or more sympathetic and so was not a threat. Only Kennedy had to die.

Was this true? Peter was more vulnerable to a conspiracy theory than the average American. First there was the question that everyone was asking. How could one crazy guy do so much damage acting alone? Yet, in the United States, it is easier for one person to commit an atrocious crime than for a group. The loner is less noticeable and seemingly more vulnerable to being thwarted. Yet it is because we do not fear the loner quite so much that his potential is greater.

Peter also had the trauma of seeing his entire world shattered, again difficult to handle if just one person created the havoc. His beloved friend, the president of the United States, had been slain. His wife and children moved back to the East Coast. Peter was suddenly alone, no longer a part of the glamour of the political spotlight, at a stage in his career when he might not regain the affluence he once had known. It was not easy to accept the idea that Lee Harvey Oswald could have so affected his life and the lives of the people closest to him without some assistance.

Peter also believed that the Warren Commission was a whitewash, though he did not say if he thought that its members were bribed or if the witnesses and experts were corrupted to some degree. Had Peter lived longer, he might have revealed all that he suspected so that it could be documented by others. But at the time of his death, all Peter left behind was the following comments concerning Judith Campbell and one aspect of the Kennedy/Mafia connection: "Judy was a mob moll and the mistress of my brother-in-law, the president of the United States.

"In 1960, Judy, then twenty-three, an aspiring actress, became the consort of Jack Kennedy. What made Judy more than just another presidential girlfriend was the other company she kept, notably John 'Don Giovanni' Roselli and Salvatore Sam 'Momo' Giancana, both members in good standing of organized crime, not to mention the Central Intelligence Agency. This is a lurid tale, and the more one probes it, the more lurid it becomes."

Peter was fascinated by the cover-up of Judith Campbell Exner's and organized crime's connections with the Kennedy White House. He noted: "Out of literally thousands of Washington lawyers, the Church Committee selected a member of Sargeant Shriver's law firm to represent Mrs. Exner." Shriver was Kennedy's brother-in-law, a fact that meant that the Kennedy family controlled the investigation into themselves. And Peter was constantly aware of such matters, either playing along or remaining silent, always aware that Frank Sinatra remained on the periphery.

Sinatra had long flaunted what, for Bobby, was an unconventional and disreputable life style. Sinatra was never a part of the Mafia. However, he was friends with many of the leaders and quite comfortable spending time with them. For Bobby, who came of age with the McCarthy hearings, even a friendship could damn you.

The fact that no one involved with these incidents was so pure as he or she liked to maintain was not a concern. Bobby had turned against organized crime because it was a good issue for the day. It would be an area where he could generate headlines that might help him with his own bids for higher office.

At the same time that there was a public display of hostility towards organized crime, behind the scenes Jack Kennedy, undoubtedly with his brother's awareness, had been negotiating with Giancana to have Cuban leader Fidel Castro assassinated. The Mafia had been involved with nightclubs and gambling in Cuba prior to the revolution against Cuba's ruling president, Batista. The United States had admitted the corruption in the country under Batista, but did not expect the harsh changes under Castro.

Fidel Castro was the son of a doctor and, in turn, became a doctor himself after studying in the United States. He was part of the middle class of Cuba, the group that thought he was leading them into democratic reforms. He was not expected to declare a Marxist/Leninist state, turning away from those who originally saw him as improving their future through democracy. Castro promised a better life, had been supported by the United States, then moved into the Communist camp so fully that Russia was given permission to have nuclear missiles on the island nation, just ninety miles away from the coast of Florida.

The Kennedys felt that the Mafia would be an ideal resource. They had contacts in Cuba and a vested interest in restoring the life style that had once made Havana far more glamorous than Las Vegas. They were also quite comfortable with the idea of using assassination as a means to achieving their business ends.

The Kennedys were obviously playing two ends against each other. They were secretly working with organized crime at the same time that they were fighting it. Bobby may or may not have been bothered by the irony of such actions, but the public image he wanted his brother to have did not allow any connection with "mobbed up" figures such as Sinatra.

Despite all this, Bobby was determined to not allow his brother to stay at Sinatra's place in Palm Springs. He could not acknowledge the real reason, so he declared Sinatra's home a security risk.

Technically, Bobby's statement was true. Access to the Sinatra home was fairly open. Someone determined to kill the president had several approaches from which to make an attack. However, what was not said was the fact that Sinatra himself required security. There were people hostile to him, and the singer had to assure his own protection. The fact that he had not been attacked at his home, plus the changes in the dwelling and the increased protection the Secret Service provided, should make it safe.

Despite all that, a decision was made to obtain a house that was strategically better located. The one that was rented, along with a house on each side to better secure the area, was located at the base of a mountain that provided natural protection from attack. There was only one road in and out. However, there was one serious drawback. The house was owned by a Republican party stalwart and well-known singer named Bing Crosby.

This action showed great insensitivity on the parts of both Kennedys—especially Jack. Sinatra and Crosby had been rivals as far back as 1941, when Sinatra knocked Crosby off the number-one position on the music charts. Peter and Sinatra were in business together. For the president to place Peter in the middle of something that was none of his doing and that could only cause him problems was unthinking and insensitive to the man who cared so much for him. Yet Peter could never call his brother-in-law to account, nor could he argue with Kennedy's request that he handle the matter.

Peter was frightened of what Frank would think when Kennedy asked him to call the singer to explain the changes made necessary by security considerations. He and Jack Kennedy had been joking about Sinatra's building of the western White House. They knew the changes that had been made to Sinatra's home, including extra telephone lines and special communication equipment that would be essential, and enjoyed what was happening. There was even going to be a flagpole to fly the presidential flag when Kennedy was present. Frank had seen one at the Kennedy compound in Hyannis and liked the idea of having one for when the president stayed with him.

No one had ever encouraged Sinatra to make such changes. Neither Jack nor Peter had ever said that the plans fit with the president's desires. Yet no one had ever stopped Sinatra or told him there might be a problem. In fact, neither Peter nor the president ever thought that there would be any difficulties. If anything, Kennedy was probably looking forward to relaxing with Sinatra, being briefed on the latest show business gossip and introduced to new women.

Jack told Peter the truth: Bobby had convinced him that, as president, he could not go to Sinatra's house and sleep in the same bed and under the same room as had Sam Giancana. The situation would look terrible politically.

Peter finally made the call to Sinatra, telling him the situation. Perhaps Sinatra would have understood the image problem. Perhaps something could have been worked out. But the fact that the president was staying in the home of Republican singer Bing Crosby after Sinatra had been a major Democratic party fund-raiser since the days of Roosevelt was too much. He was irate.

Sinatra's anger extended even beyond Lawford. He stopped speaking to Jimmy Van Heusen, the songwriter who lived next door to Crosby and whose house was rented for the Secret Service's use. However, he made up with Van Heusen a few weeks later.

Peter told me that Frank was livid. He knew that Bobby Kennedy was behind the "security" excuse and was the real reason for the snub. Sinatra was irrational in his anger toward Peter, completely out of control, blaming him as though Peter had greater influence than he did.

When Kennedy arrived in Palm Springs on the weekend of March 24 to 26, Peter explained how upset Sinatra had been. The president agreed to call, telling Sinatra the situation and asking him to not blame Peter. Kennedy said that it was a security decision and nothing more.

Sinatra knew better and seemed to hate both men for covering up Bobby's vendetta. He never spoke to Peter again, cutting him out of the movies they had been scheduled to make together, including *Robin and the Seven Hoods* and *Four for Texas*.

And the problem was all the result of Jack Kennedy's not having the common courtesy to make the first telephone call himself. No matter how close to Peter he might have been, he remained just another user of others. He knew what might happen, being aware of Sinatra's feelings and temperament, yet he allowed Peter to be hurt. The relationship with Sinatra was over.

Peter would later become obsessed with Sinatra's reaction. He came to the conclusion that the singer had blacklisted him in Hollywood. He felt that after Jack Haley, Jr., used him in the film history of MGM, *That's Entertainment*, the only reason he wasn't used in the sequel was because Sinatra refused to appear in it if Peter filmed a segment. In truth, according to Haley, he never had any intention of using Peter or any other MGM star who served as a segment narrator for more than one of the films. He wanted the sequel to be a separate screen event with different personalities appearing to talk about the clips.

Talks with other producers and directors in Hollywood revealed that at no time did Sinatra try to keep Peter from working. One producer, who asked to remain anonymous, laughed when told of Peter's allegations. He said, "A lot of us hate Sinatra's arrogance. If that son of a bitch ever tried to keep anyone from working, I'd have hired that actor for that reason alone. And I can name a dozen other major producers who feel the same. But seriously, Sinatra's just not that kind of guy. I may hate him, but he's not so mean spirited and petty as to try to keep anybody from working, except maybe on his own projects, and that's his right."

The break with Sinatra was shattering for Peter. The men had traveled the country together. They had played with the same women, gone drinking together, performed on stage, and been in movies. Peter admired Frank's singing, respected his abilities as an entertainer, and enjoyed the work they did together. Suddenly he was excluded from that world. There would be no more Clan for him. There would be no more playing in nightclubs with Sammy, Joey, Frank, and Dean.

Peter would still play Las Vegas and other locations, but he would be doing it only with Jimmy Durante, who used him for twelve weeks a year and hired him as a guest on his television show. Peter loved Jimmy like a father, yet the joy of that relationship could not ease the pain of losing the other. He was deeply hurt.

Peter could not have anticipated the events he was to face almost immediately after his break with Sinatra. Two more important relationships in his life were about to end, the next one being his friendship with Marilyn Monroe.

Marilyn Monroe was an intelligent woman who understood show business and self-promotion. She liked to dazzle columnists with titillating lines that were never so naughty that they could not be quoted.

> What do you wear to bed?
> Just some Chanel No. 5.
> Is that all you have on?
> Oh, no.
> What else do you have on?
> The radio.

It was great copy, though it was not original. Marilyn used old vaudeville routines to help her maintain a controlled image while being interviewed. She had a quick wit, but she did not leave matters to chance.

Most people focused on her body and the sexy image that she cultivated. Yet Marilyn was more intelligent than many people realized. However, she was self-educated. She kept hundreds of books in her home, including volumes on human anatomy and works such as those by Sigmund Freud. Some of her acquaintances told of discussions where she seemed to show expertise concerning the human anatomy that would rival that of someone who was trained in medicine. Others found her shockingly ignorant in many ways, making jokes that she was unable to spell the simplest of words.

Marilyn was born into poverty, her mother both mentally ill and extremely abusive. She was raped as a child and spent time in an orphanage, where she used to call the woman who ran it her mother. The woman told her that she was not to call her Mother because she was not Marilyn's mother. She just ran the place. That rejection occurred at age seven and haunted Marilyn for the rest of her life.

Marilyn was married several times and had several lovers. Toward the end of her life she was rumored to have taken a new lover every time she was depressed. Since she was frequently depressed, sex became a casual activity, many men becoming one-night stands for her.

Joe Naar talked with me about the time he spent the night on the couch in Marilyn's home. They had been out together and he was too tired and had had too much to drink to want to return home. He was fond of Marilyn, found her extremely erotic, and shared what seemed to be every male's fantasy in those days of wanting to take her to bed. He also knew that she had given him signals to indicate that if he made a move she would happily respond.

That night he stayed in her house, they both acted as though it was completely innocent. He was given the couch, Marilyn going into her bedroom. Yet she seemed to make a few passes at him, and he was aroused by her.

"It was like a fantasy," Naar later explained. "I was lying on the couch and Marilyn was in the next room. I knew that if I got up and went in there, I could go to bed with her. But I was so scared, I did nothing. I just lay there, hoping she would come out to me. She didn't and I didn't. I don't think most men would believe me but I just didn't have the nerve."

Many others did have the nerve, including baseball great Joe DiMaggio. DiMaggio was probably Marilyn's best-known lover and husband. He was considered one of the nation's greatest athletes and she was America's reigning sex symbol when they met in the 1950s. She rebuffed his early attempts at getting a date, then called him to ask him out. Their marriage lasted less than a year, a stormy relationship that was also highly publicized.

Another of Marilyn's husbands was playwright Arthur Miller, considered one of the great intellectuals of the day. She was impressed with Miller's mind and accomplishments, his gentleness, his being totally different from any of the other men she had known.

Marilyn was defensive when asked why Arthur Miller never wrote a play for her, yet he explained that he was not that type of writer. George Bernard Shaw had been able to write a play around the skills of a particular actor or actress. Likewise, contemporary playwrights have been able to produce vehicles for the women they love, most notably Neil Simon (*The Goodbye Girl*, *Chapter Two*, and similar works were created in part as vehicles for Simon's then wife, Marsha Mason). However, Miller did dedicate a collection of plays "To Marilyn."

The latter caused Monroe to comment that the dedication was the best thing that ever happened to her. Then she amended her comment by saying "No, the best thing was when he married me."

Marilyn also briefly dated billionaire Howard Hughes, a man who was known for bedding some of the country's most beautiful women. Hughes became extremely possessive during the courtship phase, to the point of assigning bodyguards to prevent other men from going into her home. Joe Naar remembered one incident when Marilyn had asked Peter to stop by: when he and Peter arrived outside her home, the guards refused to let them in. The fact that the call was social, not sexual, did not matter. They had orders and there was no way that Peter and Joe were going to be admitted.

It is interesting to note that Marilyn always wanted the respect of a man, yet chose men who were extremely possessive. DiMaggio, Miller, and the others were all smothering in their dominance. The first one who did not try to possess her was Jack Kennedy, whom she met through Peter, yet her liaison with Kennedy proved to be the most brutal, destructive relationship she would ever endure.

When Kennedy decided that he wanted to have an affair with Marilyn Monroe, there was no reason why she should have been surprised. She was the most desired woman in the United States. She had been married to a leading athlete and a leading intellectual of the day, so why not the leading politician? What she did not realize was that Kennedy did not want to have sex with Marilyn. He wanted to have sex with the greatest movie star of the day. He wanted to fuck her. He didn't want to dominate her. He wanted her because of her image, not because she was a woman whom he respected. What she was about to experience would be little better than "friendly" rape, yet because of her fantasies it would be months before she understood what was taking place. And when she did, the realization would destroy her.

Jack Kennedy was imitating his father when he asked Peter about meeting Marilyn Monroe. Joe Kennedy had enjoyed the favors of Gloria Swanson, the greatest star of her day. Jack was simply taking on the reigning woman of the screen for his generation.

I think, at the time, Peter went along with the request because he saw nothing wrong with it. Jack and Marilyn were adults. Marilyn was his friend, and he saw no reason to not introduce her to the president. If the relationship went anywhere, that would be their business. And if it didn't, again there was no problem.

Yet there might have been more to what took place than Peter understood. I say this because of what happened later between myself and Ted Kennedy.

There was something perverted about the way Peter maintained emotional ties with the Kennedy family. He had been hurt by them and they had been hurt by his divorce from Pat. His children were being raised as Kennedys and the family was estranged. Peter had great love for the kids, but he neither knew how to raise them nor how to show his emotions, a situation that will be described later in this book. The important point is that he had been broken by the family, or so it seemed to me, his spirit crushed, his morality twisted.

For me, the incident that revealed the sick side of that connection happened many years after Marilyn's death. It was when comedian Richard Pryor set his body on fire while freebasing cocaine. He was in the hospital burn center in critical condition.

Peter and Richard had been friends, so we called his wife to see what we could do for him. His wife explained that there was not much that could be done. He was unable to have flowers or any of the usual gifts that might be sent to someone in the hospital. However, she explained that Pryor had always been a fan of Ted Kennedy. It would give him great pleasure to have an autographed photograph of Kennedy.

The request seemed a simple one. Peter was at work, preparing voice-overs for a commercial, so I took out his address book and looked up Ted Kennedy's telephone number. I had the listings for Hyannis, Virginia, Georgetown, New York, and elsewhere. I finally settled on a listing for Washington because I knew that Congress was in session.

I was put through to the senator's office immediately. An aide answered, and I explained the request from Pryor. I was twenty-two years old at the time, nervous, and not certain what I was doing.

Suddenly I was put directly through to Ted Kennedy. "Hi, kid, how are you?" said the unmistakable voice at the other end of the line. "I hear you're the young one. You have big tits."

I thought to myself, nothing's changed, nothing at all. Now it was Teddy doing what Jack had done all those years.

"When are you coming to Boston?" Ted asked. Not "What do you want? Why are you calling?" Just a question about when I would be in Boston.

"Well, I think you should definitely make some plans to go there."

The more he talked, the more I realized that he wanted to have sex with me. I was expected to go to Boston and service the patriarch. I was shocked, outraged, experiencing something I could not fully comprehend. "I live with your former brother-in-law," I reminded him. "What is your problem?"

But the appeal to his respect for Peter, in fact, an appeal to any sense of morality or reason, was meaningless. He wanted me to come to Boston so he could have sex with me. I was the new Kennedy woman. I was the young one with the big tits. I was the woman he was going to have because he had not had me yet. What was even more shocking to me was the fact that Teddy was in the midst of what would prove to be a serious effort to run for the presidency.

The conversation continued, with the talk staying on me and my possible involvement with him. He mentioned that Chris Lawford, Peter's son, had said that I was cute. He asked about my age and was thrilled to learn that I was twenty-two. Apparently he liked them young.

Finally I was able to get him around to the reason I was calling. He agreed to send an autographed photograph to Richard Pryor in the Sherman Oaks Burn Center. Then he said, "So what time's your plane coming in?"

I told him it wasn't. I wasn't going out there. Then I thanked him for saying he would send the photograph and hung up.

I was shocked and livid. Peter had talked about the womanizing Kennedys and I had found his anecdotes to be humorous. But listening to the dirty little secrets of the president of the United States and discovering that the family reputation was not only deserved, it was seemingly without moral limits, was extremely upsetting. I guess everything became different when it happened to me. All I know is that I wanted Peter, needed Peter, had to talk about what happened, had to try to put it into perspective.

I called Peter at the recording studio only to find that he was in session. This was not an emergency where I could interrupt him. This was something that would have to wait, though admittedly I called him every hour or two, always leaving messages.

Finally Peter returned home, wondering what had happened. He was irate with me. "What the fuck was that calling the studio every five minutes when I'm busy working. I got five hundred messages. What's your damned problem? I told you not to interrupt me when I'm working."

I was livid. "Your damned brother-in-law . . . He's such a beast!"

"What's wrong?" Peter asked. "Didn't you get ahold of him?"

And then I told him everything, including the fact that Teddy had essentially insisted that I fly to Boston to have an affair with him.

I expected Peter to be angry, enraged. I wanted him to explode against the Kennedys. I wanted him to berate their pathetic character, the games they played, the disgusting indiscretions. At the very least, I wanted him to be as shocked as I was.

But he wasn't.

Peter was not close to Teddy Kennedy. He and Jack used to make funny remarks about the way Teddy seemed to mess up everything he did. But now he was not talking just about Teddy. He was talking about the last surviving male of the first generation of children to follow Joe Kennedy. He was speaking of the new patriarch of a family that at times was called American royalty. What a Kennedy male wanted, Peter would provide.

"We haven't been getting along all that well lately," Peter said. "Maybe it would be a good idea for you to go see Teddy."

I didn't think Peter understood what was involved. This would not be some business trip. This would not be my introduction into the Kennedy family. This would be a sexual liaison with his former brother-in-law.

But Peter did understand what would be involved. Peter knew that the only reason Teddy wanted to meet me was to have sex with me. Peter hated Teddy Kennedy the man, yet Peter felt compelled to go along with the head of the Kennedy family. It was an emotionally devastating situation that caused me to feel both pity and disgust for both men. They were both weak, pathetic, and without any sense of morality toward women.

Knowing this about Peter, the story involving Marilyn Monroe can be placed in a more realistic perspective. She was living with the fantasy that every man in America wanted her and that she could have the most desirable among them. Her life had proven that fantasy, at least so far as DiMaggio and Miller were concerned.

Peter and Jack were schoolboys, bragging about the number of women they had seduced. They were cavalier about sex and their relationships. They were also living with the knowledge that both of them, but especially the president, had always been able to have anyone they wanted. No matter how prominent a woman might be, she would always yield to the advances of Jack Kennedy. He had used his cock like a sword, cutting a wide swath through the beauties of Hollywood. Marilyn's prominence had simply elevated her to number one on the Penis Parade.

It is doubtful that Peter believed that Marilyn could be hurt by her affair with the president. She was relatively promiscuous as well as being a savvy adult. She was not naive, but she was hurting and vulnerable in a way Peter was unable to admit, despite his own history of childhood abuse. Based on my experience with Teddy Kennedy and Peter, I suspect that even if he had been sensitive to the possible outcome, Peter would still have gone along with the affair. He would not say no to Jack.

Marilyn was seduced more by her fantasies than by promises made by Jack or Peter. After the affair began, Marilyn was excited by the romantic intrigue necessary for the relationship to continue without interruption.

Peter told me how he used to dress Marilyn in a brown wig, dowdy clothing, and glasses, then hand her a legal pad and pen. She would be sneaked into the Carlyle Hotel as Peter's personal secretary, Peter ordering her to take notes. He said that she used to whisper to him, "Don't do this to me, prick," but he would just laugh her off. They both knew that the ruse was critical to avoid discovery, even though a number of reporters who had covered the Kennedy administration later talked to me of the trick (some admitted that they had been fooled). Marilyn would take notes furiously wherever they went, those who recognized her refusing to say anything publicly about what was taking place. The majority truly did not realize who she was.

The secretary trick was most effective when Peter took Marilyn on Air Force One or some other plane. The public was curious about Peter and focused their attention on him. Marilyn would frequently go unnoticed, no one interested in someone with so menial a position compared with that of a movie star.

Marilyn was given Kennedy's private number. This was a line that rang in the personal quarters of the White House, a fact that reinforced Marilyn's belief that she was something more than a casual sex partner. Frequently Jackie answered the telephone when Marilyn called the president. She brazenly asked for Jack and was able to talk with him despite the presence of his wife. What was said during those conversations is unknown, though it can be presumed that the president's side was somewhat guarded. However, the mere fact that she had the telephone number and used it caused Marilyn to create the fantasy that Jack Kennedy was going to divorce his wife. In her mind, she would be married to the president before the end of his first term in office. Then she would be first lady of the United States during the final four years he was destined to serve.

There was only one public moment in the affair between Jack Kennedy and Marilyn. This came during a birthday celebration for Kennedy that was held in Madison Square Garden on May 19, 1962. Twenty thousand people attended, the entertainment to be provided by such notables as Maria Callas, Henry Fonda, Peggy Lee, Jack Benny, and Marilyn, who would sing "Happy Birthday" to the president.

Marilyn was notorious for being late, including times when she was needed on the set of a film. Some stories claim that it was because of her insecurity. They talked about her terror of not being properly attired, not looking her best. Yet Earl Wilson, the late columnist, once wrote of an incident when his wife went to check on Marilyn after she was more than an hour late for a party. His wife found Marilyn fully dressed but admiring herself in the mirror. She was delighting in looking at her own reflection.

Whatever the reason for Marilyn's persistent lateness, Peter decided it would be fun to use her reputation as the basis for some humor. With Kennedy sitting, watching the show, Peter went to the microphone and announced: "Mr. President, on this occasion of your birthday, this lovely lady is not only pulchritudinous but punctual. Mr. President—Marilyn Monroe!"

The audience, cheering, turned to watch her entrance. She did not appear.

Other acts followed, then Peter said, "A woman of whom it may truly be said—she needs no introduction." There was a drum roll, heads turned, and again nothing happened.

Finally, after several more acts, Peter said, "Mr. President, because, in the history of show business, perhaps there has been no one female who has meant so much, who has done more . . . Mr. President . . . the *late* Marilyn Monroe!" And then she was pushed from the wings onto the stage.

Marilyn stood by the microphone, taking time to collect herself, to look at Kennedy and the audience, before softly, almost hesitantly, singing "Happy Birthday." Than, after the applause, she began singing with more fervor a song specially written for the occasion by Richard Adler. It was to the tune of "Thanks for the Memory," comedian Bob Hope's theme song.

> Thanks, Mr. President,
> For all the things you've done,
> The battles that you've won,
> The way you deal with U.S. Steel,
> And our problems by the ton,
> We thank you, so much.

Marilyn then led the crowd in a rendition of "Happy Birthday" before turning the microphone over to Kennedy. He said, "Thank you. I can now retire from politics after having had 'Happy Birthday' sung to me in such a sweet, wholesome way."

Later that evening Marilyn introduced Kennedy to her former father-in-law, Isadore Miller. She also attended a party hosted by some of the Kennedy aides.

The public display of affection was seemingly nothing more than a show business salute to a president who enjoyed the entertainment world. However, Bobby Kennedy, the family moralist and protector of the presidential image, realized that Marilyn was going too far. She had lost any sense of discretion with the way she was making telephone calls. Soon there would be a chance that the affair might be revealed publicly. Kennedy's image could be tarnished. His second term might be jeopardized by a woman who was, in reality, just another of Jack's "fucks." Bobby was determined to stop her.

Although it was extremely risky to Kennedy's image, during this period Marilyn moved into the beach house owned by Peter and Pat. There were times that Jack would be there having sex with Marilyn, separated from the Lawfords by only a dividing wall. Yet this was tolerated and, seemingly, encouraged.

Peter also acted as the official recorder of these events. There was a beautiful marble-and-onyx bathroom serving the extra bedroom. Jack liked to get into the tub, then have Marilyn climb on top of him while they had sex in the water. Peter would be asked to take photographs, the president delighting in having his activities recorded.

Such semivoyeuristic tendencies on Jack Kennedy's part were an open secret among some family members. After the president's death, as many of the photographs as could be found were destroyed. Since no one knew who had taken all of them or where they might have gone, there was great fear that some might have remained unrecovered. Peter, for one, was not asked to destroy his, apparently because no one realized he had some, and he retained them after his divorce. He did not want to look at them. He did not want to use them for blackmail or to titillate others. They were simply not that important in Peter's mind, and so they were dumped into a box and forgotten. Thus, to this day, the Kennedy family is quite concerned that one or more such images might turn up.

Pat grew fond of Marilyn, being comfortable with Marilyn staying in the house after Jack returned to Washington. However, Marilyn seemed troubled by the affair and the circumstances of her life at that time.

Peter said that on many a night he would be awakened by Marilyn's coming to the bedroom he shared with Pat. She would open the door, then stand at the entrance in her robe. Peter would feign sleep, looking at her through slitted eyes. He said she would just stand there, watching the couple sleep in bed, or staring through their window at the ocean view just beyond. She thought that they were the perfect married couple, devoted to each other, completely happy. Marilyn did not know about Peter's affairs or the fact that the marriage was essentially over. It was as though they were a role model for her to study, a picture of happiness she desperately wanted and was uncertain she would ever achieve.

One morning, as Peter lay in bed with Pat, Marilyn watching, Monroe abruptly turned and, before leaving the room, quietly said "How come I can't be as happy as you two?" It was a statement that haunted Peter.

What happened next has been the subject of countless hours of debate and more nonsense than any other issue related to the Kennedy presidency except his assassination. This is the story of the death of Marilyn Monroe. Even the so-called facts revealed in numerous books have been distorted.

The major story has Bobby Kennedy helping to murder Marilyn to shut her up. The most outrageous of the frequently quoted versions of this story has Bobby and a doctor going to see Marilyn. Suddenly Bobby grabs her while the doctor fills his syringe in preparation for the "fatal injection." Then Marilyn is jabbed in the armpit, where no mark will be visible to the coroner. From that point on, death is a foregone conclusion.

There are many counters to the story about Marilyn's "murder," including the lack of physical evidence. However, the critics all say that such a dearth of proof only helps to show the accuracy of the charges. The CIA must have been involved because they can fake anything. They are the supermen among the good guys/bad guys who are America's secret agents.

There was also a story that Marilyn's body was removed after death, rushed to a hospital, then returned to the house when it was obvious that nothing could be done for her. However, a homicide detective familiar with the scene the night Marilyn died said that the body could not have been moved. When someone dies, blood pools in the body based upon the way the corpse is positioned. Any movement of the body causes that pooling to change in an extremely obvious manner known to all homicide detectives, coroner's investigators, and similar professionals. Marilyn's body, at the time it was officially removed from her home for autopsy, showed no signs of having been previously moved. She could not have been taken to the hospital or anywhere else.

The truth is quite simple and much less dramatic. The easiest counter is to point to the dozens of women who are still alive. If Marilyn was murdered, why not the legendary Fiddle and Faddle? Why is movie star Angie Dickinson still alive? Why was Judith Campbell Exner, a woman who was not only Kennedy's lover but someone who could and did link him with singer Frank Sinatra and alleged Mafia leader Sam Giancana, allowed to live? If there was reason to kill Marilyn Monroe, there was greater reason to kill several others, all of whom are either leading normal lives or are dead, dying of natural causes long after their affairs had been revealed.

So what did happen? An unstable woman was pushed beyond her limits by the unfeeling actions of Jack Kennedy, Bobby Kennedy, and, in a sense, Peter.

The situation started when Bobby had a talk with Marilyn concerning her constant calls to the private quarters of the White House. She was told that she was not going to be first lady. She was not even a serious affair for the president. "You're just another of Jack's fucks."

Peter confirmed the harsh reality that Marilyn was facing. There was no effort to let her down easily. Shock therapy was best for the playboys of Capitol Hill. Tell Marilyn the truth and watch her fall to pieces.

Right after Bobby talked with her, Marilyn went to the Cal-Neva Lodge, a resort in which Frank Sinatra had had an interest at one period of time and a popular place for entertainment figures to both rest and play. There she proceeded to overdose on prescription drugs. Her stomach had to be pumped and she returned to her home.

If there was any effort by any of Marilyn's friends to help her through her suicidal depression, that information has not been uncovered. Certainly Peter took no action toward helping her.

She had been suicidal so many times in the past, always being saved at the last minute, that no one took her seriously. They saw the overdoses as a cry for attention, a chance to be on center stage without going so far as to really die. No one thought about the fact that she was emotionally disturbed, essentially alone despite the loving support of her secretary and housekeeper, and that death was a way to prove her seriousness.

There are conflicting reports of what happened just prior to Marilyn's final overdose. Many of these came from people who simply lied. A woman who knew Peter for a few weeks claimed Peter told her everything about that night, then proceeded to relate a story that contradicted everything Peter said and documented for me during our ten and a half years together. The fact that the woman was paid exceedingly well for the information is further indication of her lack of credibility.

Then there were the private investigators and security experts, the medical professionals, and others. If you could get your name in a book, a newspaper, or a magazine article, if you could appear on a television show, then you "knew" what happened the night of the death. The people who truly knew what happened—for example, Peter, Marilyn's secretary, Pat Newcomb, and several others—simply avoided the press. They had their own grieving to handle. They also felt that discretion was best because they did not want Marilyn abused in death as much as she had been abused in life.

One story even has Peter telling Marilyn, ". . . pull yourself together; but, my God, whatever you do don't leave any notes behind." Such a statement was so out of character for Peter that no one believes it, with the possible exception of the person who originated it. The statement implies that Peter realized that she was going to kill herself and deliberately let it happen, his only concern being the avoidance of scandal.

Peter was not all that different from other men his age. He understood men, could sympathize with their wants and needs, yet had an emotional blind spot when it came to feelings about women. He had no conception of how they might react to something a man might do, especially when intimacy was involved. It was only when she died that he recognized that her relationship with Jack Kennedy had not been perceived by Marilyn the way Peter had accepted it. As a result, he realized that he had been partially responsible for Marilyn's death. It was knowledge that helped destroy him.

Then there is the issue of where Bobby Kennedy was that night of August 4, 1962. Bobby had gone with his family to San

Francisco, allegedly traveling briefly to Los Angeles in order to see Marilyn. There are conflicting stories related to this trip, and no documentation has been uncovered to confirm or deny such a visit. However, Peter claimed that Bobby did come down briefly in order to talk with Marilyn, returning before that evening. Reports that Bobby stayed over with Peter are inaccurate, especially since there were numerous witnesses to the activities of Peter and others involved, none of whom remember Bobby staying in Los Angeles. Regardless of whether he did or did not delay his trip back, and witnesses to the family's activities in San Francisco seem to confirm that he had returned there well before the calls to Peter preceding her death began, he was not involved with any murder or cover-up.

Peter was holding a quiet dinner party involving a few friends, including Joe and Dolores Naar, Bullets Durgom, and others. It was a typical Lawford party: Chinese carry-out food being eaten out of the cartons. Everything was casual. Just a few friends had been invited, including Marilyn, who Peter knew was depressed over having to face the end of her relationship with the president.

Marilyn was despondent when she and Peter talked on the telephone around 5 P.M. He wanted her present, but she would not come. As Peter explained to Naar, Marilyn claimed to be tired, to want to stay home.

There was another call around 7:30 P.M. This one was of greater concern because she said, "Say good-bye to Jack, say good-bye to Pat, and say good-bye to yourself, because you're a nice guy."

This call was upsetting, but not to the degree that might be imagined. Peter commented to one of the guests, "It's phone-dangling time again." He knew that Marilyn was making one of her dramatic suicide gestures, though he had no reason to think she was trying to kill herself for real. He had been through this type of thing with her before, a fact that left him far less concerned than someone else might have been.

The reality is that Marilyn Monroe was a drug addict. That is something many people, including doctors who would like to consider conspiracy theories, tend to overlook.

A drug addict is not just someone who is using heroin or cocaine. A drug addict can be someone who is psychologically and/or physically dependent upon prescription pharmaceuticals. You can be addicted to sleeping pills, to tranquilizers, to any number of "harmless" drugs.

Even seemingly safe drugs may have a fatal dose. For example, suppose your normal prescription of a drug is for five milligrams. You take the drug for weeks or months, then develop a tolerance level for that amount so, either on your own or with your doctor's approval, you start taking ten milligrams to achieve the same effect. Two pills instead of one seems harmless, especially since the reaction is no different as far as you can tell.

The ten-milligram dose suffices for a few weeks or months, then no longer seems to work. This time you try three pills—fifteen milligrams—and again find that you are having only the same reaction you had when you first started with five milligrams. You assume that you are safe when, in reality, you are creating a dangerous chemistry problem.

Suppose that no matter how much of a tolerance you seem to be developing, the moment you take thirty milligrams of the drug you will die. You do now know this for several reasons. One is the fact that you feel no different taking several pills than you once felt when you took a single pill. A second reason is that either your doctor never mentions this possibility, trusting you to not consider taking six times the prescribed dosage. And a third reason is that you might have a conscientious doctor who does tell you about the fatal dose, but because you cannot conceive of yourself ever violating the low prescription dose, you forget the warning.

Over a period of months or years you keep taking the medicine in doses far greater than the doctor knows. Then, one day, you find that twenty-five milligrams is not enough, so you do what has become habit under such circumstances. You take one more pill—thirty milligrams. Then you lay down for a good night's sleep and never wake up. Unless your doctor or someone else knows that you have been gradually increasing the amount you take in excess of the approved dosage, your death may be listed as suicide. You never intended to die. You may have had every reason to live. But because you took more of the drug than the level at which it was possible to survive, you die.

There have been several people in the entertainment world who have died in this manner. They did not understand that there could be a toxic dose of a seemingly safe prescription product they had been taking for years. They thought that their increased tolerance would protect them, much as ancient rulers used to take tiny amounts of poisons such as arsenic for very long periods, gradually increasing the dosage over many months and years, so that when someone tried to kill them with that poison they would be immune to its effects.

Marilyn Monroe was an addict who had increased her use of pills to levels where it would not have been hard for her to cross over to a toxic dose. While she was undoubtedly suicidal during the period when she was wrestling with the end of her relationship with Jack Kennedy, she could easily have taken an overdose of pills without intending to do so.

The other important point about drug addicts is that the drugs they take become as comfortable for their digestive systems as familiar food. When someone experiences simple indigestion, it is generally because the food is not one they eat regularly. The unfamiliar food is not passed easily into the intestines. Familiar food, eaten regularly, passes through smoothly.

The same situation is true with drugs. An addict's stomach becomes familiar with the regularly used drugs. They are rapidly digested and passed into the intestines. The true addict, taking a familiar drug, routinely dies with no trace of the pills in the stomach, according to coroners and drug experts.

Marilyn's autopsy confirmed this. The report read, in part: "The esophagus has a longitudinal folding mucosa. The stomach is almost completely empty. The volume is estimated to be no more than 20 cc. No residue of the pills is noted. A smear made from the gastric contents examined under the polarized microscope shows no refractile crystals. The mucosa shows marked congestion and submucosal petechial hemorrhage diffusely. The duodenum shows no ulcer. The contents of the duodenum are also examined under the polarized microscope and show no refractile crystals. The remainder of the small intestine shows no gross abnormality. The colon shows marked congestion and purplish discoloration."

Coroner Thomas Noguchi, who handled the autopsy of Marilyn Monroe, felt that the findings were consistent with an addict or heavy drug abuser's overdose of a familiar drug. Other doctors, who claimed that the results would have had to have shown traces of the drugs if she ingested pills instead of being injected by "outside forces," were not familiar with the autopsy of an addict.

Peter realized that he should go to see Marilyn, but Peter had become a weak man. He tried to reach Marilyn several times after she talked with him, the line always busy. He lived approximately four miles from Marilyn, yet he did not go over. Instead, rather than calling the police, a doctor, or even a friend of Marilyn, he called his manager, Milt Ebbins.

This was one of several instances when Peter used his manager as a father figure to avoid personal involvement. He did not particularly like Milt, and their relationship was frequently strained, yet he was so weak that he was willing to sublimate his better judgment for whatever advice Milt might give him. And to Peter's relief, that advice seemed to free Peter from responsibility at the moment.

"You can't go over there," Ebbins told him. You're the brother-in-law of the president of the United States. Your wife's away. Let me get in touch with her lawyer or doctor. They should be the ones to go over."

The advice was brilliant. A woman might be dying, so her lawyer should be called? The situation would have been humorous if it had not been so tragic.

Peter made other calls, including one to Joe Naar who had arrived home. The Naars lived a short distance from Marilyn. Joe could easily walk over there and check on her, breaking into the house if something was wrong.

The Naars had left Peter's house before eleven, and were getting undressed when Peter called to ask Joe to check on Marilyn. Then he thought better of it, especially with the comments of Milt Ebbins, so he called the Naars again and told Joe not to bother.

No one called the police or any other agency that might have been equipped to handle an emergency such as an overdose. Each person tried to pass responsibility on to someone else, with the exception of Joe Naar, who simply thought Peter had things under control. By the time anyone arrived who could truly do something, so much time had elapsed that Marilyn was dead.

Could Marilyn have been saved through earlier action? Peter certainly thought so. He was haunted by her death, maintaining a sense of personal responsibility for her loss for the rest of his life. He spoke of that responsibility to Pat Newcomb and others. He might also have led himself even further along the path of self-destruction as a result of his reactions to that night.

The truth is that if anyone "killed" Marilyn Monroe, it was Peter and his manager, who failed to act in a constructive manner. Her death might have been a suicide. It might have been a plea for attention. And it might have been an accidental overdose caused by Marilyn's not realizing that she had taken too much of a drug with a lethal dosage level she had avoided in the past. Whatever the case, her death was *not* ordered by the Kennedy family, members of organized crime, Bobby Kennedy, or anyone else who has been the subject of one of the conspiracy theories. It was a tragic situation made all the more horrible because of the human inactions surrounding it.

Peter was reeling in reaction to the events happening all around him, over which he seemingly had no control. He was seeking regular sex outside his marriage, a fact that greatly troubled Pat

Kennedy. She realized that their relationship was coming to an end, though the combination of her Catholic upbringing and the fact that a divorce in the family could destroy John Kennedy's hopes for a second term prevented anything from being made public. However, Peter had a private talk with his brother-in-law at the White House, explaining that the marriage existed in name only.

Yet life continued for Peter. He worked less and less, though his popularity was still high. The money was still coming in from residuals, commercial voice-overs, and other sources, and he was still in the midst of the good life. In addition, he was doing nightclub work with Jimmy Durante for several weeks a year, an activity that delighted him. In fact, it was while Peter was playing Harrah's Club in Lake Tahoe that the president was shot on November 22, 1963. As Peter later discussed with Jerry LeBlanc, a reporter for the *Southland Sunday* publication in Long Beach, California: "I was working at Harrah's Club with Jimmy Durante. I used to go on the road with Jimmy twelve weeks a year, playing Vegas and other big clubs. It was an act I enjoyed. I danced and sang and did bits with him like 'Accustomed to Your Face,' a fun thing.

"The second show ends at four A.M. so you sleep late. And that's where I was when it happened—in a sound sleep. I remember waking up that morning. Somebody was shaking me and I thought, 'They aren't supposed to be shaking me. Why are they shaking me?'

"The first thing my eyes focused on was an SS button—the Secret Service—and I said to myself, 'What the hell is he doing here?' You know, I didn't have the Secret Service following me. Nowadays, it's different, if you're closely related to someone who's running for the presidency or vice presidency.

"I didn't recognize the agent. He was from the Reno detail, and he said, 'I think you better get up.' I got up, and of course I immediately knew something was terribly wrong. Then he just said flatly, 'The president's been shot.'

" 'How bad?' I remember asking immediately. Actually at that moment Kennedy was already dead, but the Secret Service man didn't officially want to tell me. It wasn't his place to. The country didn't know it yet. If you recall, it was all over in the car.

"I got on the phone with Pat and Harrah's lent me their private plane and I flew to meet her. The rest, it was like a terrible dream. Those days, right through the funeral in Washington, which was like an Irish wake. You know, everybody was up— drinking, smiling, and trying to make the best of it. There were even bad jokes about what costumes we were wearing. Not being Irish, I tried to get into the swing of it, but I was thoroughly destroyed. Looking back, I realize the way President Kennedy's death was handled was really the best way, even with the bad jokes.

"I think John F. would have looked on too much grief as unproductive. I'm sure of that. But my initial feeling was shock and sorrow—the obvious things—and an immediate resentment, yes, against the people who live in Texas. But you can't go on like that. To have taken an attitude that everybody in Texas stinks is stupid. Ridiculous.

"Oh, if you want to dig deep, they're a part of it, but so many other people were, too. Texans weren't the force behind an assassination movement. It wasn't Texans in the Ambassador Hotel [the Los Angeles location where Bobby Kennedy would be killed almost five years later]. I think the violence that killed the Kennedys goes back to the Adlai Stevenson thing, where a woman hit him with a picket sign, an incident like that, political emotion gone crazy. There was a terrible political fight going on down in Texas and that's what brought Kennedy there."

Peter added: "John F. rang me up in Tahoe two days before the assassination—that was the last I'd heard from him—and he said, 'Guess what? Jackie's finally decided to go.' She hadn't been planning to go. She was angry about something. He was pleased she changed her mind. 'Isn't that terrific, we're going to go, we're off,' he said. And I remember he asked when I would be going back to Palm Springs—things like that."

There was more to the Kennedy assassination than just grief for the man Peter loved as a brother. Peter's world fell apart. Marilyn was dead because he had been too weak to do more than call his manager about her warning that she was in trouble. Sinatra was no longer speaking to him, a fact that might not have been so bad personally, but that affected his relations with other men who he admired, such as Sammy Davis and Joey Bishop. It also affected his plans for future films. Then Jack Kennedy was killed, and Pat Kennedy Lawford gathered their children and returned to the East. She was through with Peter, through with the California life style, anxious to return to the familiar surroundings of New York and Hyannis.

Camelot was dead and Peter was fatally wounded. Yet more than ten years would pass before anyone knew it, and even then, those of us who loved him wanted to deny the obvious signs of his unstoppable decline.

7

The Limbo Years

"When I was making *Son of Lassie*, I had my first run-in with the star system. First of all, the dog had a dressing room, but I didn't. When we were shooting scenes in Canada of Lassie and the rapids, they had the dog all wired and roped so that they wouldn't lose him, and I was floundering around in the water with very little protection. Lassie was insured for a million dollars, and I had the suspicion that if I was insured at all, it was for a substantially smaller amount."

—Peter Lawford

THE FILM INDUSTRY WAS ROUGH ON ACTORS AS THEY ASCENDED the ladder of success. It was even tougher when they were perceived to be on the way down.

Peter's friends felt that he went into a decline following the deaths of Marilyn Monroe and John Kennedy, and the shattering of his business and personal relationship with Frank Sinatra. It was not obvious at the time, though there were changes in Peter's attitude and life style. He invested in a restaurant and nightclub. He bought a Nehru jacket and became part of the disco scene. Yet all this was oddly out of character.

Peter was never one to go along with the dictates of fashion. He liked to be comfortable, and that meant going about in his beach attire. Jeans, an old sweatshirt, a surfboard . . . that was Peter's style, even near the end when he was barely strong enough for the surfing he loved until his death. The idea that he would become a part of what was a variation of the hippie scene, wearing trendy clothing and a necklace known as "love beads" was out of character. It was as though the old Peter Lawford had failed at everything that mattered to him. Friends were dead, his career was on the decline, his marriage was over. Peter Lawford's way had not worked, so why not join with the masses? Become laid-back in a room where the decibel level of the music could shatter your eardrums. Smoke a joint, drink some alcohol, look like everyone else, and mellow out.

Jack Haley, Jr., commented on what seemed to happen to Peter professionally from the period when he was gradually fading from the MGM star system through the 1960s. He said: "They were letting everyone go out there [at MGM]. . . . You know, one by one they dropped them except William Powell. William Powell

170

approximately 6 or 7 P.M. until approximately 8 A.M. of the following day.

"2. That you limit or restrict your visits to hospitals, either as a visitor or as a patient. In the event that you should require emergency medical attention, you should obviously use either an emergency hospital or notify the police department.

"3. That you remain out of strange neighborhoods.

"4. That you select your place to eat with some degree of care. Although we understand that you are now having your main meal at the Ontra Cafeteria where you are able to select your own choice of food. This seems to be all right.

"5. That you refrain, as much as possible, from any trips by plane, train, or boat.

"6. That you hold little or no conversations with strangers or people that you do not know well.

"7. That you be very careful about eating or drinking at any afternoon parties which you may attend.

"Basically we believe that the above are no more than common sense safety rules to be helpful in preventing unusual incidents such as those you have advised us have happened to you heretofor. We hope the suggestions will be helpful to you."

Lady May had become a joke to Los Angeles newspaper reporters. She had begun to report unidentified flying objects (UFOs) with such frequency that she was the butt of editorial cartoons. There were stories about her sightings that were written with less than respect. One story, dated March 23, 1968, was headlined CANDELABRA UFO and read: "Lady May Lawford spied a beautiful candelabra UFO at 5 P.M. with sparkling lights hanging all around it before it sped away at terrific speed through a hole in the sky. Mother of Peter Lawford, a Hollywood star. Tomorrow she'll see a flashing saucer."

By the time she died, conspiracy theories were rampant in Lady May's mind. Yet no one had any reason to cause her harm. She was a lonely woman, seemingly without intimate friends, who had estranged herself from her son and all others who knew her.

Peter found work wherever he could during the 1960s. Unfortunately, there was little market for a handsome male lead with a British accent. Friends say that he increasingly was drinking and smoking pot, though not losing control, seeming to put his life on hold while he waited for the movie industry to change. His "type" was out of favor and would not be popular again until the rise of the prime time soap operas. Tragically, that was too many years away for him.

Rather than face the fact that the casual charm, good looks, and

British accent that had made him a star in the 1940s now worked against him, he lashed out at those representing him. Times had changed; the movie industry moves in cycles. Yet, had Peter lived, he would have again found his place, this time starring in the classier soap operas. However, Peter did not live to see that happen and, instead, he decided to change agents.

Peter was then represented by the William Morris Agency in Beverly Hills, the largest talent agency in the world and, at the time, the most respected. Peter felt that they should be getting him work, something that was not happening. In a letter to Abe Lastfogel of William Morris, he told of the work he was getting and the fact that it was only coming through friends. He said, in part: "Since my return from Europe (which has been exactly thirteen months) there has not been even a glimmer of creative or constructive philosophy forthcoming in connection with my future from any member of the Morris office complex. Any activity which I have experienced in terms of films during the past few months came through totally unsolicitied sources, i.e. Jerry Lewis for *Hook, Line and Sinker*, Stuart Rosenberg for *The April Fools*, and Otto Preminger for *Skiddoo*, which evolved from my original deal with David Picker and United Artists.

"The area of television has been good what with the usual guest shots for buddies such as Jerry Lewis, Carol Burnett, Rowan and Martin, etc. and four very exciting nights when I guest hosted for Johnny Carson which was David Tebet's notion and I must say came off quite well.

"I bore you with the aforementioned data simply to illustrate where 'it's at' and from whence the bread is coming! In view of all the facts which I have stated and my position today which has been considerably strengthened since my first letter to you, I feel the desperate need for the help and benefits of an imaginative force to work for me and with me. Therefore, I have made the only decision left open to me (and as you are well aware it has not been a hasty one) to move on to other fields—perhaps a little greener with interest.

"Dear Abe, please know how fond I am of you and there are many moments that I will cherish from my long association but I must, in closing, gently say to you that your Motion Picture Department sorely needs a refresher course in selling!"

Peter's guest television appearances included several on "Laugh In," which followed a new and different concept for the time. It was a cross between vaudeville, the old Ziegfield Follies, brief sketches, and one-liner monologues. There were regulars, including such talent as Goldie Hawn and Lily Tomlin who would go on to become major stars in their own right, and there were guest stars, including national politicians. The hosts of the show were comedians Dan Rowan and Dick Martin, and Peter was asked to be a guest. It was there that he met Dan's daughter, Mary Rowan, who had the minor role of a dancer in one of the ongoing production numbers.

Peter and Mary Rowan fell in love. It was 1971, and Peter was almost fifty to Mary's twenty-two years. But he was not marrying her for her youth. A reading of the correspondence that Peter saved indicated that he truly adored her, a fact confirmed by his friends. However, Peter's life style involved odd hours, intense drug use, and companions who liked Peter because he had greater access to cocaine and other stimulants than they did. Three years later he and Mary were divorced, though Peter felt that he hid his problems well during this time. He would later write: "I remarried in 1971 to a lovely girl many years my junior. We were very happy for about three years and then I'm afraid she got restless, needed her own 'space' and had to leave me. So there I was, alone again."

Much of Peter's time was spent with friends around the world. His income was on the decline, but he was still working and able to afford his life style until his drug habit became too expensive in his last few years.

Many of his friends were experiencing their own crises. Elizabeth Taylor, one of his closest friends, was fighting drink, pills, and weight gain. Her lover and two-time husband, Richard Burton, was in danger of dying from alcohol. Members of rock bands Peter "adopted" to share drugs with him were having difficulty handling their own success. And all of them were behaving in ways that were raucous, riotous, and/or tragic.

For example, there was the time Peter went to Elizabeth's home in Gstaad, Switzerland, to spend Christmas with Elizabeth and Richard. This was the early 1970s, and Elizabeth realized that Richard, an alcoholic, was drinking too much. His liver was in danger of being destroyed, and since she could not keep him away from drugs, she thought that if he switched to marijuana he might be able to recover his health.

To further help Richard stay off alcohol, Elizabeth alerted all the bartenders in Gstaad that Richard was not to be given anything strong to drink. He liked lemonade and that is what he was to be given.

Richard was trying to live up to Elizabeth's desires, but he wanted a drug of some sort and found that he hated smoking marijuana. Peter also tried to encourage him, but Peter would try anything and Burton knew it. Peter made a very poor role model.

Finally Richard had had enough. He wanted to go into town, where he could easily get a drink. Peter would accompany him but Elizabeth would stay at home.

Elizabeth took Peter aside and warned him that he dared not let Richard have even one drink. She had a vicious temper and Peter was frightened of crossing her. He also knew that there was no way he could stop Richard from doing anything he wanted to do.

The two men stopped at the Palace Hotel's bar, where Peter ordered vodka and Richard, much to Peter's relief, ordered lemonade. They sat and talked, Richard finishing one lemonade, then going on to the next.

By the time Burton finished his fourth lemonade, Peter noticed some changes in his behavior. He was not certain what was happening, but the changes worried him. Then, when Burton finished his eighth glass, Peter realized that Richard was, as Peter put it, "shit-faced drunk."

Laughing, Richard looked solemnly at Peter and said, "I'll let you in on something. I have all the waiters paid off. Elizabeth told them not to serve me, but I pay them to spike my lemonade with vodka."

Peter was suddenly terrified. He knew Elizabeth's temper and was certain that she would blame Peter when she saw the obviously drunk Burton.

Richard was calm. "I know how to make that bitch shut up," he said rising from the table. He led Peter to the Gstaad branch of Van Cleef & Arpel, a jewelry store that has extraordinarily valuable merchandise. He then purchased a piece of jewelry costing several hundred thousand dollars.

Drunk, happy, the two men went strolling back up the hill to Elizabeth's home, falling in the snow, singing and laughing. Then, at the top, they had to face Elizabeth, whose first words were "Peter, you cock-sucker, I told you not to let him drink. . . ."

Burton gave Elizabeth the present, which calmed her a little. However, he also explained that Peter "made" him drink, refusing to tell her the truth about the waiters.

There was also a Christmas dinner where Elizabeth behaved in a manner that Peter thought was crude. Her domestic staff could not speak English and could not understand most of the words she used. They knew the names of the food that was being served, but they were lost beyond that. As a joke, Elizabeth deliberately used the crudest possible language, knowing that they would not understand. "Give me the fucking roast beef," she would say.

The staff, knowing only the term *roast beef*, would bring the platter of meat to her, their language extremely polite. "Now pass the fucking peas," she would add, again the staff aware of nothing out of the ordinary. It was a situation she found hilarious and Peter felt was in poor taste.

Richard was a man who was frequently "onstage," even during dinner parties. Peter said that Richard frequently did speeches from *King Lear* at the dinner table. The guests were always on the edges of their chairs, so powerful were his abilities. But Elizabeth, who had heard it all too many times before, would coldly say "Would you shut the fuck up?" They were enraptured; she was bored.

Elizabeth also became friendly with Peter's son Christopher, when the boy was about the same age Peter had been when he went to MGM. They went to Disneyland and other places together, either as friends, as she claimed, or as lovers, as the rumors indicated. As I mentioned earlier, Henry Wynberg felt that the rumors could not be true. However, he did not really know her then. Peter introduced Elizabeth to Henry because he was concerned about her relationship with Christopher.

Peter was in awe of Cary Grant, a man who was a major success in both film and business. Grant did not have the style in real life that he created on the screen, yet he was handsome, brilliant, and as Peter found out, cheap.

Peter told me of the time he visited Cary at home, having been invited for dinner. He did not know what to expect, though he realized that with Grant's wealth, the meal would only be the finest.

That something might be wrong with Peter's reasoning first occurred to him when he toured the house. Grant had huge wardrobes filled with clothing, but his wife had only a few dresses. Then they went into the living room to have dinner. To Peter's amazement, Grant, his wife at the time, and Peter each had a freestanding tray placed in front of his or her chair. And on each tray, the aluminum foil still in place in order to keep the food hot, was a TV dinner. Such a meal was Grant's way of saving money when he invited a friend over to eat.

Peter later laughed about the incident, telling me that the only actor he had ever met who seemed as cheap as Cary Grant, whom he otherwise greatly respected, was Fred MacMurray. MacMurray was under contract to MGM when Peter was there, and he was an established star.

Peter said that he used to have a dressing room near Peter's, where he would bring his lunch. Fred would not spend the money for lunch at the commissary even though he was quite wealthy. Instead he carried a brown paper sack.

One day, after Easter, Fred had hard-boiled eggs for lunch. To Peter's amazement, the eggs were all colored. Peter said that apparently MacMurray had taken them during what was supposed to have been a children's Easter egg hunt.

Peter was extremely close to Cass Elliot, the overweight, drug-abusing singer with the group The Mamas and the Papas. Cass Elliot would eventually die from a heroin problem, though the officially released cause of death was that she choked to death while eating a sandwich.

Mama Cass, as she was called in the singing group, was a friend to Peter, who felt sorry for her. Despite her financial success as a singer, she was a troubled woman who used obesity as a protective shell against others. However, she thought that there might be more to the relationship than there was. When they were together in Peter's apartment one evening, she suddenly leaped on his body, wanting to have sex with him. He not only did not want to go to bed with her, he was so thin and she was so heavy that he could barely breathe when she attacked him. He laughed about it later, but at the time he apparently thought he would suffocate.

John Lennon and Peter were quite friendly with each other during this period. Peter was enamored of the Beatles, who were still together, and he often hung around with Ringo Starr.

Lennon, the truly talented Beatle, was also rather immature. At one point, when he had temporarily broken up with Yoko Ono, whom he eventually married, he, his date, Peter, Tom Smothers of the Smothers Brothers comedy act, and a few others went to the Troubador. It was a club where Tom and Dick Smothers were having a reunion show. The brothers were frequently breaking up, then getting their act back together, and that night they were having a big show.

John was very drunk and very stoned that night after Tom left the group to go onstage. He looked at the waitress, who was wearing a uniform that included a Dixie cup–type of hat and short skirt, and said, "What's that you've got on your head, a Tampax?" There were other comments as well, all made in a loud voice while Tom and Dick were trying to perform. His actions were rude and disruptive, something that Peter could not tolerate. Peter was a gentleman when it came to other performers, a man they considered a good audience. He would delight in their success during an act, laugh at their jokes, and show them respect even when they were bad. The idea that Lennon would act so rudely appalled him.

Peter was not a big man, but he was extremely strong when angered. He became so irate with Lennon's disruptions that he grabbed him and bodily threw him into the street. Then, outside, he said, "You're a rude son of a bitch! If you can't sit there and be quiet and courteous, get out."

Lennon started yelling back, but did not go back inside. The next day, Peter received a huge basket of flowers from Lennon, asking for forgiveness.

Peter wrote a note back, easing the situation. But their friendship was somewhat strained after that.

There were women, of course, but nothing serious other than Mary Rowan. It was more a time of drifting, his work on the decline, his friendships changing, his family situation pained.

The relationship Peter had with his children was a difficult one. He had had two bad role models of parenting. First was the fact that he had been raised in the classic British tradition, where the child was cared for by nannies and seen by the parents only when properly cleaned, dressed, and well behaved. Parents were somewhat distant figures, family outings never involving close interaction between parent and child.

Peter was also a child abuse victim, a fact that made normal parenting difficult for him. His father was a distant hero to whom Peter could never measure up. He was also the passive abuser, not stopping his wife from actions that were emotionally destructive to their son.

May Lawford actively hated her son. She caused him deep pain, yet when he had children of his own he had no idea what to do with them that might be better than his own treatment. He wanted the children to call him Peter instead of Dad or Father or some similar term. He maintained his distance from them, not knowing how else to behave.

The divorce from Pat Kennedy went uncontested by Peter, who respected Pat's abilities as a mother. She was the one who had come from a large family. She was the one who knew what it was like to live with brothers and sisters, Peter having been an only child. He felt quite comfortable with her being the primary person to raise them, providing them, through the Kennedys, an extended family.

Pat needed male support in Peter's absence. The children would later talk of the fact that she would frequently mention Uncle Jack or Uncle Bobby and the things that they had done. She was trying to provide a strong male role model, a healthy goal that should have been beneficial. But in making mention of their late uncles the children were constantly reminded that they were without a father. They were not a normal family unit, and most of their friends and cousins did not come from broken homes.

There was unquestioning acceptance into the Kennedy family for the children. Jack Kennedy, upon learning of Robin Lawford's birth, sent her a telegram that read: "Your entrance is timely, as we need a new left end." Bobby helped Chris learn to ski at a time when the boy was afraid of the unfamiliar sport. And always the children were considered members of the Kennedy cousins, not objects to be discarded because Peter divorced their mother. Yet there was always something lacking, a fact that undoubtedly contributed to Christopher's turning to drugs during the time I was living with Peter.

Sadly, as will be explained in the next chapter, Peter never was able to show his children the deep love he felt for them. I doubt that any of the children ever understood how much he cared. He just did not know how to reach out.

Peter also was damaging his body during this period. There was a point after the deaths and the divorce when Peter stopped taking care of his body. He ballooned from 163 pounds, the natural weight he carried on his six-foot-one-inch frame, to over 210 pounds. He was bloated from alcohol and a lack of exercise. He was a pathetic figure to see compared with what he had been. In addition, his liver was getting so bad that even before I knew him, one doctor told him that he could die if he went so far as to eat rum cake. He was dangerously reactive to alcohol.

Peter had reached the end of the life he had known. He was at a crossroads, the last period where he might have had a choice in his future. But he would take none of the warnings seriously, a fact of which I would be unaware when I first came to know him.

8
The Last Years

"It was Friday night, two days before Peter entered the hospital for the last time. He was drifting in and out of a deep sleep, the precursor to a coma he would soon enter, when he managed to talk on the telephone with Milt Ebbins, his manager. 'Peter, where have you been?' Milt asked, concerned when Peter sounded as though he was passing through conscious awareness. Peter replied, 'I've been to heaven.' Then he drifted back to sleep."

—Patricia Seaton Lawford

PETER WAS A DYING MAN WHEN I MET HIM. HE HAD HAD A serious pancreas problem in 1969 from which he could fully recover only if he stopped the drinking and the drugs. The fact that he continued with both pleasures meant that his days were numbered. Yet he had the attitude that if his weight was down and his tan was fresh he was in perfect health. He could be dying of heart disease, cancer, diabetes, and the plague, but if his skin was tan, he was certain everything was all right.

On the outside, Peter looked in perfect health when I first met him in On the Rox. This was a private club on top of the Roxy Theater, then an extremely popular entertainment night spot on Sunset Boulevard. On the Rox was an exclusive hangout for the stars appearing at the Roxy, who were invited there to unwind by the handful of members who owned it. If you knew the right people in show business connected with the Roxy, you could also become a part of that scene. That was how I happened to be there the night I met Peter.

Being in On the Rox was like being in someone's private living room. There was a dance floor so small that if more than two couples tried to use it at the same time they would constantly be bumping into each other. There were intimate tables and a feeling that you were always among friends. No one would ask a star for an autograph. No one would disturb you if you just wanted a quiet drink while you thought over the performance you had given earlier that evening. And no one thought it odd if you wanted to cut loose a little after having been onstage for a couple of hours.

The bathrooms of On the Rox always had a supply of cocaine available, and the liquor flowed freely in the main room. The place stayed open until three, four, or five o'clock in the morning, much like an after-hours joint.

The night I was there, a girlfriend of mine and I had gone to see Al Jarreau and George Benson perform. We both loved jazz, and she had the connections to get us into the club when the show was over. We had champagne, the owner talking with us because he and my girl friend were interested in each other.

Suddenly the door flew open and up the stairs came Peter, Ringo Starr, and Keith Moon (the drummer for the then internationally famous rock group The Who), along with Peter and Ringo's dates. Peter and I noticed each other in the mirror, each intrigued by the other. I found him extremely attractive, and he was obviously taken by me. However, the latter might have been caused by a rather unusual circumstance.

I was born with a bone problem that affected my jaw. There had been degeneration that required major surgery, which I had completed a short time before. In order to allow for the reconstructive work to heal, my jaw had been wired shut by a doctor who was sensitive to the life style and self-obsession common for any teenager. He had thus done the wiring in such a manner that it was not apparent when looking at my face in any casual circumstances. This was a blessing for a seventeen-year-old, my age at the time. However, there was no way to reduce the physical impact of the wiring. I could not open my mouth wide enough to take in solid food. I had to limit my intake to anything that was liquid or could be put through a blender, then sipped through a straw.

My girl friend caught me flirting and asked me what I was doing. "Who is that good-looking man?" I asked her, but she had no idea.

You have to remember that I was very young at the time, my familiarity with actors being limited to those men who were making a name for themselves right then. I knew who Al Pacino was. I would recognize Robert Redford. But Peter Lawford? I had my glimpse of him at twelve and had never seen one of his movies. If my mother watched "The Thin Man" on television, I would not have remembered, having been only a year old when it was running. All I knew was that the man was handsome and seemed to be attracted to me.

Peter sent a bottle of champagne to our table, then came over to speak with us. "What are you doing?" he asked.

"We're just sitting here," I told him.

"Here's a bottle of champagne for you," he said.

"Thank you," I replied. "Have a nice night."

"Yeah," he said. "We're just coming out for the evening."

And that was it. He went back to the girl at his table, a woman I later learned was Deborah Gould, who, for an extremely brief period of time, would become the third Mrs. Peter Lawford. My friend and I left the club, still not knowing who he was.

During this period I was seeing Henry Wynberg, who was also dating Elizabeth Taylor. For some reason, Elizabeth and I often had affairs with the same men, though usually at different times. I had even had a brief fling with Richard Burton, a fact that led Elizabeth to one day comment with some exaggeration, "You and I seem to have the same men in our lives. The only one you didn't fuck was Mike Todd [Elizabeth's third husband] and that was only because you were still in diapers when he died."

Elizabeth was out of town, filming overseas, Henry staying in her home and using her Rolls-Royce. I would frequently stay with him at the house, keeping enough clothing in the closet so I could spend the night or return to my apartment above the Sunset Strip.

At the time, though I was only a teenager, I was working for a London insurance group, underwriting aviation business. I was taking flying lessons and had learned the business through my father. I was also going to school.

Three days after meeting Peter, Henry mentioned that he was planning a dinner party that he wanted me to attend. He said that there was someone he wanted me to meet.

The night of the party I arrived early so I could dress in some of the clothing I kept at the house. There was a woman already there who was sitting down, wearing a T-shirt that read PHOTO PATROL. Henry introduced us, saying "You know, Patricia's got great boobs." And the woman said, "Show me your boobs."

I didn't know how serious either of them was, but it was a statement that made me extremely uncomfortable. I didn't know if they were having fun with me or if they wanted to get involved with something kinky. Either way, I was a seventeen-year-old kid who had lived a very straight life, and I was certain I didn't want to be involved with any of this.

Then Henry said, "Deborah has a great ass."

I could see where this conversation was heading, and I wanted nothing to do with it. I excused myself, went to get my clothes, and put on an outfit I frequently wore during that period. It was a black silk top, black slacks, a Cartier watch on my wrist, and a solid gold Quaalude around my neck. I thought I looked special in this unusual outfit, and I knew that it showed off the figure I had acquired as a result of living on liquids while my jaw was wired shut.

The party was delightful. Handsome, eligible men were there along with beautiful women. Everyone was open, friendly, getting high. They wandered through the gardens with their lovely view of the city. Music was playing and the liquor flowed free. I turned to Henry and asked him where was the person he wanted me to meet.

It was three o'clock in the morning when the door opened and in walked a man wearing jeans and a casual shirt, looking tanned and gorgeous. It was Peter, the man I had met just the other night.

I was at the bar. He came over, looked at me, and did a double take. We spoke for a minute, then separated, and I went to Henry, asking him who the man was.

"His name's Peter Lawford," Henry told me.

"What's he do?"

"He's an actor," said Henry, annoyed by my naïveté.

"What movies?" I asked.

Henry started rattling off a list of the films in which Peter had starred. "I don't know any of those movies," I said. "Where did they make them?"

"Here," he said, really annoyed. "In America."

"Oh," I said. I returned to the living room an "expert" on Peter Lawford. Then he made his way over to where I was standing and said, "You know, there's something about you I like."

"Thank you," I replied.

"You can't be all bad. You're dressed in black, you have a gold Quaalude, and you have a Cartier tank watch."

"Is that what counts with you?" I asked.

"Oh, so you're a smartass too? I really like that."

"So?"

"What are you doing?"

"I don't know but I'm getting very tired and I'd like to go," I told him.

"Would you like to go now?"

I said yes, and he said, "Can I take you somewhere?"

"I have a car," I explained.

"Fuck the car!"

"Sure, I'll go," I said, taken aback.

Peter went to see Henry for a few minutes. The party was beginning to dwindle down, people drifting out. The woman I had met earlier, Deborah, was seated near me. She looked at me and said, "What are you doing?"

"I'm leaving," I told her. "I'm just waiting for someone."

As I said that, Peter walked from the back room. He greeted

me, asked me if I was ready to go, and I said yes. Then, as I rose, Deborah stood up quite angrily. Coldly she said, "You're going to leave with my husband?"

I was stunned. I had no idea what to say so I just said nothing. We left, got in his car, and he said he would take me to Hugh Hefner's Playboy mansion, where he spent a lot of time.

I sat in the car, saying nothing, staring straight ahead, not certain what to do. As Peter used to say about Frank Sinatra, I was barreling through life, going full-speed like a dynamite truck that has no problems until it hits a pothole. Still, this incident took me by surprise.

Peter leaned over to kiss me along the way. It was only then that he noticed that something was not quite right with my face. He stopped the car, turned on the inside light, and that was when he discovered he had picked up a woman with her jaw wired shut. "Oh, this is great. I find a girl and her jaw's wired shut," he said. "I pick you up. You're nice. I thought you were kind of British through the clenched teeth with those . . ."

Peter was beside himself. We went to Hefner's, took a Jacuzzi, then went to the guest house and spent the night.

The trip to the Playboy mansion was impressive. I had been there once before, but not in any way that was meaningful. This time it meant driving through the gates at four o'clock in the morning, being greeted by an employee saying, "Good morning, Mr. Lawford. How are you? What can I get you this morning?"

I thought the situation was wonderful. The guest house room was mirrored on the ceiling and walls. The room was black, the bed with a built-in stereo console. There was a velour robe on the door, a small bathroom, and piped-in music. The room was soundproofed to provide privacy, with endless electronic games just outside the door. It seemed to reflect our host, Hugh Hefner, who was well known for being nocturnal.

There was a telephone in the room on which you could dial the number thirty-three and the butler would bring you anything you wanted. I had to keep ordering milkshakes because I was limited to those foods I could take through a straw.

For the next three days I led a rather odd life. I had half my possessions in an apartment belonging to a girlfriend of mine, but I spent each night with Peter. Then, on that third night, he told me to move in with him.

I was overwhelmed by Peter, especially when he suggested we stay together. I had no idea what I should do. I hated living in the apartment I was sharing with another girl, yet I knew it was wrong to just walk out, sticking her with the entire rent each month. At the same time, I had a tremendous need to be wanted by a man, and here was someone who was famous, certainly wealthy and respected, who wanted me with him. Finally, too excited to say no and too immature to face all the issues honestly, I decided to move out while my roommate was still at work.

I called my parents to tell them the news. I had always been independent. Even when I had all my problems with my family, I simply moved out on my own. I did not create a scene or let my schoolwork slack off. This was the first thing I had ever done that got their attention, my father announcing that he was going to kill Peter, my mother telling me that the decision was great.

For the first time in my life I felt powerful. People were taking notice of me. I had done something others felt was out of character and they were paying attention. I was moving in with Peter Lawford, the actor, the movie star, the handsome man I barely knew.

I had just started living with Peter when a friend called and invited me to a party at the Beverly Hills Hotel. The hotel has a combination of rooms, suites, and cottages on the grounds. The party was in one of the cottages and, to my surprise, one of the guests was Deborah Lawford. She took one look at me, slipped the wedding ring from her finger, and threw it at me. "Here!" she yelled. "You might be needing this, *cunt!*"

The ring struck me in the side of the face, then fell to the floor. I casually picked it up, studied it for a moment, then said, "I'm sure I can do better."

It was an odd scene. Deborah had moved in with Henry Wynberg and I knew it. Under the circumstances, I was unable to feel bad. She and Peter were married in name only. I did not feel as though I was stealing her husband.

Later I learned the truth of that third marriage. Peter was stoned when he was dating her, using drugs heavily and apparently convinced that she had access to a better supply than he did. In his mind, such a circumstance was an arrangement made in heaven. He immediately wanted to marry her.

The marriage, as such, lasted less than a week, and they were separated almost immediately. Peter sent her over to Henry Wynberg's to live until arrangements could be made for her to go back to her family. It was an incident that was undoubtedly painful for them both, yet it was not a tragic love affair.

Later I felt that Deborah inappropriately capitalized on their relationship. She was paid for at least one interview concerning Marilyn Monroe, supplying details that I found were generally incorrect. She gave the impression that Peter had shared extensive information with her during their few days of pillow talk. While it would have been possible, knowing both his condition at the time and how long it took for him to cover all that information with me, even after he started making notes for his book, I doubt seriously that it happened. I suspect that she repeated common gossip of the day instead of anything he said. Yet her words were accepted just as Peter's would have been.

One week to the day after I began living with Peter, there was a knock at the door. Peter went into the bedroom, shut the door, and told me to answer. It was Milt Ebbins, Peter's manager.

I had met Milt and thought of him as a kindly old man. I never realized that he was the person to whom Peter turned whenever he wanted to run away from an emotionally difficult decision. Peter was a coward in many of his relationships, choosing to turn to Milt, who, at times, was also unable to act effectively. Most likely this was because Milt was suddenly thrown into situations for which he was unprepared and of which he knew little.

I told Milt that Peter was in the bedroom but that he would be out in a minute. I did not know this was a setup, not even when Milt said he wanted to talk with me.

Milt told me that I would have to leave Peter right away. There was to be no delay. I had to go.

I stared at Milt in shock. I had left my apartment. I had hurt my former roommate. I had told my parents I was moving away. And now this. My actions would seem even more foolish because everything I had thought was my future was being taken from me.

I went back to the bedroom to get my things, but Peter could not look me in the eye. He got up and left, driving away so he wouldn't have to talk with me.

I gathered my possessions and made the most difficult call of my life. I telephoned my mother to tell her that I had to come to her place.

I was ashamed, devastated. I had been hurt, my adolescent dreams shattered. I felt that I was humiliated in front of people whose respect I had gained for the first time in my life. My entire world was altered in ways I could not understand. Unable to face anyone, to deal with what was happening to me, I went to bed and refused to get up except to go to the bathroom. I didn't want to die, yet I didn't want to live. I wanted to will myself into emotional limbo.

Eight days after I had taken to bed, the telephone rang for me. Peter was calling, telling me that everything was okay and asking if I was ready to come back. He sent a limousine for me and I returned to his home.

The next night we went to the Palm restaurant to celebrate our being back together again. There were some other friends with us, and they all ordered lobster. I protested that I could not eat it, but no one listened. Instead, a pair of telephone cable cutters was brought to the table and they snapped my wires so I could eat. Fortunately, I was far enough along in the healing process so no damage was done. The joke, of course, was a double entendre.

I learned several things from that incident. One, of course, was Peter's weakness. He was in the process of getting his divorce from Deborah. He knew that there was no reason it would not be granted, yet he felt that he might have some problems if she could point to the fact that he was already living with another woman. The fact that she was living with Henry Wynberg would not alter his involvement and might cause financial difficulties for him.

The second thing I learned was how much I was willing to degrade myself in order to change my life. I had been hurt so much that when someone wanted me, even if I would be taken for granted at times, meant more than my self-respect. I had felt unwanted for too long. Someone who would pay me the attention that Peter was paying, even though his actions had been rude, unthinking, and cowardly, was more important than anything I had known.

And I also learned just who Peter Lawford was to this country. When we left the Palm there were reporters and photographers everywhere, climbing on our cars, on other parked vehicles, on anything they could use to get a different vantage point. This man was a major star. His actions were considered to be national news. His impending divorce was known and I was the new woman in his life. We made gossip column headlines, our pictures everywhere.

I learned something else that night. I learned that the press is not always accurate in checking information. When I saw my photograph, I was listed as a twenty-two-year-old unemployed Beverly Hills secretary. Only the city where I was living at the time was accurate.

There was one other surprise awaiting me. My wires were completely removed a few days after all this, and I expected to settle down into a normal intimate relationship. But it did not happen. Days went by, then weeks, and finally Peter and I had been together three months without having intercourse. There had been extensive touching and intimate fondling. There had been oral sex. Yet there never was intercourse.

At first I blamed the wires. I figures that my wired jaw was a turn-off for him.

Then I wondered if I wasn't sexy enough for him, if there was something about me that did not please him. I rejected this idea because there was too much intimacy to conclude that he did not want me.

Only later was I to learn the truth about Peter. The drugs and alcohol had taken their toll. He had gone from being a stud who could have several women in a day to a man whose body would no longer respond to his mind's desires. Prolonged oral sex could still bring him pleasure. But Peter's drug habits resulted in his becoming a voyeur more than a participant. It would be my longing for a normal sex life that would eventually drive me to several affairs during the time we were together. I never stopped loving him. I never wanted a divorce. At the same time, I also could not continue without periodically experiencing a relationship where everything was rational and all parts of both participants worked as they were intended.

There was so much to experience in our new life together. Peter still had money, so we were able to travel wherever the whim might take us. I thought nothing of being with Peter on a chartered jet just because he decided that he wanted to catch a show in Las Vegas. He would pay a cabdriver to do our grocery shopping. We would take a limousine for a weekend retreat, the hired driver sleeping in an extra room so he would be constantly available. The fact that Peter no longer had the income or earning power that would make such a life style possible was ignored. I had no idea that we were slowly drifting into financial trouble and that Peter's live-for-today attitude meant that he did not care.

Suddenly I was living in a world that I never thought I would know. It was a world of glamour and excitement, of seemingly unlimited wealth, of power and adoration. It was also a world of fans, of people who knew Peter from television and the movies.

There was a moment early in Peter's career after MGM when his entire image might have been different. This was when the James Bond movies were first under consideration. The Bond books were extremely popular, a copy of one of the novels was frequently by John Kennedy's bed when he was president. It was felt in Hollywood that a movie based on the Bond character might be popular with American audiences, and Peter was asked to play the lead.

Peter thought about the film and talked with his manager, Milt Ebbins. As usual, Peter's judgment left something to be desired and Milt's was no better. They felt certain that the story line would be too lightweight, the film unsuccessful. There seemed no reason to link Peter with something that would obviously be destined to either fail or be forgotten. Peter turned down the opportunity to play a part that would have turned him from a romantic comedy performer to a man considered the role model for macho sophistication. The film was given to the then little-known actor Sean Connery, who became both successful and quite wealthy as a result of the series.

Thus, Peter was typecast as the boy next door to some, the handsome song-and-dance romantic lead to others, and a good-looking lightweight comedy/suspense actor to still others. And the fans who adored him believed he matched these images.

The most frightening fan was a woman I encountered when I was first living with Peter and he was hospitalized at UCLA Medical Center for one of the numerous times his body was failing him. He had had a nineteen-and-a-half-inch nonmalignant pancreatic cyst, which resulted in his failure to manufacture the enzyme critical for the digestion of food. As a result he had to take from one to six enzyme tablets whenever he ate anything for several years until the enzyme condition corrected itself. He also had numerous other problems, most of them related to his drug and alcohol abuse.

Peter was on the celebrity floor of UCLA, where the rooms were large and there was a place for spouses to stay. He had both the regular nursing staff and private-duty day and night nurses, one of whom was fired for smoking marijuana with Peter.

I came to the hospital one night when the room was dark and Peter was sedated after having undergone some extremely painful procedures. When I entered, I saw a woman in a white uniform awkwardly unplugging his tubes.

At first I was not certain I should say anything. I was just a teenager, not someone with any medical background. The woman did not seem to be acting right, yet who was I to judge that?

I was quiet for a moment, standing without saying anything. I had always been respectful of the nurses, letting them do whatever they had to do without my interference. Yet this time something was not right.

"Excuse me," I said. "I'm with Mr. Lawford and I'm just wondering what you're doing."

I moved toward the woman, who suddenly turned slightly and angrily said, "Get out of this room!" To my horror, I realized that her face was reflecting what can only be described as madness. I also realized that she was ripping the IV lines from Peter's body.

I leaped at the red button on the wall, the one that would call the nursing staff. They were supposed to come on the run but it was 11:15 at night, a time when most visitors were gone and routine became more casual. No one responded instantly, so I began screaming into the hall for help.

When nursing and security staff finally arrived, we learned that the woman had been a hospital employee. She worked in records and had become obsessed with Peter. She was convinced that she was Peter's wife. It turned out that the woman was also an escapee from the UCLA psychiatric section, where she had been undergoing treatment. Whether she was planning to kill Peter, kidnap him, or just make him "more comfortable" by removing the tubes, I never knew. The staff subdued her and returned her to the ward.

I was irate with UCLA's security staff. Peter was in the most expensive section of the hospital. He was a celebrity in a room reserved for celebrities, a fact that should have resulted in increased security. Yet this woman had been able to walk into the room, and had I not been there when I was, she might have killed him.

Peter returned home three weeks after this incident. I awakened one morning to find the woman who had attacked him at the hospital asleep in the bushes. She had been released because her actions had not warranted her being held any longer.

Letters began arriving from this woman, who signed her name Beverly Lawford. She named all four of Peter's children and told him that they were doing well, that their grades were good. She refused to acknowledge my existence or that of his previous three wives. She knew the names of the children's schools and wrote as though they were temporarily separated but would be reunited as a family in the near future.

Time passed and I encountered her again. I left the apartment one day to find her waiting outside. She informed me that she was going to kill me, then left. She made no physical move to hurt me, but I was scared. I had seen what she had done to Peter, the man she supposedly loved. Her statement had to be taken seriously.

I called the police, only to be told that little could be done. They could not arrest this woman based on a statement she had made. Actions that were annoying but not threatening and that took place on public property were not sufficient grounds for arrest. She would have to physically threaten or assault me before they could do anything.

This was another frightening thing I have had to learn to handle, both when I was with Peter and since his death. There are crazies like "Beverly Lawford" who become so obsessed with a celebrity that their fantasies are lived as though they are a reality. There are fans who want to assume the identity of the celebrity, then kill the star because only one person can have the name (John Lennon's killer might fall into this category). And there are fans who seek out not the star but the spouse of the star. They want to meet the spouse, emotionally manipulate the spouse, perhaps having sex with the spouse. They may be laughingly called "star fuckers" before they act. But when one of us is raped, knifed, shot, or otherwise hurt, the words stop being jokes. I have been bothered by them at times, once having been told by a member of the Beverly Hills Police Department that there was a good chance the man would try to kill me.

Yet always the reaction is the same when you are accosted by these people. Unless they commit a crime, they cannot be arrested. They can walk your streets, follow you everywhere, telephone you, send you letters, and generally harass you. They can threaten you, discuss obscene acts they are planning to perform on your body, and do almost anything else they wish. But so long as they do not physically hurt you, the police have limited power and elaborate rules to follow.

For example, when I receive threatening telephone calls, I have to log the time each call is received, what is said, and describe the person to the best of my ability (male voice, female voice, deep, high-pitched, muffled, and so on). Then, when an adequate pattern is established, a tap can be placed on my telephone in order to try to catch the person.

One detective facetiously suggested I'd be better off shooting one such man because they could do nothing until he was violent. This is a side of celebrity life I did not know, did not wish to know, and still have trouble explaining to others.

The police recognized our problem with Beverly enough to periodically charge her with vagrancy. Under that law the woman could be held for three days at a time, then released. It wasn't much, but it gave us short periods during which we could feel safe.

The situation continued for weeks, then months, then years. The woman was found in the bushes of our apartment building. She was found on the grounds of neighbors. They knew that we had nothing to do with it, yet they also knew that she was coming around only because of her obsession with Peter. There seemed to be no way we could escape.

I should never have made assumptions about Beverly. She became so much a part of our life that I let down my guard, forgetting that she had once taken an action that could have cost Peter his life.

I went to the supermarket, returning home with several bags of groceries. I set them down in front of the door, then went inside with one of the bags. When I returned to pick up the second bag, Beverly suddenly slashed at me with a large knife.

I blocked Beverly's attack with my arm, the groceries flying down the steps. We fought until help came. Beverly was arrested for attacking me.

We continued hearing from Beverly for a while, notes even being sent to us from jail. Then, three years before Peter's death, Beverly disappeared from our lives. We never heard from her again.

There was a more humorous, if still troubled, fan. This was a young man who was homosexual and had focused on Peter as his lover. He attended the game shows Peter was on in New York and wore shirts that read I LOVE YOU PETER LAWFORD. He also carried signs declaring his love.

I felt sorry for the youth when I'd see him in the audience of the New York shows, so I was willing to talk with him. Then, one day, he asked if I could get Peter to sign some photographs. I saw nothing wrong with that, agreeing to his request. That was when he handed me a stack of dozens of photographs.

Eventually this fan realized that because Peter lived in Los Angeles he would have to leave his home and come west. He saved his money until he could afford the trip, then began showing up around our home. He knew every movie Peter had made, every television show he had made or appeared on, every song he had sung.

For hours he sat in front of our home with a sign, his shirt, and a stack of photographs. He would be there from around eleven in the morning until well after midnight, when we would finally call the police and have him moved. We felt as though we were prisoners in our own home, yet he was harmless. Fortunately he returned to his home on the East Coast and we only received fan mail from him.

Most of the others were more rational. They were people who said that they wished Peter would work more, make more films. A few would come up to him and say, "Do you remember me? I slept with you in Indiana [or Ohio or wherever]." Peter didn't remember, but he admitted that it was possible. He had been with many women during the USO tours and the MGM promotion tours, as well as picking up attractive women whenever he traveled without one of his wives.

I also received letters from women in their eighties who said that he had had an affair with them. Since Peter was fifty when I met him, their stories were doubtful.

The other surprise I had in those early days was the realization of how gentle and kind Peter was. There are people who are suckers for a pitch by a beggar. They will reach into their pockets and hand the beggar their change or, in some instances, paper money. But Peter went a step further. He would bring them home for dinner.

I was shocked to discover my bathroom once being used by a stranger. The man was a wino whose clothing was filthy, whose body smelled foul, and whose social graces were nonexistent. Peter had him shower and clean up in my bathroom because "it's nicer than mine." Then he expected me to cook a meal for this person, something that upset me. I kept wanting to tell him to stop, but Peter would not. He wanted to help, a fact that was as touching to me as it was annoying.

The same was true with animals. He found a stray dog so near death from old age and starvation that the dog could barely move, even after Peter cleaned him and we began feeding him. There was so little life left in the dog that Peter called him the Rock. He had to carry the Rock everywhere because the dog could no longer walk very far, yet Peter did not care. That dog was going to be loved until he died.

At various times we had a squirrel, a miniature goat (housebroken to a kitty litter box), dogs, a cat, and numerous other creatures. It was a strange, exciting life that kept us close.

The one area that was a continuing problem between us was our sex life. Don Brown, a close friend of ours, said that he felt Peter had developed a fantasy sex life. Peter had been one of the great studs of Hollywood at one time until his drug abuse caused the impotence that plagued him by the time we got together. Whether or not stopping the drugs would have also corrected the problem is academic because Peter was unable or unwilling to stop. Yet Peter still insisted upon having his women, frequently getting two together for sex acts. When he could achieve an erection, the effort took hours and was always orally stimulated. Most of the time he was part voyeur and part oral participant, a thoroughly unsatisfactory arrangement for me. But so long as he could attract the women and convince them to perform, in his mind he remained one of Hollywood's greatest lovers.

Eventually Peter's addiction made having any sort of sexual feelings extremely difficult for him. He needed to be physically stimulated literally for hours, something no woman could ever handle. However, he solved this need through a purchase at the Pleasure Chest, a store selling everything from sexually oriented magazines to a wide variety of sex toys. One of these was a product called Acujack.

Acujack was an electrical device that became Peter's best friend and companion. The device is a male version of a woman's vibrator. A man attaches it to his penis, turns it on, and it is meant to stimulate him to orgasm. The sound it made was much like that of a kitchen blender, but Peter did not care. He would attach himself to it at night, turn it on, and let it go literally for hours at a time until he eventually achieved some sort of climax.

This new relationship was almost as disgusting as his women, except that it looked ridiculous. After several months of listening to that motor whirr far into the night, I threw the machine out with the trash, hoping it would be gone before Peter awakened. Unfortunately, he discovered it missing before the garbage collectors arrived and he was able to retrieve it.

There was an accident on the freeway when a man used an Acujack he had plugged into his cigarette lighter. When he reached orgasm, the machine short-circuited, electrocuting him and causing the car to go out of control. It crashed into a pole. He was killed instantly, and I showed Peter that his "friend" could be deadly. Unfortunately, he continued using it the rest of his life.

Peter was not alone in all this. I later learned of women whose husbands had never shown much enthusiasm for sex but who purchased Acujack and used it regularly. Several of them became so disgusted that they filed for divorce, successfully claiming that Acujack had destroyed their marriages.

With all his oddities, especially in areas that women feel are essential to a relationship, it may seem strange that I stayed with Peter for so many years. However, sex was not critical for me. I had seldom known normal sexual relations. The men in my life had used my body out of ego, for domination, or to cause me pain. Peter's eccentricities in this area were at least meant to achieve some sort of pleasure for himself and his partners.

What mattered to me was that Peter cared about me. I know he loved Pat Kennedy and Mary Rowan. I know he tried to make those marriages work. But he was younger then, stronger, able to bed hop and play games that were highly destructive to his relationships.

I met Peter at the perfect time in both our lives. He was older, slowed by the physical deterioration caused by drugs and alcohol. He needed companionship. He needed a friend. He wanted a woman with whom he could play sexually, who he could introduce to his "friends," the drugs; but this was all secondary to the fact that he wanted a genuine companion. He was at a point of reflection, needing to talk about the past, his experiences, his feelings. He desired a friend in the truest sense and was just immature enough that someone my age who was prematurely older than her years was perfect for him.

For my part, I needed to be needed, to be wanted. I needed a friend who had the wisdom to guide me, the compassion to try to understand me, and the maturity to treat me as a person in my own right.

Peter wanted to be a teacher for me, especially in the field of history, which he loved so much. He would suddenly shout "1066" and expect me to know that it was the date of the Battle of Hastings. Or he would say, "the Battle of Britain" and want me to tell him what happened there.

And Peter wanted to be able to adore me, to love me in ways that were gentle, touching, intense, and have me accept them. Not a day went by that I did not receive a love note or a love letter. If he arose early and I slept in, I would awaken to a note telling me he was gone, where he could be reached at the studio, and that a limousine would be arriving to take me to the set. He would also tell me he loved me.

Peter and I were not married for the first few years we were together, yet to Peter we were married from the start. He constantly referred to me as his wife. He introduced me to others as either "my wife" or as "Mrs. Lawford." He never thought of himself as "shacking up" with some young girl. He committed to me more completely than he had ever done with anyone and that touched me deeply.

Peter bought me presents even when we could not afford very much. I remember one time coming home when we were practically broke. We were barely able to cover the cost of food and shelter. Yet there was a note saying "Present for you in the bedroom." I went into the bedroom and there was a small potted plant with a flower in bloom, a plant sold in the supermarket where he had purchased a few essentials. At that time it was an extravagance greater than if he had purchased a Mercedes Benz for me when he was still wealthy.

There were other signs of his affection. I would go to the set to watch him work on a movie or television show. I would slip quietly into an area reserved for spectators, watching him perform. Even if he was in the middle of a take, where film would have to be reshot, if he saw me his face would light up with pleasure. As soon as he could, he would rush to my side and talk with me as though I was the most important person he had ever known. We would slip into the dressing room and either talk or I would read the script with him so he could go over his lines.

Think about it. Here was Peter Lawford, a man who had walked with royalty and presidents, a man who was a welcome guest in the White House during the Kennedy administration, a man who had talked with some of the great leaders of the world, anxious to listen to me.

Certainly the sexual problems were difficult. But Peter never related sex and love. One was a recreation in which he had long indulged at every opportunity. The other was commitment, something he had avoided in many ways until we came together. In almost every way, I knew happiness and love for the first time in my life. We cared for each other more than either of us ever thought possible.

But Peter taught me something else during that period. There were periods when I craved a normal sexual relationship. I had love, affection, and tenderness from Peter. But I did not know the feeling of a man and woman coming together to have intercourse, something I periodically desired to such a degree that I chose to be sexually unfaithful to him.

My decision was not an easy one. Peter had no qualms about having sex with someone if we were separate, though I deliberately kept myself from thinking about just how often that happened. I knew that he felt such actions were all right. However, I had wanted sex to evolve only from love. Unfortunately, I realized that I had wants and needs that forced me to rethink that position. Several times I had brief affairs, not because I cared for the men but rather because I needed to experience normal intercourse. I wanted to be able to go to bed with a man without having to play out some fantasy or remain intimately untouched for the night. As strange as it may sound, and I am surprised by my own words as I write this, I periodically cheated in order to save our relationship, not destroy it. I went outside the home for the one thing Peter could not give me, so that I would not grow to resent him and eventually lose so much more that we did share.

There was no problem in finding willing men. However, there was a problem with being able to continue with the same partner. The friendlier I became with a man, the more comfortable I was talking about what I enjoyed in life. The problem was, what I truly enjoyed was Peter. I talked about him incessantly, the men regularly telling me that they didn't want to be with me because they could not stand hearing about my "husband."

What I did not realize is that Peter understood this. Perhaps

THE PETER LAWFORD STORY   199

there was hurt, deeper hurt than I knew, that he never showed and never expressed. Or perhaps Peter understood that a woman can use casual sex in much the same way as a man. Whatever the case, we never discussed the situation, though I later learned to my embarrassment and shame that Peter knew what I was doing.

I had met a man while Peter and I were on location in Hawaii for his TV movie "Island of Beautiful Women." (If you didn't see it, please don't. If you did see it, you know why it was an embarrassment for everyone.) He lived in New York, a city where my father had business and where I occasionally had to go for trips related to that business. Since I liked the man and wanted to see him again, I thought that it was the perfect cover for having an affair.

The circumstances of my existence at that time are hard for me to accept now that I am out of it. I was a teenager who had been used by men. I was in love with Peter, deeply in love with him, yet rebelling against him at the same time. He was incapable of what I considered normal sex. He was a drug addict, so heavily addicted to so many different things that he had come to see money only as a vehicle for buying more drugs. So long as there was more money than the cost of his addiction, then we would have food, shelter, and a housekeeper. But nothing was so important to him as the drugs.

Even worse, there was no one to whom I could go to discuss the drugs. When interviewing people who were friends and/or co-workers of Peter I found that none of them realized how addicted he actually was. He hid it well, even for a time from me.

For example, I had been living with Peter for a while when I could not find any shampoo. I began looking for it in the medicine cabinet, then explored the counter under the sink. Finally I found a bag and thought there might be some in there. To my shock, the bag was filled with hundreds of needles for drug injections. They were all sterile, all identical to those you would encounter in a doctor's office or a hospital. They were used by Peter to inject Talwin, an intramuscular painkiller, a painkiller he took around the clock.

The injections went into his rear end in a place that made it easy for me to not see any marks. He did not let me know he was taking the injections and he certainly did not want me to know how often. I had no idea that he would carry filled syringes to parties and anywhere else we might go, using the bathroom when he needed an injection. He never showed signs of the drug, or perhaps no one had seen him for years without his being on the drug. Whatever the case, it was a shock.

Later, Peter would get me addicted to the same drug. I had severe menstrual problems during that time, the pain becoming so intense that I might be doubled over on the floor, unable to move until the cramping stopped. I was in the midst of one such experience when Peter suggested I try the drug. He gave me a shot and it eased my discomfort. Then, when I had more pain, he gave me another shot and I enjoyed the peace it brought. Gradually, over time, I came to like the feeling of the drug regardless of my "need" for it.

That was what happened to Peter. The drug, used in quantity, was self-rewarding. It gave us pleasure just to use it. There was no need for us to have pain to be "killed." It was something to which we looked forward, becoming addicted without realizing we could become addicted.

Eventually there came a time when Peter and I both began carrying the syringes so that we could share the pleasure wherever we went. And still no one knew.

Some of the drugs we took were illegal substances such as cocaine, where the market could vary, though usually the prices were high. Others were prescription items, sometimes expensive, sometimes cheap, but needed in such quantities that the bills mounted. At one time we were using a dozen legal pharmaceuticals each. We had to worry about different prescriptions, different doctors, and different pharmacies to keep from being discovered. Though there is a chance that, even if we had been discovered, we could have continued to get the drugs somehow.

There are a number of unethical doctors and pharmacists in Beverly Hills and the surrounding area of Los Angeles. They like having celebrity clients. They enjoy having a "name" in their waiting room or their drugstore, depending on their profession. They will look the other way when they write prescriptions or fill them. They will accept obvious lies about the need for such medications. They inadvertantly destroy patients to feed their own egos.

Peter had been a drug addict for more years than I had been alive, and he also understood the fact that the first thing an addict must do is maintain a source of supply. When he was working regularly, money was no object. By the time I met him, the cash reserves were dwindling and he would do anything to get money. He would fail to pay taxes. He would ignore bills. He would borrow from friends and he would steal from his "wife."

The latter incident I discovered after I received a gift from my father. The money was placed in a bank account to which Peter had access.

I went to the bank one day to get some money from the account, but the teller informed me that the check I wanted to cash was too great. I thought that I had a sizable amount from which to draw. The bank showed that I actually had $34 and some odd cents. Peter had withdrawn the money in order to buy drugs.

I was furious. The closest thing to affection my father had shown was when he gave me that money. He was not trying to buy my love. He was not trying to shut me up to cover the abuse. He actually wanted me to have an inheritance while he was still alive, and he had given me the money in the way a normal father might if he wanted to assist his daughter to assure her future security. Thus, that money not only represented financial benefit for me, it also was one of the few decent things my father had ever done. Peter had every right to share in that money, but he had no right to steal it. Taking it without consulting with me was theft.

I returned home enraged. Peter was in bed, under the covers, watching a game show on television. "What happened to my money?" I demanded.

"What money?" he said blithely.

"My money. My dad's money. The money that he gave me."

"Don't be so common," said Peter, acting as though I was an interruption in his day's pleasure.

"There's thirty-odd dollars in that account. The three had some extra zeroes on it before, if you will recall," I said.

"I don't want to talk about it now," he said. "If you're going to bitch, leave this house."

That was it. I informed him that unless he came up with the money that night, I was going to leave.

Peter ignored me and went back to watching television, pulling the covers up higher on his head like a little boy who thinks that if his head is hidden, no one will know where he is. I went out, withdrew $1,500 from another account to which I had access and that had not yet been looted, and returned home. The next day I decided to go to New York to be with the man with whom I had been having an affair.

I don't know what I felt at that point beyond rage. I considered Peter my husband. I wanted to please him, doing things I found repugnant even then, though I would often "anesthetize" myself with drugs so I could tolerate his requests. (Today, my heart is damaged enough from past drug use that to use something like cocaine would be potentially fatal.) Still, he was my father figure, guiding me into adulthood in ways that were constructive for the most part. We had mutual respect, something I had never known before.

For example, I am a very private person. I like having my own room. I like thinking that there are objects, such as my purse, that can be used to hold whatever I desire, safe from prying eyes. All other men in my past thought that there should be no secrets. They were comfortable looking in my drawers, my purse, reading any mail that happened to be lying about.

Not Peter. I knew that even when I was occasionally having a sexual affair and Peter was aware that phone numbers and other details could be found in my purse or in one of my drawers, he would not look. If it was important for him to know, he would ask me. If I chose not to tell him, he would respect that decision.

However, taking the money for something that related to his drug abuse and not our relationship filled me with a sense of betrayal. I was angry, hurt, in an adolescent rage. I wanted someone to hold me, to comfort me, to not steal from me. I would go to New York and move in with the man I had been seeing even though, if I analyzed things objectively, his attraction was not so powerful as to make me want to ever leave Peter.

The next morning Peter had to go out early. He went to the recording studio at 5 A.M. to do a voice-over. It was my chance to get away.

I took a steamer trunk from the closet and packed everything in the house that I knew had meaning for Peter. Cigarette boxes with John Kennedy's name on them went into the trunk, as did items from Peter's wedding to Pat Kennedy in 1954. If it had physical or emotional value, I wrapped it in a towel and packed it in the trunk.

Meanwhile our housekeeper had arrived and could only stare at what I was doing. "What am I going to tell Mr. Lawford?" she asked.

"You're going to tell him to go fuck himself," I replied coldly.

"I couldn't tell him that," she said.

I told her, "Tell him whatever you like."

She was shocked, finally lapsing into silence, watching me strip the house.

I loaded my clothing, the trunks, and everything else I could carry into a cab and headed to Air France in the international section of the Los Angeles airport. I checked most of the baggage, tipping the porter who arranged for storage. Then I made my way to American Airlines and flew to New York, paying cash to avoid leaving a paper trail.

I was clever. I knew how to cover my tracks. Peter might

follow my trail, but all he could assume from it was that I went overseas, probably using a false name. It would be days, weeks, or months before he found me.

New York was a relief. I was welcomed by my lover and taken to his apartment. I could relax, ease my anger.

The first day I was constantly waiting for the telephone to ring, hoping that Peter might magically find me. The second day I was there, still not hearing from Peter, I became cocky. He must be suffering, I told myself. He has no idea where I am. If anything, he thinks I'm wandering around Europe. He must be eating his heart out with misery.

It was midnight when I took pity on Peter. I called him in California, waiting for the anguished voice of the spurned lover to barely croak his greeting. "Hello?" he said, a lilt in his voice as though he had just won the lottery and the first prize was a lifetime supply of his favorite drugs. I hung up the phone.

At six A.M. I tried again, knowing that it would be only 3 A.M. in Los Angeles. "Hello?" The same damned voice. Happy. Carefree. Not suffering in the least.

It was my fourth day in New York and I still had not spoken with Peter. He had spent my money and all I had were the stupid cigarette boxes, ashtrays, and other things that meant nothing to me. I was in the midst of what was supposed to be a great escape but that was actually occurring for all the wrong reasons. I was lonely, miserable, and irate that he was not suffering. My housekeeper hated me. Nothing was as it should have been. Even worse, California had been warm when I left, while New York was covered with ice and snow.

While I was brooding, there was a knock at the door. It was a delivery man, obviously exhausted, surrounded by boxes. My lover was a dancer and dance instructor, so as strange as it seems, I assumed the boxes contained dozens of pairs of ballet slippers. Yet when I took a closer look, I realized that there were more than a few boxes. The private elevator to the apartment was filled, floor to ceiling, with boxes. The hall was filled with boxes. The area surrounding the door was filled with boxes. There was a narrow little area through which the delivery man had passage from an exit to the apartment door, yet there was so little space that he had to slip the receipt form over the top of the lower stacks.

"What is this?" I asked.

"Lady, I just got a job to do. Will you sign the paper?"

Not knowing what else to do, I signed, then stared at the boxes more closely. Each was marked "Aqua Chem," a name with which I was familiar. Aqua Chem is a brand of swimming pool water we used for our swimming pool in California, as did many of our neighbors. It was a commercial product meant to provide safe water for swimming. We'd buy hundreds of gallons at a time, though there was no reason why such a product would be sent to my lover's New York apartment. Somebody must have used the boxes to send the toe shoes.

Then the delivery man paused and said, "By the way, lady, I got something else for you." With that he managed to throw a letter over the top since he could not physically reach me through all the boxes.

The envelope was one I recognized immediately. It was the exact same gray stationery that Peter and I both used. The note, and the boxes, were from him.

I was shocked. I had so carefully covered my tracks. I had utilized Air France. I had paid cash. I had . . .

I opened the envelope and read the letter. It said, "Darling Patricia, you forgot the fucking pool!" Peter had literally sent me all the Aqua Chem from the swimming pool. It was the only thing of his, other than his clothes and the furniture, that I had left behind.

Now I knew why Peter sounded happy as a clam when he answered the telephone. He wasn't enraged that I had left him. He understood or at least tolerated my lover since he knew that my commitment would only be physical, not emotional. He had played what for me was the ultimate joke by sending me the pool water.

At that moment I knew that I would never again leave Peter. His sense of humor touched something in me that kept me with him until his death. There were periods of abuse, and the lack of sexual intimacy never changed. There would also be one more nightmare period in 1982, a situation that would radically change both of us, but that was a long way off.

Peter's greatest pain during our first years together seemed to come from his trying to come to grips with his children. Peter not only did not know how to love his children, he was afraid of the feelings that, at times, seemed to overwhelm him. He had difficulty being vulnerable to the emotions the children created for him.

I never knew why the children were a problem for him, though there are a couple of possibilities. One was the fact that he was raised without nurturing love. His parents never had the physical bonding with him that comes from frequent touching and sharing. Instead, Peter had nannies as he was growing up, surrogate moth-

ers who provided for his needs in every way, including his introduction to sex.

A second possibility related to his own insecurities. Peter had
difficulty accepting himself as worthy of love.. He had trouble
with healthy adult feelings, especially with women and children.
He seemed frightened to be emotionally vulnerable and tried to
keep a wall around himself. Sometimes he made his wall through
avoidance. At other times he created it by leaving himself in a
drug-and-alcohol-induced haze. You have to be able to accept
yourself to love another, and Peter seemed to fear that he might
be found wanting.

Peter tried to be a pal to his children because he could not bring
himself to be a father. He wanted to be called Peter, and he liked
to take me and the children to "fun" restaurants such as Trader
Vic's in New York when we were visiting there. The children
frequently stayed with us when they came out to California,
sometimes bringing other members of the Kennedy family. In
fact, it was not unusual for me to come home and discover one of
Peter's children and several Kennedy cousins sprawled in the
living room and around the house. We had only two bedrooms,
the overflow of Kennedys often fanning out around the Los Angeles area to sleep with friends. I once jokingly said that the Kennedys never travel alone. They travel in packs.

It was through the children that I met Pat Kennedy Lawford, a
rather embarrassing experience. Peter and I had been living together for only a few months, and the kids had been staying with
us from time to time. She would call them at the house and they
would call her. Frequently I would be the one who answered the
telephone so I got to meet her first that way.

I was always respectful when I talked with Pat Kennedy,
referring to her as "Mrs. Lawford" and treating her with deference. She was larger than life to me, both because of the Kennedy
name and because she had been the president's sister. She was
also Peter's wife of eleven years, the mother of his four children,
and seemed to be extremely tough.

My actual meeting with Pat Kennedy Lawford came when
Peter and I were in New York. I was eighteen years old, and we
were temporarily living in the Delmonico at 502 Park Avenue, in
an apartment owned by a friend of mine who was out of town.
Peter was appearing on a game show that was deservedly short-
lived. It involved two-part questions and was produced by the
same man who produced "The $20,000 Pyramid," a successful
program on which Peter appeared as regularly as possible.

Quiz shows were a delight for Peter. He would pick up around

$5,000, get a trip to New York, and be able to see his kids. He was also usually quite good on them and gave the performance they sought from a celebrity guest.

Peter and I arrived in New York the evening before his appearance, then went out partying to all the clubs. He had an early call the next morning, but we got in so late that he only had two hours of sleep. He was still able to function effectively, the lack of sleep not phasing him, even though I was exhausted when he left for NBC.

I stayed in bed, drifting off to sleep, when the door buzzer rang. I figured that Peter had forgotten something, so I put on an old, rather tattered robe, did not bother running a comb through my hair, and answered the buzzer. I was a wreck, black mascara under my eyes because I had been too tired to wash it off the night before. And there standing in the hall was Pat Kennedy Lawford and the three girls.

"What's all this fuss about this young one?" said Pat Kennedy. "You don't look so red hot in the morning."

I said, "Oh, Mrs. Lawford, I'm so sorry. Let me get you some coffee." I began blithering, taking them inside, trying to figure out how to work the coffeemaker. I was shaking, a wreck.

"Get dressed. We're going over to the studio."

I didn't know what to say or do. I was in shock and realized how Peter would feel when all of us showed up at the studio. But there was no arguing with this forceful woman who stayed up late, got up early, and had a way of dominating everything. Thoroughly intimidated, I was showered and dressed in twenty minutes, a record.

The five of us took a cab to the studio, Pat being extremely nice to me. However, I also knew that Peter had warned her to leave me alone. He had told her that I was a nice girl. He certainly never expected for us to get together.

We entered the studio and Peter spotted me from the stage. He smiled and mouthed "Hi, babe," then caught a glimpse of his ex-wife and three daughters. "How the fuck did that happen?" he mouthed, his face in shock.

Peter knew that Pat had wanted to meet me, but he had warned her away from me. He was surprised that she had come to see me and even more startled by our presence in the studio. However, it did not affect his performance. He was winning regularly, his partner a woman from New Jersey who was excited equally by being on the show and being with Peter.

Finally Peter and his partner reached the big question. This was the one where they would win the top money and prizes. The woman was extremely excited because she, like all noncelebrity contestants, did not get a flat fee for her appearance. She went home only with what she won, and it looked as if she would get everything they had that day. All they had to do was answer a two-part question.

The host took out the question which was: "Famous singer named John. City in Colorado."

Peter smiled in recognition, slammed his fist on the buzzer, and said, "Boulder! John Boulder!"

The woman was horrified, her look one of pure hatred toward Peter. Pat leaned over to me and said, "Let's get out of here. We're going to lunch and we're going to have a few drinks."

Peter had no idea that he had done anything wrong. He had not made a deliberate error. His interest in music primaily jazz, was such that he had barely heard of John Denver. His guess was a serious one, but when he learned the truth, he saw the humor of it. From then on, whenever he saw John Denver on television, he'd say, "There's that Boulder chap again."

The relationship between Peter and his children would have been happier than it was had it not been for the drugs. Christopher, who was three years older than myself and looked exactly as Peter had when he was young, began using drugs with enough frequency to eventually become addicted. He also enjoyed having sex with many of the same women as his father; in at least one instance Peter insisted on watching as his son and the woman made love.

When Christopher turned twenty-one, a party was held in New York that Peter flew out to attend. Pat Kennedy Lawford decided to have some fun with Peter. He had on a new pair of jeans and Pat wore the same size pants. They were both slim-hipped, so it did not surprise him when she asked to try on his pants. However, the moment she put them on, she immediately went back to the party, leaving Peter in an upstairs bedroom with no pants and no change of clothing. He finally wrapped a towel around his waist and ventured down to the party to locate another glass of vodka and his ex-wife. She did not return his pants until the end of the evening. He was forced to send someone out to buy him a new pair.

The lighthearted joking hid a more serious problem at Christopher's birthday. Peter's gift to his son, a gift he thought was a proper present, was a container of cocaine.

Later Peter received a thank-you note from his son that read: "Dear Pedro, Thanks for making it cross country for my birthday. You were a surprise and the most honored guest of the evening. You made the party and I thank you. Oh, thanks for the gift. Unfortunately it was not one I could hold on to for very long."

What is sad is that it was obvious that each was reaching out to the other as best he could, yet nothing seemed to work. I became disgusted by what was taking place. We were in New York one evening, both Peter and I carrying cocaine on us for our own use later, when Christopher asked Peter where he could score some coke. Peter had a connection whose name and location he gave to Christopher. Then Peter spent a part of the night snorting cocaine with his son.

I felt that his snorting cocaine with Christopher was the worst possible example to set for his son, and I told him so the next day when Christopher was not around.

Peter was angry with me, constantly complaining about my Catholic morality. I had been educated in Catholic parochial schools until I was a senior in high school, and the Kennedy children had also been raised in the Catholic Church. Peter disliked my sense of morality because, as loose as it may have seemed at times, there were limits I could not cross without feeling great guilt.

Apparently Peter took my comments to heart. However, he did not have the strength and maturity to correct the relationship with his children, so he chose to avoid contact with them as much as possible. Unable to be a "pal" in the destructive way he had developed, Peter became cold, distant, desperately wanting to reach out to his kids and always holding himself back. It was an attitude that caused his children great pain and made them feel that he did not care for them. The truth was that he cared beyond his ability to cope with such feelings.

The result of all this turmoil was rather brutal. The children were always welcome to visit us and continued to do so. He seemed to like seeing them. But he deliberately cut himself off from them in other ways.

For example, Peter and I once took a trip to New York and made no effort to see the children. We were there for two weeks without telling the kids, then Peter sent each child what amounted to a form letter telling them that he was in good health, that he was happy with me, and that he loved them but wasn't going to see them there.

I was upset with Peter. I felt it was a very cold action. Small children who fail to get love and affection from a parent feel hurt, and, at times, guilty for somehow failing as individuals. They think that if they had done everything right they would have the parent's attention. They don't realize that an adult can be cruel.

Adult children, such as Peter's four, also feel the pain of rejection. However, they also understand the cruelty. They know that it is not something they have done. They recognize that it is a deliberate, hurtful act for no logical reason. As a result, their pain is also great, and only slightly eased because they are capable of more sophisticated reasoning.

Christopher was in his early twenties, his sisters in their teens. How terrible their pain must have been. How ironic that the man who freed me from my own suffering stemming from early child abuse could commit such emotional violence on his own children.

Unfortunately, withdrawing from responsibility and feelings was a common reaction for Peter when faced with emotional demands. He had done something just as cold to me when he had Milt Ebbins throw me out of the house during the period when he was divorcing Deborah Gould. There had been no mention of what was taking place or any of the underlying reasons. This was much the same, the form letter serving to avoid the feelings that seemed to be overwhelming him.

The children's pain from their rejection was best articulated by Peter's daughter Victoria. She sent him a letter that expressed her feelings in an eloquent manner. The letter was sent from her Aunt Ethel's home in McLean, Virginia, on July 11, 1978.

Dear Daddy,

I really don't know how to tell you this or how many times I've said this and meant it, but I love you. I don't know if you believe this but I hope to God you do.

I've never really had a chance to sit down and talk to you as father to daughter, but I guess I feel just as close to you as if I had. I guess the circumstances leave it difficult to get to know one another, but I hope this changes in time, Daddy.

I have to tell you I am very upset this year because last year I felt we got really close and then this year that all just fell apart. The reason I call so often is just to say hello and hear you because I do miss you.

When I heard you were ill from Patty, I wanted to go see you so badly and yet couldn't tell you over the telephone. I wanted to see you when you were here simply because I've waited all year. I know you're busy and I understand. I guess I just ask for things too far in advance; things I know I'll never get, but maybe that just takes time, too.

I didn't understand what's going on this year when you sent us all a typed letter trying to explain that you were happy, busy, and in good health. All of that makes me happy, but I still don't understand it.

I love you, Daddy, and I never want you to forget it.

Your daughter, always.

Victoria.

The letter was deeply moving. It also sat unopened until I removed it from the envelope. Peter did not have the courage to look at the mail that came from his children. Perhaps he feared their rejecting him. Perhaps he was frightened that they could touch his heart in ways he did not want to deal with.

He deeply loved his children. He wanted to be a father they could respect and care about. Yet there was too much turmoil, too many emotional changes caused by his fears, the alcohol and pill abuse.

I also think that Peter was shocked by the fact that he was living with a woman who was younger than his oldest child. He had to face an aspect of his life that he had never considered before; his own mortality.

There were occasional discipline problems with the children that Peter also did not know how to face. The Kennedy money, like many great family fortunes, became diluted by the tremendous number of Joe Kennedy's grandchildren. The money from the trust funds allows them an above-average income compared with that of most Americans, but it also requires them to hold jobs if they are going to be able to play in the manner with which they were raised. Yet the children could be and were spoiled, so many of their desires were so easily met that there were times when they showed a lack of self-restraint.

I remember one time when Peter and I were away and Christopher stayed at our house. During this period we were both abusing prescription drugs, a habit we were able to "enjoy" because we had dozens of doctors treating us without any of them being aware of how much the others were prescribing. This gave us access to legal prescriptions and also enabled us to have a running charge account at a pharmacy that was delighted to have our large volume of business.

Christopher knew about the account and took advantage of it while we were gone. He purchased whatever he wanted that the pharmacy sold, charging it to Peter. When we returned we discovered that we owed $1,300. In addition, Christopher forged a prescription for a Darvon compound, getting arrested for that action. Then, a week later, Christopher was in Aspen and again was arrested for forging a prescription.

Peter was not overly concerned that his son might be an addict or be heading into a life of crime. Peter was upset that Christopher's actions might hurt our credit. We had the perfect setup for drug abuse and needed the pharmacist's trust as well as the credit line.

The first time Peter had to face the seriousness of his son's problem was when we returned from a trip and came upon a large number of emergency vehicles parked near our home. There were drug agents' cars, sheriff's department cars, paramedics, and other law enforcement personnel. Lights were flashing and a crowd was gathered just outside the apartment.

We looked up and saw Christopher on a ledge, clutching a bag, preparing to jump. He had overdosed on heroin and he was no longer rational. He had no intention of trying to commit suicide. His brain was so confused at that moment that it seemed perfectly natural for him to walk off the side of the building. The fact that the fall could kill him was of no concern.

Then we saw another figure on a different ledge. He was a friend of Christopher's who had taken PCP ("angel dust"). He was also unable to reason logically and had decided to join Christopher in his trip over the side.

We had arrived in a limousine, gotten out long enough to see that the place was completely surrounded, trained individuals trying to talk the two youths back to safety, then gotten back into the car. Peter was terrified not only of what seemed about to happen but also of having to deal with it. He had been running from life for so long that he wanted to tell the driver to go on, that he could not handle being there with the crisis taking place.

We sat in the car, watching. Our apartment had been entered and searched, officers coming out with bags marked "evidence." They had confiscated our private stock of pills and marijuana plants. This was at a time when possession of marijuana was a criminal offense, even if the amount was so small that it was obviously being used only personally. That law has since been changed, but at that time every emotion we could have was taking place. We were frightened for what might happen to Christopher, who easily could have gone over the edge. We were concerned about whether or not we would be linked to the drugs that were being confiscated. And we were angry that our main supply had been compromised because, when the crisis was over, that would be the way we'd want to relax.

They even discovered the marijuana plants we were growing inside, plants we lovingly nurtured to provide us with a good source of "natural" drugs. About the same time that the agents were able to talk Christopher and his friend back far enough so that they could be grabbed and safely subdued, we watched our largest plant be carried out. Peter turned away from the handling of his son and said, sadly, "Oh, no, not that plant." It was our most beloved plant, thriving more than any of the others. He was more concerned about the loss of that plant than about the danger to Christopher.

Somehow Peter found both the courage and the maturity to get into the ambulance with his son. I stayed back to deal with the law enforcement officers, pleased that Peter was showing some maturity.

It was very late when Peter returned, his face ashen. Christopher had come near to death. The drugs he had taken were depressants. His respiratory system had slowed to the point where, without treatment, he would have died.

The doctors had had to inject Christopher with stimulants to combat the effects of the depressants. Then he had regained awareness of his surroundings, seen his father, and said, "Dad, how come you never yell at me? How come you never yelled at me?"

Peter said, "What do you want me to tell you? Not to do this? Don't do this? Don't do that? If you wanted a father who was going to go after you, you came to the wrong window. I'm not going to do it. I'll talk with you quietly but I'm not going to yell at you."

Christopher was longing for his father to show some authority, to set limits, to show that he cared. I don't know if Christopher started with drugs in order to get Peter's attention, to force Peter to react. He may have been like Peter, hurt, running away. Or he may have started with innocent experimentation, then discovered that using the drugs could mask the pain he was feeling. But as the problem progressed, he wanted Peter to stop him, to act as he felt a father should.

There would be other times when Peter would be with his son when Christopher was in trouble. Peter's love was intense, obvious to all who saw them during one of the crisis periods before Christopher sought help and began to gain control of his life.

Yet when the crises were over, when Peter and his son were together, he was unable to express his feelings. Peter could not tell Christopher he was loved. He had no idea how to talk to his son, holding in his feelings, going through life in a way that hurt the person he did not wish to hurt.

In the end, Christopher never realized that his father loved him.

The great sorrow was what might have been had either of them been able to break through the walls they both erected.

The drugs were a constant problem for us. Peter was a major star in Australia when we first got together, and one of his jobs was to promote a brand of Scotch whiskey in that country. We were flown overseas, traveling first-class, all expenses paid. We also made certain that we took a supply of cocaine with us because we had no idea whether or not we would be able to get any when we arrived.

Shortly before landing, Peter began talking about the Australian drug laws. At the time the Australians were extremely harsh to anyone attempting to bring drugs into the country. They were willing to jail anyone, regardless of how famous or important that person might be, if he or she violated the drug laws. As a result, Peter became increasingly worried about what might happen to us if we were caught with the coke.

Finally, Peter decided that the answer was for me to hide the drugs. I protested, explaining that with his celebrity status and family history, there would be no problem for him. He might be arrested, but they would let him out fairly quickly because of the scandal. I, on the other hand, would be jailed until I died of old age.

Peter wanted to hear nothing of it. He was the one earning the money for the family. It was better for me to try to bring them in. Besides, I had better ways to hide them. He was wearing kilts as part of the promotion, so he could not place something in a pocket. There was nothing he could do.

I gradually realized what he was trying to tell me. He wanted me to slip the tiny packages of drugs into my vagina. He tried to say it was no different from using a tampon, but I was disgusted. At the same time, I was as frightened as he was about being without the drugs. I did not think we could function for a prolonged period without being able to get high.

Finally I agreed, going into the lavatory on the plane in order to fit the drugs into my body as best as I could. They were extremely uncomfortable, and I was lucky that I did not cut myself trying to do it. However, I succeeded, landing with several grams of coke between my legs.

We walked outside to throngs of people. The whiskey company had arranged for everything for us. We had the finest possible treatment from everyone, including customs. They did not bother with a search of our possessions, waving us on to where a representative of the whiskey company was waiting with the limousine.

We got into the car and I was extremely uncomfortable. The

drugs had moved deeper into my body as I walked. I wanted them out and figured I could reach inside and remove them while we drove.

Just as I thought I could relax, the representative of the company got in the back, lowering the jump seat so that she could sit facing us. The drugs would have to remain until I could gain some privacy.

By the time we got to the hotel, I was furious with Peter. There had been no search. Others coming through had been subjected to a much more thorough check. And I was in pain. I felt that Peter had betrayed me, and I could not wait to remove the small packets.

Suddenly I panicked. The drugs were too firmly lodged for me to reach them with my fingers. I could not remove them. No matter what I did, they remained embedded. We had to arrange for a sympathetic doctor to take them from me, an extremely painful and embarrassing procedure.

On a trip through Rome's Da Vinci Airport, the drug problem was easier. That time Peter was convinced that the police used drug-sniffing dogs of all types. He stressed to me that the Italians were smart. They used specially trained dogs without regard to size, or so he believed. The obvious police dogs—large German shepherds, giant schnauzers, and the like—would not be there. But any dog, no matter how unlikely, could be an undercover narc. That was when we saw the Chihuahua.

Chihuahuas are the smallest dogs I've ever seen. They were named for one of the states in Mexico where they are bred. They are frequently high-strung and do not have the instincts for special training. Even if they could do the job, their temperament makes their use impractical. However, in his paranoid state, Peter decided the dog was working for law enforcement. We had to get rid of the drugs quickly.

As quickly and quietly as he could, Peter made his way to a trash can. There he quietly emptied all the hashish, cocaine, and marijuana he was carrying. Then he slipped back in line so we could safely go through customs. The Chihuahua sniffed his leg, Peter looking down, smiling smugly, knowing the drugs were gone.

We were both rather depressed as we made our way to the limousine. Then, just as we were getting inside, we saw a woman with the Chihuahua. The dog was leaping into a limousine directly ahead of us, the woman and the animal obviously going to a hotel or some other location, not the police station. For the first time Peter realized that the animal was a pet and that he had tossed the drugs for no reason.

"Don't go anywhere!" shouted Peter, racing back inside. He made a straight dash for the customs area, leaping benches and baggage as startled passengers stared at him. He breathlessly grabbed the trash can, then glanced up. There, a few yards ahead, was a man calmly emptying cans into a large container.

Peter moved the can he was holding. There was no sound.

He shook the trash can harder. Still no sound.

Then, slowly, he opened the lid and looked inside. The drugs were gone, taken by the trash collector and now covered by the waste from several other cans. If he ran to the man and began going through the large container, someone would become suspicious. There was nothing to do other than go back to the limousine and be driven to our hotel, where Peter berated me for not telling him how foolish it was to think so small a dog could be trained to work for the police. I just smiled politely.

I was frequently stoned on drugs during those early years together, yet I recognized what was happening in our lives. Peter was being used by people because he was generous with drugs. Major entertainers were constantly in our home—John Lennon, Keith Moon, Mick Jagger, and others. But they were there not for brilliant conversation, impromptu sessions with their instruments, or casual fun. They were there because drugs were available, liquor flowed, and Peter was the perfect host.

I would make the drinks, prepare the drugs, then feel as though I had to spend a couple of hours cleaning the house before the maid came in the next morning. I didn't want her to see the evidence of what had been taking place most of the night. Traces of cocaine were cleaned, liquor-stained furniture was scoured, pills were hidden away. And I was a wreck.

I remember one night when we had a party and I had to go to bed. A popular young comedian was present. He had just turned forty and he was feeling full of himself, impressed by his celebrity status, and expecting any woman he desired to want him with equal fervor. As a result, he walked into the bedroom and announced that I was going to have sex with him as a present in honor of his birthday.

I was indignant, yet he had had just enough of Peter's "private stock" that I don't think he recognized how serious I was about saying no to him. The next thing I knew he was trying to get my clothes off, not realizing that my objections were genuine. I began screaming, but between the loud music and the stoned guests, no one seemed to hear at first. I was facing being raped by a man who thought my protests were part of a game, not a serious attempt to tell him that he was going too far. He had come to expect anything during his visits to the Lawfords. Why not a sexual experience with Peter's woman?

My friend Don Brown heard my screams, came in, and grabbed the comedian. Don hit him and threw him out of the house.

The comedian had no idea that he was trying to do something I did not want. He was upset about being manhandled and never spoke with me again. After all, he had been in the Lawford's home, where anything you wanted you could have. Or so it seemed. I had become just another object, even though I never let myself be used.

There was another time when I briefly left Peter in disgust with the way we were living. I went to a nearby hotel, informing Peter that I would not return so long as I had to constantly be a drudge to freeloaders. When he talked me into returning, he had a special treat for me. The living room furniture had been rearranged so that there were lines of cocaine to snort, champagne, and a foam pad on which we could have sex.

Such a return would have made for a wonderful reconciliation for us except for the fact that Peter never quite knew when to stop. We had a beautiful marble fireplace, and he wanted the evening to be as romantic as possible. He had placed logs in the fireplace, then managed to start the blaze without properly fixing the damper. Partially burned pieces of paper rose up the chimney and then dropped onto the awning outside the window, setting the fabric ablaze. As I stared out the window, I saw a small amber light that grew in intensity until I realized what he had done. Instead of getting stoned, drunk, and having the sex Peter antici-pated, we had to place an emergency call for help, then watch the fire department put out the blaze.

The way I chose to live back then is something I continue to fight to this day. I enjoyed the drugs, the way they numbed my senses and dulled my mind so that I could accept whatever was taking place, do whatever Peter wanted. I liked traveling by limousine, by helicopter, by private jet. I never thought about how much money was going out and how little was coming in. I laughed when our friends called us "The Jetsons," a reference to a children's futuristic cartoon show where everyone always traveled by jet. And most of all, I reveled in the fact that my mother called me to talk.

There had been so much stress between my mother and myself, so much pain she had endured as a result of the split with my father, and so much isolation for me, that I desperately wanted her approval. She seemed to never telephone me after I first moved out of the house. If anything, she seemed angry because I was not around to help raise my half-brother.

But after I moved in with Peter I was "somebody." My mother would call me. My mother would take me to lunch. My mother would wonder what it was that he saw in this ugly duckling daughter of hers when she was more beautiful, more worldly, and quite successful. Being with Peter got me her attention and, I suspected, both her envy and approval.

In a way my mother and I are like Christopher and Peter. I don't know if we love each other, hate each other, or feel some combination of the two. I think we are each jealous of the other. I think we each long for the respect of the other, for a sense of mutual approval. Yet it seems impossible for us to express our true feelings. When I am in trouble, I want to run to her for help, for comfort, for advice. Yet I am afraid of rejection, fearful of scorn if she sees weakness, terrified of any perception that she might have that I "owe her" for her kindness. Neither one of us is willing to be vulnerable to the other. We are two strangers who lack the courage to discover our potential as mother and adult child.

I can express such feelings now, even though I am still wrestling with those overpowering emotions so many years after I left home. At the time I moved in with Peter, I understood none of my subconscious motivation. All I knew was that when I lived with Peter I also gained attention from my mother. When I was apart from him I seemed to never hear from her.

Fortunately, part of the time with Peter was filled with joy. I lived with Peter during the most destructive period of his life. Even today, while remembering the past and reading his writing in preparation for this book, I am haunted by dreams of the way he looked at the end, his body emaciated, incontinent, decaying. Yet when I look past all that I remember the suave, debonair, loving, brilliant, and witty gentleman who was the best friend I had ever had.

I was lucky. Although I was rebelling against my mother when I moved in with Peter, I did not live with him only to gain my mother's approval. I would have stayed with him no matter what because Peter was the first man to care about me. He loved me and wanted me to overcome the pain I had known in the past.

I still remember the time he bought me a teddy bear, for example. It was a rather adolescent wish, but I was an emotional adolescent for most of our life together.

The teddy bear was a large one, a toy meant for adults, not children. It cost $350, an outrageous price.

Peter pointed out how frivolous such a purchase would be. He hated the bear to begin with, and the price tag made it seem all the more foolish. In addition, he was beginning to be strapped for money, something I did not realize.

I begged and carried on, acting childish over this bear, yet I was serious about wanting it and would not give in. Reluctantly, he purchased it for me, complaining the entire time.

We were out late the night we made the purchase, and Peter had an early morning call for a show. As was my habit, I slept in after he left, rising later. It was then that I saw the bear hanging from the bedpost, a noose made from one of Peter's neckties around its neck. There was a "suicide note" from the bear saying that it could not handle the stress of our constant bickering and so it had chosen to end it all.

At first there were many good times, yet always there was an air of impending tragedy. He was constantly reminded that he was not the man he once had been.

There was the night that Don Brown came by our house unexpectedly. We were having dinner with some friends when he dropped by, thrilled because he had closed a business deal that had made him a large sum of money. To celebrate he announced that all of us were going to fly by private jet to Las Vegas, where we could catch Frank Sinatra's act at the Sands.

Don and I knew of Peter's falling out with Sinatra, yet that didn't matter. Sinatra has always been one of my favorite singers. He is a stylist without equal and Peter and I had many of his albums. The evening would be delightful.

We flew to the Sands, went in to the room where Sinatra would be appearing, and waited eagerly for the show to begin. Naturally Peter was recognized when we entered, and word must have gotten back to Frank. All I know is that the show did not start as scheduled. Instead, two very large men came by the table and explained that Mr. Sinatra would not perform as long as Peter was in the room. Either we left or there would be no show for anyone.

Peter was deeply hurt. We left, did some gambling, and returned home. It was an incident he did not wish to discuss, another devastating blow to his ego.

Then there were the people in Peter's life whom he trusted and depended upon for work. He was frequently being led to believe that there would be a terrific job that was just right for him, and that the job would be offered "next week." The trouble was that "next week" never came.

Creative people live on hope. They may be out of work and of no interest to the media today, but tomorrow they are going to be offered a starring role that will put them on top. Or maybe they will only be offered a bit part, yet they will handle that part so brilliantly that not only will the critics notice but so will producers and directors. Again their careers will turn around and soar.

Every creative person is hurt by rejection. That is only human. Yet creative people also have courage, facing failure after failure because they sense that their skills are improving or that their luck is about to change for the better. However, sometimes this only means that they are going to be shot down again and again and again, wounded so frequently by rejection that the wound eventually destroys them.

Perhaps people such as Peter's personal manager, Milt Ebbins, meant well when they told Peter about possible work that did not come through. Perhaps they believed what they were saying and were as shocked as Peter when the work did not materialize. But they were not the ones who had to endure the rejection. Peter was, and for him the experiences brought him to a point of despair.

Perhaps if he could have held out longer. Perhaps if he had been able to hang on until the soap operas became prime time programs and a handsome, older man with a British accent would have been in demand, everything would have worked for him. But it did not happen. And the drugs were taking their toll.

I began to think that there were as many different Peter Lawfords as there were different types of pills in our medicine chest and hidden around the house. He could be charming, gentle, sensitive, and kind. He could be a lover of animals and see joy in all the creatures God created. He could be the sex-mad director, a sort of Otto Preminger of the bedroom, who would arrange two naked women with special lighting and props, touching them, moving them about, and generally putting on a production whose climax was never satisfactory. And he could be the crazed madman who seemed destined to one day kill either himself or someone else.

We had an argument one day and I decided to walk out and go to a nearby hotel to meet a friend for a drink. It was a way to calm myself with someone whose companionship I enjoyed.

I was not gone for long, but it was long enough for Peter to take one of his "madman" pills. (I never knew what drugs would cause an adverse reaction, and neither did he. In general, he could flip out one way on Monday and a different way the following day, both times with the same drugs.) I returned home, went into the kitchen, reached into the refrigerator, and took out a bottle of grape juice.

Before I could close the door and pour myself a drink, I felt something cold against my head. Peter was holding a loaded revolver, threatening to blow my brains out for leaving him. He had decided that I must have had a rendezvous with some lover. Fortunately, somewhere deep inside his troubled mind, he knew that what he was saying was not true. He eventually put away the gun and, when his mind sufficiently cleared hours later, was horrified by what had almost happened.

I was desperate to get Peter help. We had been warned that his liver was deteriorating, that he was in danger of dying if he did not stop drinking.

The damage to Peter's body was so obvious that he dared not deny what was happening to him. Yet Peter kept insisting that a few years earlier, when his pancreas had gone bad, a doctor told him that he could never drink again. Yet he had survived and, in his mind, flourished by drinking and taking drugs.

Peter's daily routine was becoming one of drinking, taking whatever drugs he could afford, and watching television game shows and soap operas all day. He was existing, not living. Our money was almost gone, and he was beginning to borrow from friends.

Finally I tried to get out. I left for five months, trying to sort out my life, yet always recognizing that I loved Peter and that I wanted the man who existed underneath all the layers of drugs and drunkenness. When I came home, I found a sick shell of a man.

Peter had not cut his hair or his nails the entire time I was gone. He was incontinent, yet had not bothered to change the sheets. The floors were disgusting. The entire apartment looked as if wild animals had been penned up inside.

I was frightened, disgusted, wanting to lash out and weep at the same time. I mourned the loss of Peter Lawford, my friend, my father figure, my lover. I was angry at Peter Lawford, the little boy who was unable or unwilling to handle his own survival. And I was terrified of this living dead man who was so sick, so strange, so unlike anyone or anything I had ever known.

I helped Peter clean up. I began ridding the house of his vodka and pills. I fed him healthful meals. And I began attending meetings of Alanon, the Alcoholics Anonymous program for individuals who are living with alcoholics. There I learned about tough love, where the greatest love of all comes from not pampering someone who has become a dependent personality.

As I worked to help Peter, I remembered something that had happened a few years earlier. I was traveling abroad with a girl-friend, driving on a road that paralleled the ocean, when a truck suddenly appeared. We were knocked over the edge of the cliff, landing upside down in the water. There was no reason we should have lived, yet, miraculously, we both survived. My friend was paralyzed, and she is still in a wheelchair. My back was broken, though I was in enough shock that there was no pain until I reached the hospital.

I was placed in a full body cast, unable to walk for many weeks. Peter was horrified by my condition and changed his life so that I would never be alone. He stayed by my side for the next three and a half months, even carrying me into the bathroom and helping me.

Peter was so gentle and understanding that I did not feel humiliated. He cared for me selflessly. His only concern was my comfort, my healing. I needed someone desperately, and he never left my side. Seemingly close friends were uncomfortable with me in the cast. Only Peter stood by me.

Peter seemed to make an effort to regain his health as I cared for him. He tried to stop the use of the drugs and alcohol. His mind cleared, and he was his old charming self. He was on the rebound and doing much better. Still there was no work. He could not face some of his former friends. Some of them had never been friends but drug-using hangers-on who wanted nothing of a sober man. And some were too busy with their own careers to think much about Peter.

Peter's last movie was a rather pathetic gathering of brilliant "losers"—men who had been major stars but had not been offered good roles in several years. There was Peter, Orson Welles, and Tony Curtis. The film, which mercifully opened and closed within four days, was called *Where Is Parsifal?* The plot should have been a clue to its potential for success, because the story was about a man who invented a skywriting machine that could save the world. It was filmed in England in an old mansion called Hamden House that had originally been owned by a Lord Hamden, whose one major distinction was that he assassinated a king. Many horror movies had been filmed in the house, which had been only marginally modernized over the years. The toilet seats, for example, were oversized and made of wood that was not properly sanded. You had to sit carefully to avoid falling through. You also had to position yourself with caution because there were splinters.

The bedrooms were no more appealing. There was a single light bulb in the ceiling, a wardrobe rack, a small cot, and the bathroom down the hall. We stole a down comforter from the girl down the hall, yet we were still cold at night because the walls were poorly insulated.

The grounds were enormous. I was told that it was thirteen miles from the main gate to the front of the house. It would have taken half a day to get there by horse-drawn carriage.

The house was magnificent despite the problems. The dining room could seat two hundred people. I imagined a group of Middle Ages diners throwing food around and wiping their hands on passing dogs during the orgies.

I wanted to be useful on the set and kept trying to find some job I could do. What I did not expect was that I would be hired to feed Orson Welles.

The catering for the cast and crew was done by a company that served heavy food. There was shepherd's pie, steak and kidney pie, roast beef and mashed potatoes, and other things all meant to be quite filling. Every time we ate, we felt as though we should follow the meal with a three-hour nap. The one exception was Orson Welles.

Orson Welles was one of the greatest actors and directors of his time, with a voice that was riveting. He had achieved great fame for projects such as his radio presentation of "The War of the Worlds" and the movie *Citizen Kane*, yet he never reached the heights predicted for him. He was a genius who was underemployed, working on too few films over his career. He was also a rather troubled man who seemed to turn to gluttony for solace in his later years, ballooning to grotesque size.

Orson was late arriving in England, having taken the wrong directions and somehow ending up in France. A special plane had to be dispatched to Paris because his several hundred pounds of weight did not enable him to fit in a normal first-class seat. Then he had to be conveyed by a London cab to the movie location because he could not fit in a limousine.

Orson played Klingsor, a magician, who was supposed to first be seen arriving in a Daimler. However, they found that he would not fit, nor would he fit in a Rolls-Royce or other luxury vehicle that would have been logical for the film. Thus, they had to use the London cab for shooting the scene as well. The cab, which normally can seat six, was filled with just Orson and the driver.

I was hired to feed Orson, a job that seemed a little odd. Peter laughed at me, but because he sat with the crew, not the actors, he never realized what was to be involved.

Orson was kept in the basement of the house because the steps to the upper floors, where everyone else was eating, would not hold his bulk of at least four hundred pounds. My job was to take him his food.

I took him a plate. I figured that he had a healthy appetite, so I gave him a little of everything. I gave him some slices of prime rib, some Yorkshire pudding, plus plenty of vegetables to create a heaping full plate.

Just then the director came over, irate. He called me a twit, berating me for not doing my job.

"There's no reason to be abusive," I explained. "I'm just doing what you asked."

As it turned out, my idea of feeding Orson Welles did not match the man's appetite. The director handed me a platter of a size meant to hold an entire turkey. "Fill it, and repeat same in fifteen minutes."

I stared at him, then realized that he was serious. I heaped food on the platter, took it down to the basement, having to turn sideways to get down because the platter was so large.

The director said, "Now I want you to knock lightly on the door, say, 'Mr. Welles, your dinner is here,' and leave it for him. Then go back upstairs, because by the time you're done, you'll have to do it again."

I did as he said, then walked up six steps to the landing and glanced back. Suddenly the door opened, a hand shot out, and the plate was jerked inside so rapidly that it made a whooshing noise. When I looked back down the stairs a few minutes later, the platter was out, piled with bones. I repeated the process with a fresh platter, a pattern I was to follow the entire time we were there.

Orson Welles had been close to Peter from the time that Peter did *Othello* in London with Orson, and the two of them hung out together. They also had another connection—Peter had had an affair with Rita Hayworth, and Orson had married her. Peter said that going to bed with Rita showed him why the two would get along so well together. He said that after having sex, Rita got up, went to the refrigerator, opened the door, sat on the floor, and ate everything she could find. The sex act was foreplay for her gluttony, somehow she managed to keep her weight at a level where she remained beautiful.

I was shocked by the image, but Peter assured me it was true. "She was the worst lay in the world," he said. "She was always drunk and she was always eating."

Orson Welles did not know that Peter and I had been living together when he saw the two of us together on the set. He looked at Peter and said, "So there you are, Lawford, a man who knows no shame." His voice was deep, rich, like melodically rolling thunder, the tympany section of a celestial orchestra. "What are you doing with this young one?"

"I've been with her now for about nine years," Peter said.

"Oh, dear God, help us!" commented Orson.

"I'm the one who's been shoving those barrels of food in front of your door, Mr. Welles," I told him, though I don't know where I got the nerve. Everyone on the set was afraid of him except Peter. He was brilliant, imposing, and not a little strange.

Welles resided in Hollywood and did not live for very long after the movie was made. What touched me, since both Peter and I loved animals, was that he willed his beloved French poodle, Fifi, to his neighbor. It was his first bequest and, I'm certain, in his mind the most important.

Except in England, where the quarantine laws were too strict, Orson carried Fifi everywhere. They went into his favorite Los Angeles restaurant, Cafe Moustache, together, Fifi sitting obediently on a chair while he dined.

Peter's drinking began again, and I was desperate to find a treatment center where he could get help. I felt certain that there had to be a place where someone would be able to get through to him, say something that would convince Peter to stop his self-abuse. I sensed that he hated himself, but I thought he could learn to see the potential that I felt was still within him.

Eventually I thought of the Betty Ford Center in Rancho Mirage, California. This is a center named after a former alcoholic and wife of Republican president Jerry Ford. Mrs. Ford had been a substance abuser even during the White House years. She had had the courage to face her addiction, go in for treatment, then tell the public what had happened to her. She dedicated herself to helping others with the same problem, the center being a tribute to her caring.

I had been told that the center might work for Peter, but I was also told something else, something I did not wish to hear. A man who was a former alcoholic and worked with alcoholics told me that Peter might be one of those people who had to die.

There is a saying among addicts that you have to hit bottom before you can recover. "Hitting bottom" means many things to different addicts. Sometimes it is the threat of losing a job or a spouse that causes the person to decide to get help to become sober. Sometimes the person simply has a minor traffic accident when he or she thought no one would notice the liquor for lunch. No one is hurt in the accident, but it is enough of a shock for the person to admit that there is a problem. And sometimes hitting bottom means losing job, family, home, and self-respect, sleeping in a gutter until forced into a treatment center where there is the first taste of sobriety the person has had in years.

But there is another type of hitting bottom. This occurs when nothing seems to reach the individuals involved. Their careers end, their relationships fail, they use all of their money. But whatever the specifics, the person refuses to quit even as body organs are damaged and then cease to function, loved ones beg for change, counselors speak to them, and everything that can be tried is tried. Nothing works to stop the drinking except the person's death. It is the final form of hitting bottom, and the counselor I consulted believed that that would be the fate for Peter.

The idea that Peter might have to die was not something I could contemplate. Peter was going to live and I was going to ensure that he made it. He *had* hit bottom. He was not going any lower. I had given him mouth-to-mouth resuscitation in the past—literally the breath of life. Doctors had written him off as a dead man before and he had proven them wrong. I was going to get that man well no matter what it took.

The Betty Ford Center did not share my enthusiasm. They were not comfortable accepting Peter. They were a serious treatment facility, they wanted me to understand, not a place that could be a three-ring circus with show business people in and out of there.

The trip to Betty Ford in December, 1983 would have been a comedy had Peter's life not been at stake. First we flew to Palm Springs, California, the nearest airport to the center. Peter consumed little bottles of vodka throughout the flight, becoming quite drunk by the time we landed.

Then we got into a car and drove to the center, something Peter did not quite understand. "Where are we going?" he asked.

"To Betty Ford's," I told him.

"That's wonderful," he said. "I've always liked Betty Ford."

Peter was as happy as a clam, prattling on. We were obviously going over to Betty Ford's house for dinner. He was certain of that. It came as quite a surprise when he entered the medical facility.

I stayed with Peter during the days of detoxification. The situation was rough for him, his body having become chemically dependent on a poison. Withdrawal caused extreme discomfort, yet was necessary for his survival. Fortunately, he seemed well, and I felt comfortable returning to Los Angeles. However, as soon as I returned home I found out that he had made an attempt to escape out into the desert, looking for a liquor store.

Part of the Betty Ford program involves Alcoholics Anonymous. They use special booklets published by Hazelden Educational Materials that provide a guided entry into the AA program. This series of booklets, around which the center's therapy sessions were built, begins with the first step: "We admitted that we were powerless over alcohol, that our lives had become unmanageable."

In the back of several of the booklets are self-analysis questions to be answered. The notes Peter made are interesting, sometimes painful, and sometimes quite revealing. For example, when discussing the topic of selfishness, he admitted: "There is no question, I want what I want now!" Then he added something that showed how insensitive he was toward both me and the friends who tried to help him along the way. He said: "I only hurt myself, not others that I am aware of."

More revealing was Peter's writing about resentment. He stated: "I resent where I'm living right [sic]. I had to move from my old place because of lack of funds. It makes one rather frustrated watching one's life going down instead of up—especially at my age. . . ."

Peter was not the most cooperative patient at first. He was rebellious against the authority of the center, an attitude necessary to maintain discipline for people whose lives have long been out of control. Eventually, however, Peter went from being belligerent to being extremely cooperative. The staff and I thought that a breakthrough in Peter's attitude had finally occurred. The reality was quite different.

I was taking an increasing interest in our finances at this point. I had gotten into conflict with the man who worked with Peter on financial matters because we were in so much trouble. I thought that he had failed to warn Peter. Instead, he was upset with me for living so lavish a life style when he was certain I knew we could not afford it. When we both realized that I knew nothing of our financial situation, I took the trouble to begin to carefully check what was happening to our money. That was why I noticed what seemed to be an odd charge on our American Express credit card bill.

The charge was for plane and helicopter charters during the time when Peter was in the Betty Ford Center and I was at home. There was no way Peter could have flown, and I certainly had not used the card. Since no one else had access to our cards, I assumed that a mistake had been made.

There was no error. Peter had had enough of life in the slow lane. Sobriety was fine with him, so long as someone else practiced it. He managed to contact a drug dealer who regularly supplied him with whatever he needed. He had the dealer fly cocaine to the Betty Ford Center using the chartered aircraft. The pilot of the helicopter landed in the desert behind the center, an area where no one would normally think to check. A patient searching out there will find nothing to drink except the juice of a cactus. The center is so isolated that Peter's wandering off caused no concern at all. They did not realize that he met his dealer, did a few lines of cocaine, and felt wonderful about everything and everyone. He was much more willing to work in the program once he found he could do it and not abandon his old ways.

The center's program lasts for five weeks, but Peter stayed six weeks at my request. The first week he was not truly involved, cheating at every opportunity.

For example, all patients who go to Betty Ford must be fully responsible for their own care. Many have had servants and lived in pampered luxury, but while at the center they have to do their own wash. They must vacuum the halls, make their beds, and generally be useful.

Peter rebelled against doing his own laundry that first week, even though the patients are provided simple clothing, such as sweatsuits, so that the task is an easy one. He waited for me to come and visit, then brought me his clothing, insisting I do the wash for him. Only after the second week did he begin taking care of himself and, by the time he was finished, he actually discovered that he liked to vacuum.

I still remember the day he came home, complaining because I had never told him how much fun it was to vacuum. I said that it was boring, but he disagreed. He bragged about the straight lines he could make with the vacuum and he did it at every opportunity. In fact, later, when he returned to drugs and would alternate between vacuuming and going into the bathroom to snort a line of cocaine, I called the Betty Ford Center, irate. "I sent you Peter and I got back a fucking maid who gets high," I complained. "You were paid my last five thousand dollars and Peter still snorts drugs. But he does clean the house."

Peter's first few days back were delightful. He emerged from the Betty Ford Center looking wonderful. His body chemistry had stabilized, and he had been off alcohol the entire time he was there. I thought that I had found the miracle cure for Peter, only to get a call from a bartender three days later. Peter was so drunk he had to be brought home.

I am not bragging when I say that Peter and I were probably closer than he had ever been with any other woman in his life. I

was with him during a time when he was able to settle into a
relationship more than at any time in the past. He loved me
deeply, committing to me more than he had with anyone. And
this belief was shared by those interviewed for this book who had
known him over the years as he went from wife to wife and
girlfriend to girlfriend. Yet such a relationship was not enough to
overcome the drug-induced stupor that prevented him from helping me when I was raped.

It was 1982 when the incident occurred, less than three years
before Peter's death. I was extremely naive when it came to
understanding my body and what I should expect from the medical profession. Despite the seeming wildness of my life, I was in
some ways a rather sheltered girl who had been educated by nuns
in a strict Catholic environment. There was little health information provided and no sex education, other than learning that sex
was for marriage and procreation only. Sex as fun was a mortal
sin, and no one discussed the normal biological concerns a woman
faces. After all, going to see a specialist in obstetrics and gynecol-
ogy might mean having to take your clothes off while a stranger
examined your body.

I needed a checkup, and chose a doctor who had an excellent
reputation and was working with many women in Beverly Hills.
He was extremely conservative in appearance and demeanor, so I
thought nothing special about him.

The first problem, though I did not realize it at the time, was
that he saw me alone. There is nothing illegal or unethical about a
male doctor being alone with a female patient. However, considering the woman's vulnerability and the intimate nature of the
various tests that have to be performed, it is normal for a nurse or
other female employee to be present. This serves to comfort and
protect the patient, who may be uneasy about being naked and
alone with a male doctor. This also protects the doctor from
allegations of sexual misconduct. Even female gynecologists usually follow this procedure. Yet I knew nothing of this and simply
accepted that I was seeing him on my own.

The doctor had to perform a minor procedure on me and was
meeting me before he began to work. He had some questions, one
of which was "Do you masturbate?"

I was embarrassed and a little shocked, though I realized that
this was undoubtedly a routine question that all such specialists
asked. He was speaking quietly, the question no different than if
he had said "Do you have any pain in your side?" Still, I was
reluctant to answer.

"It's a good idea to masturbate before this procedure because it helps you relax."

I explained that I was fine, that I was certain it would be unnecessary. I wondered at how naive I was to not have known about this. After all, in a way what he was saying made sense.

"I could do it for you, if you like," he said. Still his expression and tone of voice did not change. There was nothing seductive about it. He was offering me nothing more than a mild tranquilizer in a completely safe form. Or so his voice indicated.

The procedure was handled without masturbation by either of us. There were no complications and I thought nothing of what had happened.

Since he never did anything out of line, I simply assumed that his seemingly odd question was standard. If I had asked any of my girlfriends about their visits to their gynecologists, they undoubtedly would have said, "Oh, of course, questions about masturbation are a routine part of all exams. You mean you didn't know that?" And then they would have laughed at me.

I didn't see him again until I had some problems with severe cramping that made me realize something was not quite right. I called to ask if I could see him and he told me to come to his home, where he had an examining area.

This time there really was nothing unusual about what he was saying. It is common in Los Angeles for professionals to buy a large home or apartment, then establish a separate office area. His office was quite separate, and the furnishings completely proper. Nothing was out of line.

Time passed and I had learned to trust the gynecologist. I felt comfortable telling him of intimate problems that might affect my body. That was why, when I had to go to New York and was quite late with my period, he told me to stop by his home office. He said that I simply had a recurrence of a hormone imbalance that had troubled me in the past. He would give me a hormone shot that would induce the period and I would be fine.

He gave me the shot. I explained that I normally followed a perfect schedule of every twenty-eight days and I was concerned. I made an appointment to see him upon my return from New York.

I drove to the doctor's office upon my return. It was 5:30, the end of his day, the nurse and all patients having long gone.

"Get up on the table so I can examine you," he said.

"Okay," I replied, climbing on, laying on my back, elevating my legs, and positioning my feet in the stirrups. It was the standard examining position all women take. I was positioned in such a manner that I could not easily get down. There was just enough restraint so that I was relatively helpless, a situation that caused me no concern whatever. This was my doctor and I trusted him.

The doctor kept his speculum, a metal examining instrument, in a warmer so that there would be no discomfort from a cold metal probe being inserted in the vagina. He removed it from the warmer and then shoved it inside me.

The pain was intense. He began jabbing at me, my natural instinct being to jam my legs together. I could not rise, could not strike at him, and each time I jerked my legs, I only made them all the more set in the stirrups. I might as well have had my ankles bound with slipknots.

I could feel myself bleeding. He was hurting me, saying nothing as I screamed.

I never felt the doctor enter me. I was already in too much pain. I just knew that everything was wrong as he became verbally abusive, saying, "This is what you've wanted, bitch. You needed a fuck." He zipped up his pants, moved to the side of the examining table, and struck me.

I have never before seen madness in the eyes of someone I trusted. This man was no longer a doctor, a caring healer. He was a rapist, violent, barely in control. I had the feeling that if I protested, he might kill me.

The doctor left the room for a minute and I removed my feet from the stirrups, getting down from the table. I could not think about the rape. I could not think about the violence. The only thought in my mind was "Blood."

Somehow Peter had managed to find enough money to make the down payment on a beautiful white lynx coat for me, a coat I had been wearing when I went to see the doctor. I was wearing white slacks, a white sweater, and the upholstery of my car, a Volkswagen Rabbit, was white. In my terror, all I could think about was that the blood would stain it all.

Desperately I tried to find some towels to place between my legs to stop whatever bleeding I could.

The doctor had left his office, setting the perimeter alarm so he would know if I tried to get out. Fortunately, wherever he had gone, he was not close enough to stop my escape. I got into the car, started the engine, and drove to the emergency room of St. John's Hospital. Towels were piled under me and I was in great pain.

The hospital staff was wonderful to me. They got me right in the emergency room, asking what had happened.

I wanted to tell them the truth. I wanted to tell them about the doctor who had raped me. I wanted them to know that there was a madman with a license to practice medicine.

At the same time, I realized that if I told the staff the truth there would be newspaper headlines. WIFE OF PETER LAWFORD RAPED BY GYNECOLOGIST! DOCTOR SAID SHE HAD NO SEX AT HOME SO HE HELPED. The whole idea was a nightmare.

The entertainment industry is rather strange in that there are good crimes and bad crimes with which you can be involved. If you're going to be a victim, do it in a way to which everyone can relate. Be stabbed twenty-seven times. Be mugged, beaten, and thrown off the top of the Arco Plaza Building. Get repeatedly run over by a Bentley in Beverly Hills. But do not get raped by your gynecologist and expect sympathy, understanding, or pity. I would have been ridiculed, and Peter would have had even a harder time getting work. We would both be the butt of jokes, something I was not ready to handle.

"My boyfriend did this to me," I lied, never mentioning the rape. I let them treat me for my injuries without telling them my name. I had buried all identification in the trunk of the car before arriving so they couldn't learn about me while I was being treated. I also informed them that I was walking out the moment they tried to call the police.

To my relief, the staff respected my wishes. I made a telephone call to Peter to have him pick me up. "I need you," I told him. "Something has happened that is so terrible, I need to see you right away."

"What is it?" he said, angrily.

"Peter, I'm in the hospital," I said.

"I don't understand you."

"Peter, are you loaded?" I asked, realizing that he sounded stoned.

"Fuck you!" he shouted, slamming down the receiver.

I called my girl friend Laurie, told her I was in St. John's, and she told me she'd be there in ten minutes. She took me home without questioning me, even though the hospital wanted to keep me for the night.

I told Laurie everything as she drove me home. She was irate, going into the house and telling Peter that he had better talk with me.

"What are you doing here?" he asked, unable to see or think clearly. He was so drugged that Laurie spent the night with me, caring for me while he slept.

I had still been unable to talk about this with Peter when Laurie brought an area newspaper to our home. In it was a story about my doctor, who had been arrested on eight counts of molestation. He had been caught by an undercover police officer posing as a patient. The story also gave the name of a police officer who was coordinating the investigation and was looking for other women who might not have reported their assaults.

The situation became worse very quickly. The article indicated that there were several charges against the doctor, but none were as serious as mine. There were charges of attempted rape and more mentioning molestation. He apparently was becoming more violent each time, mine being the worst, and I was keeping silent because of Peter.

Then I went to another doctor because I still had not had my period. This time there was no hormonal problem. The rape had impregnated me. I was carrying the doctor's child.

Had I told the hospital that I was raped, not just hurt by my "boyfriend," they would have given me what is called a morning after pill. This would have caused a spontaneous abortion if I was pregnant and would have caused me no harm if I was not. It is routinely given to rape victims. In my case, I knew that the pregnancy was literally only days old. There was no way I could consider carrying the child to the point where I would be aware of a new life. I agreed to a saline abortion.

All this was too great for me to handle alone. Two weeks after the rape I called the police officer whose name had been mentioned in the paper.

The officer, a woman, was kind, attractive, and very professional. However, Peter still had no idea what had happened. All he knew was that a female police officer was at the door and it aroused him. A female police officer could handcuff him and hit him with her stick. It would be the ultimate sadomasochistic experience, and it excited him as much as he was capable of being excited. He had no idea why she was there, though I could tell he hoped that she was a present for him. He had once mentioned that he thought a threesome with a policewoman would be wonderful. He felt I had finally decided to let him have his fun.

The officer interviewed me privately. I told her everything that had happened and stressed that I would not go into court. I was still worried about the future of Peter's career, not realizing that it was over. He was in the process of dying and would never be able to work again. But I still held the fantasy that he would successfully perform again.

"Do you know what happened here, Mr. Lawford?" she said to Peter. Her manner was cold, hard. I had explained everything to her, including the fact that Peter was a drug addict. The result was that she was irate, tearing into him for his insensitivity, lack of awareness, and lack of caring.

I thought I was all right. I thought I was handling things well. Then I checked the mailbox and discovered that the doctor had sent me a bill for the time when he was raping me. And Peter, his mind fogged with drugs, wondered if I had encouraged the man.

"Peter, I have to get away. I'll be gone five or six days. Good-bye," I told him, taking a suitcase and leaving our home. It was May, and I did not return until October.

I wanted a complete break from Peter. Using what little cash I could get, I changed my name, got a job, and lived in Hawaii. I wanted to be on my own, cope with my own life, and not have to experience the destructive ego of Peter Lawford. I also made some trips back to the mainland, including one to Las Vegas, where I made contact with Frank Sinatra, the man Peter still considered an enemy.

Ironically, it was Frank Sinatra who got me to call Peter after all that time. He told me that he had heard from mutual friends that Peter was hurting extremely badly. He was not doing well without me. Frank encouraged me to telephone.

Peter sounded awful on the telephone. I loved him and he loved me, that was our truth. He was an alcoholic, a drug addict, a dysfunctional Don Juan, a weak man in many ways. But Peter was my friend, the one true friend I had ever known. He was my father figure and, in the past, in his own way, my lover. No matter how upset I had been. No matter how positive a move my leaving had been for me, he still had a hold on me. We could not stay apart.

I rushed back to Peter only to find that the situation had gotten worse than anything I had ever known before. He had seldom washed or shaved. He had failed to change the kitty litter, our cat using sofa cushions on which to relieve herself. There was clothing everywhere, dirty dishes, rotting food. I was horrified as I viewed what amounted to a walking corpse. He was depressed and had lost all will to live.

I helped Peter clean himself up, then tackled the apartment. It took hours to restore the place and days to get Peter reacting more naturally. Once again he seemed to be returning from the dead.

During this time, indeed, literally through to his death, Peter was working on his autobiography. For many years people had wanted him to write such a book because of his colorful life, the people he had known, and other facets of his world. He finally decided to do it, and asked Wayne Warga, then a waiter for the television program "Entertainment Tonight," to assist him. Sterling Lord of the Sterling Lord Agency was handling the sale and, by the time Peter was hospitalized for what was to prove to be the final time, contract negotiations were under way with a large New York publisher. Peter was excited, making notes, preparing an outline, and generally showing more enthusiasm for the book than for anything he had done in quite a while.

Yet Peter was also having trouble keeping his mind on anything for very long. Sometimes Wayne would just get started interviewing Peter when Peter would declare that they had worked enough. He would change clothes and go out to use the apartment's swimming pool. Wayne would sit, stunned, trying to salvage the session by interviewing me. Thus, work on the book progressed extremely slowly.

Weeks passed, and suddenly Peter announced to me that he was bored with the way we were living. He said that we should go to Barbados and get formally married (Peter's writings over the years indicated that he considered me his common-law wife almost from the time we moved in together). It was a ridiculous idea on the one hand and a wonderful one on the other. I said yes.

We started for the airport, taking a route that, fortuitously, passed near UCLA Medical Center. As we drove, he suddenly complained of severe pain, his stomach becoming distended. He had to be admitted on an emergency basis right away. There was no way we could go any further.

Peter was diagnosed as having a bleeding ulcer that required emergency surgery. I was told that he might not survive.

But Peter *did* live, and we were married in his room the next afternoon. I wore white. Peter wore a hospital gown. And the patient in the next bed (we no longer could afford a private room) vomited through the entire ceremony. When it was over, Peter pointed to his roommate, who was dying, and said, "This is a sign of things to come."

I laughed at Peter's joke. I didn't know it was a prophecy.

Our wedding night was spent together until I finally left at 5 A.M., wondering how much longer he would live. I let his children know that their father was in trouble, but they had heard it before. He had been hospitalized eighty-five times during the decade we were together. No matter what happened, Peter recovered. In my anger, I felt that their attitude was that they were tired of his slow deterioration. If he was going to die, he was going to die. (Later three of the children did come by, they did see him, they were concerned. We were all just hurting so much that none of us was able to reach out to the others.)

Christopher came to ask for some of his father's possessions. I pointed out that he was a bit premature since his father was still alive and, with luck, would continue to be.

By the time Peter was able to return home, his body was in terrible shape. Thirty-five percent of his stomach had been removed. I learned to flush his stomach, feeding him through a tube. For the first four postoperative months Peter had to be fed through that tube every ninety minutes around the clock. I had to assist him to the bathroom (his weight had dropped more than 45 pounds to 120). His food had to be prepared according to an extremely strict diet. Yet he was improving. Slowly he was improving.

The doctors were pleased until the gastro tube had to be removed. Suddenly Peter was bleeding uncontrollably. With all the liver damage, an enzyme was not being formed that allowed blood to clot. He had developed coagulopathy, a problem that was life-threatening. Yet again he survived.

The next morning Peter was going to the bathroom by himself when he accidentally bumped his arm against the door. Although a normal person would only have been bruised from the bump, his arm became swollen to several times its normal size. Then, three days later, blood came out of the surface of his arm as though it were sweat. He had to be hospitalized immediately, and I was told that the slightest bump to his head, even during a sudden stop in the car, could kill him. As it was, Peter had to spend three weeks in the hospital recovering. He was also told that if he drank again, he would be dead.

By Thanksgiving of 1984 Peter was near death, though still so mobile that we went to dinner at the home of Elizabeth Taylor. Peter was on a restricted diet and taking large quantities of medication. This was a delicate situation because his liver was severely damaged. As a result, some of the medication needed to treat a problem affecting one portion of his body, such as his kidneys, could be dangerous to a different, weakened section of his body, such as his liver or heart. Everything had to be delicately balanced so that the cure for one problem did not cause an equally severe problem somewhere else.

I was sleeping less and less each day, becoming severely depressed. We could not afford help, though I discussed with his children that perhaps he should be placed in a medical facility where he could receive around-the-clock nursing. The children saw no reason for that.

I was increasingly angry with the children. They had access to money and could easily have helped their father.

At the same time, I was aware that they had been emotionally starved from being raised in a disturbed environment. Many of the Kennedys were alcoholics and drug addicts. Their sexual lives were such that emotional commitment was impossible. Peter had denied his children his presence through divorce, then tried to be everything except the involved father they wanted and needed.

Yet he was still their father. This was the man who had been with them during the earliest years of their lives, a man who loved them despite his inability to express that love. He was sick, disturbed, dying, and they were too shallow, too hurting, or both, to care. I was his wife. I would be the one to clean him. I would change the dressings. I would feed him, give him his medicine, and never sleep for longer than an hour or two at a time as I worked around the clock to keep him alive.

Peter had maintained his tan through sunbathing, though it was tinted now with the yellow of jaundice. He certainly looked and sounded well enough for Elizabeth to think it would do Peter good to have a job. She was going to star in a television movie called "Malice in Wonderland," the story of two infamous Hollywood gossip columnists, Hedda Hopper and Louella Parsons, and there would be a bit part for him to play. Quietly, behind the scenes, she arranged with the producer, Jay Benson, to hire Peter.

I tried to explain to Elizabeth that Peter could not handle the task. He was too far gone to be able to perform.

But Peter hid his problems well. She did not believe that he was as bad as I indicated. Jay Benson was comfortable with giving him the part as a favor to Elizabeth.

Elizabeth did warn Peter that he had better not screw up his chance. She was going out on a limb for him and did not want his addictions to interfere.

Peter only laughed. He found Elizabeth's sobriety extremely funny. She had conquered her addiction and was determined to straighten out her life. She had tapped an inner strength that she was not going to lose for anyone. I was extremely impressed with her courage, but all he could do was tease her. He would refer to when she was a drunk and say, "You used to have a personality. You used to be interesting."

Peter was terrified of going in front of the cameras again. He began to drink heavily, then telephoned his old connections in order to buy marijuana and cocaine. He was not going to disappoint Elizabeth. He was going to do the role.

I talked with one of Peter's doctors, telling him what was going on. The doctor talked sternly to Peter, yet it all seemed to be a drama staged for my benefit. It was obvious to me that the doctor was willing to go along with whatever Peter wanted. He did not like Peter's self-destructive behavior, yet he also did not want to alienate Peter Lawford, the movie star, the brother-in-law of the late Jack Kennedy. I was witnessing what I call the Hollywood "starfucker" phenomenon, and Peter was going to die because of it.

Peter collapsed again and had to be taken to Cedars Sinai, where they used vitamins and other treatments to try to lower the toxicity in his body. His liver was not functioning properly, and he was in serious trouble. However, he was able to get around again by the time he had to go on the set.

I arrived at the hospital early in the morning to get Peter, knowing that I would have to spend the day on the set with him. To my surprise, he was not downstairs waiting for me, though he had been checked out of the hospital. I left the car in an area that was improper, looking around desperately. Then I spotted him walking down the street, happy as could be. He told me he had gone for a walk, nothing more. It was only after we got on the set that I discovered his walk had been to a nearby store, where he was able to buy small bottles of vodka, the type they have on airplanes.

For the first time everyone connected with the show understood what was happening. Peter Lawford was not on that set. In his place was a pathetic shell of a man, someone who could not remember his lines, his cues, or why he was there. He was yellow from jaundice, his movements were painfully slow. Gone was the quick study. Gone was the natural movement that convinced people he was a trained dancer. Gone was the consummate professional who could be brilliant in a single take or brilliant twenty times over if it took that many times to get a scene to be perfect.

Elizabeth, extremely upset, came over and whispered that she should have listened to me. Peter could not even say "Hello, my name is Tony." The crew kept glaring at me, as though it was my fault that this pathetic creature was on the set. Finally I hid out, returning only when his dressings needed changing. Aching for him, I took him home at the end of the day, only to have him fall asleep without dinner.

Peter awakened on the next day, a Saturday, long enough for fresh orange juice. He slept the rest of the day and seemed about to sleep through Sunday when I risked taking thirty minutes to go to the market. By the time I returned Peter was incoherent and blood was all over the apartment. The telephone was also ringing, though I did not answer it, and Peter was incapable of knowing it was even there.

Later I learned that the caller had been Jay Benson. He was firing Peter from the show.

I dialed 911, but the emergency service had to ask questions before they could send the paramedics and I didn't think we had that much time. I had to half carry Peter, rushing to get him out, when the telephone rang. Ironically, it was Jay Benson again. "Pat," he said.

"Yeah, I know what you're going to tell me," I said, too tired to want to deal with any of this, yet knowing that I had to.

He said, "Do you want me to say it?"

"No," I replied. It was the first acting job from which Peter had ever been fired. I knew that I would not tell him.

I got Peter into the car with the help of a neighbor and drove him to Cedars Sinai, where they admitted him immediately. Tests were being run, and I was told it was safe to go home. However, the moment I arrived, there was a telephone call from the hospital, telling me to return at once. As I had expected, Peter was in danger of dying, yet any procedures they might have tried would have caused uncontrollable bleeding that would kill him.

I was determined to keep Peter alive. I returned to the hospital and talked with him. I wanted him thinking, fighting to stay conscious. I was going to will that man to rally and live just as he had so many times before.

Our friend Jackie Gayle came by, and I insisted he tell Peter jokes. Peter always loved Jackie's humor. Jackie could be outrageous, vulgar, or sophisticated with his comedy, and Peter would always roar with laughter. He was a great audience, and I knew that Jackie would jar him out of his coma. Peter's subconscious mind would hear the jokes and he would respond as he always did.

Laugh, Peter. God damn it, laugh!

I was angry. Peter wasn't laughing. Jackie wasn't doing his job. They were a pair of assholes. Peter was slipping further into his coma. Jackie was doing shtick.

If you're so fucking funny, Jackie Gayle, then why aren't you keeping my husband alive? You play the world and you can't keep one man from going into a coma? What the hell good are you? What the . . .

Peter was dying. My best friend was dying.

The children were alerted. Elizabeth came by to see us. A few other friends stopped by.

I was living on the eighth floor of the hospital, spending most of my time with Peter in the Intensive Care Unit. One morning I found a note taped to the door. It was from my mother. The note read: "I love you. Call me if you need me. Mommy."

We finally got together, and I took her in to see Peter. For the first time she realized what life for the "glamorous Lawfords" had been like during the previous months. She had last seen Peter when he was vital, dynamic, seemingly one of the world's most desirable men. Now she saw an aged shell, wasted away and near death, yet a shell for which she knew I had been caring. It was probably our first moment of true understanding in our adult relationship and, for a moment, we were close together.

Faces. Nurses. Doctors. Security personnel. Some were familiar. Others I had never seen before. And a few, who I was certain I did not know, were people with whom I had been close in the past.

My mind was dulled with emotion, with lack of sleep. I would eventually experience sleep psychosis, where exhaustion becomes so great that the body can no longer function normally. The more tired you become the harder it is to rest, until you somehow break the pattern and collapse.

It was almost Christmas, and the hospital was filled with reminders of the holidays. There were Christmas cards hanging in the offices, decorations wherever possible, and an effort was being made to make the stays of those who could not go home as pleasant as possible. Yet I saw none of what was around me.

Peter looked at me, said "I'm sorry," then slipped back into a coma. He never spoke again.

The children left to go to Jamaica for the holidays. Many of our friends stopped coming. Reporters and photographers were camping out by the hospital, trying to get interviews. And hovering everywhere was Ron Wise, the public relations director who was trying to help me through my ordeal by coordinating whatever was needed to make the hours easier. He handled the countless telephone calls that came in, he worked with the press, and he was available to me on a twenty-four-hours-a-day basis. He also encouraged me to look my best when I was in the midst of others, knowing that that is how I wanted to appear at those times.

Sleep was something to be gained in fits and snatches. I read to Peter. I sat by his bed. I slept in the chair. I wandered the floor and read to him some more. He was on life support equipment, yet somehow I was determined that he would make it. There had been so much abuse of his body for so many years that I thought if he had not died before he could not die now. His body must somehow be, if not immortal, at least invincible.

And then, the day before Christmas, at 8:50 A.M., there was movement. Peter's body rose, as though he were struggling into a push-up position, and suddenly blood rushed from every opening.

His heart stopped. His lungs stopped. His cell walls, damaged by the drugs, the alcohol, and the periodic malnutrition, could no longer hold the life-sustaining fluid. Peter Lawford was dead.

What happened next was like a circus. I could not leave Peter's side. I held the bloody shell of the man and talked to him for the next two hours. I reviewed our life together, laughing, crying, sharing precious memories with someone who could no longer hear. Finally it was time for the body to be removed to the mortuary, yet it seemed as though he had only been dead for minutes.

Suddenly there was a whirlwind of activity. The children had been notified before they reached Jamaica and were returning to Los Angeles immediately. They were not told of Peter's death until they landed and could be met by Stan Kamen, a family friend and the head of the William Morris Agency. The press was notified and arrangements were made to sneak me out a door where I would not have to face anyone.

The children wanted to see their father, but he had deteriorated to such a degree that he was not recognizable, and I could not allow them to see him. The toxicity in his body was so great that an expert embalmer had to be flown down from San Francisco to handle the job and, hopefully, restore Peter's appearance to an approximation of what he had looked like before poisons had overwhelmed him.

I drove with the representative from the funeral home, Peter's body in back. He was delighted to be out working on Christmas Eve. To him, it was the best possible time to be working on a corpse, a fact he enjoyed telling me, though I refrained from asking him why. We even stopped at a convenience food store so he could get a soft drink along the way.

There was a telephone call from Jackie Onassis after I returned home. She was gentle, kind, understanding of the horror that I had witnessed. She had undoubtedly arranged with the hospital to be called at the moment of Peter's death, for she apparently knew about the nightmare of blood passing from his body. She mentioned the fact that when her husband was assassinated she had held bits of his brain in her hand. And for a moment we were two women, united in grief, who shared the experience of the disintegration of the men we loved.

There was no rest that night and, on Christmas morning, I witnessed Peter's cremation. The next day, telegrams, letters, and cards began coming in from every corner of the world. There were messages of condolence from the Reagans at the White

House and from mainland China. Heads of state sent cables. Fans sent letters. It was as though the world had lost a beloved friend who was not forgotten even though his time as a star had long since passed.

Peter had no clothing for the cremation. I went to Carroll & Company, the only clothing store that was open where I could charge clothing for Peter. He had been raised a gentleman and he was going to go out a gentleman.

Christopher, who had been his father's size, was impressed with the outfit. He asked if he could have it, but I refused.

I rode to the crematorium in a van with Peter's body. I climbed into the back to look at him once more. I opened the box and touched him. Peter was with me and Peter was gone.

The crematorium was in Glendale, and it horrified me. An aide came and took the box, loading it on a gurney and rolling it up a ramp. A fireproof number was placed in the box so that, because he would be cremated at the same time as other bodies, there would be no chance of misidentifying his ashes. The number would survive.

We walked up a ramp, where I was faced with six giant ovens, most of them working. At first I panicked, certain I could not burn his corpse. Then I remembered that it was what Peter wanted. Four hours later, Peter's ashes were placed in an urn, the numbered tag assuring I had the proper remains.

On December 26 a memorial service was held for Peter. There were Kennedys, friends from the MGM days, and others. A friend of mine put something together for me to wear, and then I found myself on Rodeo Drive where some Italian man draped veiling around my hat. I had no idea who was doing what to me, and I certainly did not want to go to the service. Peter would have understood. He hated funerals.

The funeral director explained that I would have to carry the urn along a gravel area to the vault in which the ashes would be placed in Westwood Mortuary. Peter would be near Marilyn's remains, a fact that would have amused him. Then the director suggested I take a practice walk with an empty urn they apparently used for such a purpose.

Suddenly I felt as though I was participating in a perverted wedding ceremony. I was being led down the aisle in preparation for the actual "show" scheduled for that evening. It was as though there was going to be a casket filled with the remains of the best man, and perhaps a smaller casket containing a dead flower girl. It seemed perverse, a show for ghouls, even though there was nothing unusual about it.

The actual ceremony took forty-five minutes. It was pouring rain and I was wearing high heels as I maneuvered along the gravel road, carrying the sixty-pound brass urn that held Peter's ashes. The Lawford children followed. I kissed the urn, then placed it into the crypt. From there I returned to the limousine, relieved that it was over.

Stan Kamen held a gathering in a private room at La Scala Restaurant. There were numerous people from Peter's past attending, and it could have been a beautiful tribute to a man who had once been a major star. The problem was that these were primarily not people who had cared about Peter. These were people who wanted to be a part of the Kennedy mystique. They had abandoned Peter years earlier, leaving him to wallow in despair except when he could be used to make contact with Bobby or Teddy, Jackie, Pat, Eunice, or anyone else who was part of that family.

I was given condolences by people who had refused to return Peter's telephone calls. I was told of his greatness by people who looked on him as being lower than dog shit when he was no longer a major star. Peter had been self-destructive all his life, yet he had managed to maintain his professionalism, to perform with competence, so long as anyone wanted him. Many of these people had hurried Peter to a premature grave.

Finally I returned home and the Lawford children were able to continue their Jamaican holiday. The mortuary bill came to $10,000, money I no longer had. There was no life insurance. The bank accounts that Peter failed to strip for drug money had been frozen by creditors. The children avoided the issue of the bill, as did the rest of the Kennedy family. It was an omen of things to come.

I was not prepared for life without Peter. I had not been prepared for life *with* Peter, for that matter. I was a scared, hurting adolescent when we met. I had traveled. I had worked at jobs that required me to be far more responsible than my years. I had escaped from physical and emotional abuse, developing a veneer of sophisticated toughness. I had a quick mind, a faster tongue, and the ability to curse in two languages. Yet the truth was that I was a scared little girl who had lived with, loved, and married a scared little boy in the body of a gentle, handsome, sophisticated older man.

For years we had done little more than play house together. Sometimes that was fun, chartering a helicopter or private jet, traveling to Europe on a whim, experimenting with more drugs than most invalids see in a lifetime. Toward the end it was mostly a nightmare, as I changed dressings, cleared tubes, provided intravenous meals, cleaned vomit, and mopped up urine. But always we were together.

I hated Peter's impotence and the fantasies he acted out. I hated myself for accepting abuse from him as well as for cheating on him when I could no longer tolerate our life.

And so we played our game of house, getting serious only about such matters as the writing of this book. We had a symbiotic relationship, two unlike creatures totally interdependent upon one another. We experienced love and hate, joy and sadness. But neither one of us ever grew up. We were together approximately ten years, yet I was an adolescent widow.

In spite of everything, Peter had given me his respect and attention. He loved me. He left me notes. He constantly reminded me of his caring. No matter what problems we endured together, there never was any doubt in my mind that I was the most important person in his life. I was as loved by Peter as he was capable of loving anyone, a situation I wanted, needed, treasured. With all our troubles, I was angry at him for dying, for leaving me, for taking that intense love from my life.

I continued to look for notes. I continued to hear something funny and start to rush to a telephone to call Peter and tell him about it. I did not want to have him dead.

A few people understood. Elizabeth Taylor consoled me, having been widowed at about the same age when her third husband Michael Todd died. Actor Roddy McDowall was kind, providing support and another link with Peter's past. And there were others, including longtime fans.

But mostly I chose to retreat into self-pity, hiding from creditors, wanting to break with the past while continuing to cling to the name "Mrs. Lawford." I had no job, no direction, no money, and so much fear that I could not reach out and try even a tentative step toward establishing my own future.

Finally I came to realize that being Mrs. Peter Lawford only got me a better table at a good restaurant or, if I was lucky and the police officer was older, a warning about my erratic automobile driving instead of a ticket. I had an apartment filled with mementoes and memories that were rooting me to the past instead of allowing my new home to serve as a base for establishing my future. I established an archives for Peter and his things with the special collections division of the Hayden Library of Arizona State University in Tempe. Marilyn Wurzburger, the woman in charge of special collections, worked with me to pack everything and arrange for students, researchers, and others of serious purpose to benefit from Peter's life and historically important relationships. I rid myself of "things" and began using only memories to remind me of the past.

Throughout this book I have talked about how Peter and I were abused as children. There is also the fact that I was still a teenager when I began living with him. Yet those are only explanations for our behavior, not excuses.

We all make choices in our lives. For me the choices were often bad ones. Sometimes they seemed exciting, such as running off with Peter in the first place or experimenting with drugs. Sometimes they were made in anger, such as the affairs, a childish reaction to hurt. Sometimes they were made to gain acceptance, my not wanting to face the displeasure that would come from saying: "No." But I've learned from these past choices and finally, I believe, grown up.

I ask for no pity in writing this book. I certainly do not want anyone to see Peter's life or my past as the inevitable result of abusive parents. Too many healthy, mature adults have had similar backgrounds for our situation to be an inevitable one.

I must now move forward and not repeat the past. I am trying to be responsible, to think ahead, to plan, not to just react to life. I am trying to make arrangements to meet Peter's financial obligations so that I can find respite from my countless creditors. I know, in part, that I am drug-free because my health cannot survive their use. But I want to live instead of retaining the "I don't care. What will be will be" attitude that killed Peter and nearly killed me.

All I can do is live my life, doing my best and not becoming obsessed with any failures. I am luckier than Peter in that I discovered my failings earlier. I believe I now have the maturity to mould my own future instead of letting myself be manipulated by my past.

Yet I will never forget Peter Lawford, nor will I ever stop loving him.

The world lost Peter Lawford, the actor. The Kennedy family lost Peter Lawford, the loving friend of the president and key to Hollywood gossip. The children lost a father who adored them even as he could not reach out to them. But I lost three people when he died—a father figure; my dearest, closest friend; and, in his own way, my lover. I shall miss him always.

Epilogue

PETER'S FUNERAL BILLS REMAINED UNPAID INTO MAY OF 1988. The total bill came to $10,000, a sum I did not have. The estate had no money, but many debts. The IRS was owed back taxes. And my employment had been sporadic at best, never bringing in the type of money needed to pay even the interest on the debts. I was unable to handle the bill.

Eventually the mortuary changed ownership and pressure was put on me to pay the bills. This was perfectly valid because a mortuary is a business. There were expenses in just maintaining a crypt for Peter's ashes, and there was no way a business could survive without the bills being paid.

Peter's children and I were at odds over this. The Kennedy family claimed they did not know the bill had not been paid, despite the fact that I had been told around the time of the funeral services that they would handle the matter. There has been much name calling on both sides, and everyone has their own version of what happened. But this is not important. What matters is that in May of 1988 I was faced with the choice of either paying the bills or removing Peter's remains.

The mortuary was as cooperative as possible, being willing to write off much of the debt. I also was deeply touched by the generosity of a number of people who sent me cash and checks after reading about the problem. The cash and checks, totaling less than $20, was forwarded to the mortuary and appreciated by the staff there, though it really was almost a meaningless gesture compared with the debt of several thousand dollars.

I was becoming distraught over this issue. I thought objectively about Peter's last wishes. He had not cared about what happened to him. He had suggested I wrap him in a sheet and dump him in a dumpster after he was gone. He was half joking about that, yet

245

more seriously spoke about wanting to be placed in the ocean he loved.

Why hadn't I just done that at the start? I wondered. Then I realized that I had been so grief stricken that I did what many people do. I arranged for the nicest possible resting place. He was cremated, but his ashes would rest in a beautiful location near such old friends as Marilyn Monroe. It was my wish for him, not necessarily his desire. In fact, if I wanted to be objective about it all, he probably would have wanted me to take him into the ocean on a surfboard, then ridden a wave while scattering the ashes to the wind. That action would have been fitting.

I decided to remove Peter's ashes, though to do so approximately $2,500 would have to be paid, plus the cost for arranging to have them scattered over the ocean. Contact with the children was made, and they decided to pay the bills necessary to keep Peter in the crypt, a relief for me. The Kennedy family just wanted to be certain that I would not consider removing the ashes in the future if I agreed to let them pay the bill.

I could finally relax. Removing Peter's ashes was a trauma I did not wish to face. I was delighted that they were coming through with this final gift for Peter, weeping happily after I hung up the telephone following my conversation with them.

On a Friday I received an affadavit to be signed. It was an agreement that stated that once they paid the bills, I would not remove the ashes unless at least two of the children signed an agreement allowing such an action. I was annoyed at the mistrust, yet thrilled for Peter. Of course I would sign.

It was Monday before I had a chance to do anything about the affadavit, and by then it was too late. I received a telephone call from a spokesperson for the children. I was told that they had "convened" in New York City and decided that I could do what I wished because Peter just "wasn't worth it" when it came to paying the money to keep him in the mortuary.

I was shocked, angry, and hurt. There was still that great gap between Peter and his children. Even now they had not found any form of understanding. The situation was a sad and tragic one, and I wept for them all. I was also livid, resenting the sudden turnaround after being sent the form to sign.

Finally the children sent a check—$430 to cover the disinterment fee. This payment later would be grossly misunderstood by the press. The bills were *not* paid in full so far as I knew. The disinterment fee covered only the removal of the ashes-filled urn from the crypt. The urn would have to be kept in the office until the remainder of the bills were paid. Peter was removed but I was not free to take him anywhere.

I had had it with the Kennedy family, their changes in attitude, and their willingness to pay only a tiny portion of what was owed. I felt emotionally manipulated, as though it was a personal attack against me. It was time for me to take matters into my own hands and arrange for Peter to be released into the ocean.

I talked extensively with the mortuary staff and found them most understanding. We finally agreed that I could have the remains despite the outstanding fee. I just could not keep Peter in the crypt any longer.

What happened next remains an embarrassment to this day. It was a nightmare that made headlines throughout the world.

I talked about what was happening with some reporters who work for the weekly *National Enquirer*, one of America's best-selling tabloids. They realized that this was a strong story and asked if a reporter and photographer could be present. They offered to help me with transportation and other needs in exchange for the story, and I agreed.

The staff of the *Enquirer* is paid extremely well for their work and placed under a great deal of pressure to obtain their stories. Some become overly aggressive, going to any lengths to beat out others. Most with that attitude do not last, though. The long-term people, both writers and photographers, are kind, friendly individuals who, though aggressive when working, understand their paper's past reputation and work to show that they are different. As a result, when the two reporters wanted to be involved, I decided that, yes, they could have the story. I knew that they would be dignified, respectful, and that once it appeared, I would no longer be subject to intense scrutiny by the press at large.

What I did not know was that a man who had learned of the disinterment decided to call the entire Los Angeles area news media. By the time I arrived at the mortuary, there were approximately eighty-five reporters, photographers, and television cameramen; three helicopters; and countless cars. I was faced with a three-ring circus.

I was suddenly terrified. Had I done the right thing? Should I go ahead with this? Ted Schwarz, (co-author of this book) had arranged for a private investigator, a former Los Angeles Police homicide detective, to act as my bodyguard during this time. He did not think I needed protection so much as the support that would come from knowing that if I had any trouble someone would be there to help. The urn weighed almost thirty-five pounds, and the bodyguard is six feet, four inches tall. If I become too emotional or was overwhelmed with the task, he was to help. Fortunately, he was also trained and experienced in protecting someone from mob scenes.

My first reaction upon seeing the mob was to ask the driver of the limousine my friends had hired for me to take me home. I was increasingly upset about the fact that I had allowed any reporters to be present during this last moment with Peter's remains. Now I was faced with eighty-five of them, the grounds of the mortuary jammed to capacity.

The bodyguard had seen me when I left my apartment, and he knew that I was an emotional wreck. He sensed that I would not be able to go ahead with the scattering of the remains if I had to consider it a second time. He knew from talking with my co-author how distraught I was and encouraged me to go ahead. From what we all knew at the time, he was right. In hindsight, I regret the action.

What happened next would have been funny if it had happened in a motion picture, but it was emotionally devastating for me. There were microphones everywhere. Some reporters relied upon small tape recorders with built-in microphones that they jammed into my face. Others used long "shotgun" types that are on special long handles. In their rush, my skirt was caught and lifted by one mike and my blouse was caught and tugged by another. I thought for a moment that my clothing was going to be accidentally ripped from my body by their mishandled equipment.

Cameras were shoved toward my face, reporters leaped on my car and tried to get inside, and others tried to wedge-in my vehicle so I could not get away without talking. Notes begging for an interview were shoved into my hands. People were screaming questions. "How does it feel, Patricia?" "Why are you doing this, Patricia?" "Wouldn't the Kennedys come up with the money, Mrs. Lawford?" "You can tell us, Mrs. Lawford. This is really a publicity stunt, isn't it?"

I was numb. The monsignor from my church, who had accompanied me, a man who I have relied on for spiritual guidance, was weeping from the emotions of what we were experiencing. I felt as though I had disgraced Peter and cheapened what we were doing because of the mob that was present. What had promised to be an uncomfortable experience at best was suddenly a nightmare beyond comprehension.

The crypt was opened, the urn removed, the monsignor leading me in prayer. Then, somehow, we were able to get away.

Eventually we were on the boat, traveling across the ocean,

spreading the ashes. I helped with the sails. And, at times, I wept bitterly.

It ended eventually, of course. The bodyguard arranged for more than one car so that we could elude most of the press. The security guards in my building kept reporters away from me. My answering machine handled most of the telephone calls.

There were threats of physical harm, threats of legal action by people connected with the Kennedy family, threats from crazies. And everyone was embarrassed.

The Kennedy children issued a statement that the bills had been paid in full. I would like to believe that the statement is a true one. Certainly, with all the press and all the problems, they would have had no reason to tell me of their last-minute decision. Perhaps they did not realize the seriousness of the problem until they saw my situation and decided to cover everything at the last minute, not letting me know that they had acted.

The mortuary, not wishing to offend or be damned for what truly had been a proper business attitude, claimed that the bill had been paid in full and there was no reason for my removing the remains. And I looked like a publicity seeker who was trying to gain attention through the use of my dead husband's ashes. However, at this writing, the mortuary has refused to give me copies of the bills, the canceled checks, or any other documents that would prove that past debts were paid and that Peter's ashes could have remained. All I can document is that the children paid to have the ashes removed, no other bills being covered. Since the ashes could only be removed with the help of the mortuary, and since at the time everyone was claiming that there was no debt, that I had lied, no one was able to come forth with documents proving any payment other than the $430 payment, I fear that my name was smeared for simply telling the truth. Certainly I have no regrets about my actions—given the same circumstances as I knew them, I would again do exactly what I did.

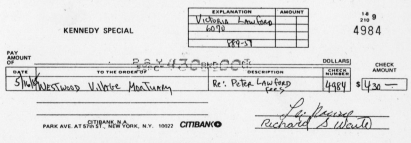

There is only so much you can fight in Hollywood and Beverly Hills, two small towns where truth and reality are perpetually twisted. Had things taken place the way they originally were planned there would have been no trouble. Peter would have wanted me to use my friends from the *National Enquirer* because he felt the same way toward them that I do. He also would have been pleased with the disposal of his ashes and touched by the people who had tried to help avoid the trauma. But he would have been irate over the media "zoo" that descended on us, whose actions were unprofessional and without style.

Unfortunately, there is nothing I can do to change anything that happened. I feel more alone than I have at any time since Peter's death, though one burden, the pressure over Peter's final resting place, has been lifted and both of us can get on with our futures, whatever that means.

And always there is the irony of the boat the reporters hired to take me out to sea for the spreading of the ashes. They knew nothing about it other than it was capable of handling the job and comfortable enough so the physical part of the ride would not be unpleasant. Yet when we left the vessel and I glanced back to see what its name might be, I was shocked by what I saw. The last boat ride Peter and I would ever share was on a vessel named *Freedom*.

Bibliography

Allyson, June with Frances Spatz Leighton, *June Allyson*, New York, G.P. Putnam's Sons, 1982.

Arnaz, Desi, *A Book*, New York, William Morrow & Company, Inc., 1976.

Bego, Mark, *The Best of Modern Screen*, St. Martin's Press, New York, 1986.

Berle, Milton, with Frankel, Haskel, *Milton Berle*, New York, Delacorte Press, 1974.

Bradlee, Benjamin, *Conversations with Kennedy*, New York, W. W. Norton & Company, 1975.

Carey, Gary, *All The Stars in Heaven: Louis B. Mayer's MGM*, New York, E. P. Dutton, 1981.

Collier, Peter & Horowitz, David, *Kennedys*, New York, Simon & Schuster, 1984.

Crowther, Bosley, *The Lion's Share*, New York, E. P. Dutton & Co., 1957.

David, Lester and David, Irene, *Bobby Kennedy: The Making of a Folk Hero*, New York, Dodd, Mead & Company, 1986.

Exner, Judith, as told to Ovid Demaris. *My Story*, New York, Grove Press, 1977.

Galon, Buddy, *Bitch*, Branden Publishing, Brookline Village, Massachusetts, 1986.

Gardner, Gerald; *The Censorship Papers*, New York, Dodd, Mead, & Co., 1987.

Gehman, Richard, *Sinatra and His Rat Pack*, New York, Belmont Books, 1961.

Goodwin, Doris Kearns, *The Fitzgeralds and the Kennedys: An American Saga*, New York, Simon & Schuster, 1987.

Herman, Gary (compiler), *The Book of Hollywood Quotes*, New York, Omnibus Press, 1979.

253

Hopper, Hedda, and Brough, James, *The Whole Truth and Nothing But*, Garden City, New York, Doubleday & Co., 1963.

Kelley, Kitty, *Elizabeth Taylor: the Last Star*, New York, Simon & Schuster, 1981.

Kelley, Kitty, *JACKIE OH!*, Secaucus, New Jersey, Lyle Stuart, 1978.

Kelley, Kitty, *His Way: The Unauthorized Biography of Frank Sinatra*, New York, Bantam, 1986.

Kennedy, Rose Fitzgerald, *Times To Remember*, Garden City, New York, Doubleday & Company, 1974.

Leigh, Janet, *There Really Was a Hollywood*, Garden City, New York, Doubleday & Company, Inc., 1984.

"Los Angeles Herald Examiner," July 6, 1973

"Los Angeles Times," December 25, 1984

Madsen, Axel, *Gloria And Joe: The Star-Crossed Love Affair of Gloria Swanson and Joe Kennedy*, New York, Arbor House/William Morrow and Company, 1988.

Minnelli, Vincente, with Arce, Hector, *I Remember It Well*, Garden City, New York, Doubleday & Company, Inc., 1974.

"Modern Screen," July, 1942

"Modern Screen," January, 1943

"Motion Picture," January 1972

"Movie Life," November, 1943

"Movie Life," February, 1944

"New Jersey Daily Record," December 25, 1984

"New York Daily News," Sunday, April 25, 1954

Noguchi, Thomas, M.D. with DiMona, Joseph, *Coroner*, New York, Simon & Schuster, 1983.

Parmet, Herbert; *J. F. K. The Presidency of John F. Kennedy*, New York, Dial, 1983.

"People Weekly," January 14, 1985.

Rainie, Harrison, and Quinn, John, *Growing Up Kennedy*, New York, G.P. Putnam's Sons, 1983.

Sheppard, Dick, *Elizabeth: The Life and Career of Elizabeth Taylor*, New York, Doubleday & Company, 1974.

Sinatra, Nancy, *Frank Sinatra, My Father*, Garden City, New York, Doubleday & Co., 1985.

Sullivan, William, with Brown, Bill, *The Bureau: My Thirty Years in Hoover's FBI*, New York, W. W. Norton & Co., Inc., 1979.

Summers, Anthony, *Goddess: The Secret Lives of Marilyn Monroe*, New York, Macmillan, 1985.

Swanson, Gloria, *Swanson on Swanson*, New York, Random House, 1980.

Thomas, Tony: *The Films of Ronald Reagan*, Secaucus, New Jersey, Citadel Press, 1980.

Turner, Lana; *Lana*, New York, E. P. Dutton, Inc., 1982.

Wilkerson, Tichi and Borie, Marcia, *The Hollywood Reporter: The Golden Years*, New York, Coward-McCann, Inc., 1984.

Wills, Garry, *Reagan's America: Innocents at Home*, Garden City, New York, Doubleday & Co., 1987.

Wills, Garry; *The Kennedy Imprisonment*, Boston/Toronto, Atlantic Monthly Press of Little, Brown and Company, 1981.

Wilson, Earl, *Hot Times: True Tales of Hollywood and Broadway*, Chicago, Contemporary Books, Inc., 1984.

Wilson, Earl; *Sinatra*, New York, Macmillan, 1976.

Filmography

Motion Pictures in which Peter Lawford appeared

1931 *Poor Old Bill*, BIP/Wardour, produced by Walter C. Mycroft, directed by Monty Banks, starring Leslie Fuller, Iris Ashley, Syd Courteney. Running time: 52 minutes.

1938 *Lord Jeff*, M-G-M, produced by Frank Davis, directed by Sam Wood, starring Freddie Bartholomew, Mickey Rooney, Charles Coburn. Running time: 78 minutes.

1942 *A Yank at Eton*, M-G-M, produced by John W. Considine, Jr., directed by Norman Taurog, starring Mickey Rooney, Edmund Gwen, Ian Hunter, Freddie Bartholomew Running time: 88 minutes.

1942 *Mrs. Miniver*, M-G-M, produced by Sidney Franklin, directed by William Wyler, starring Greer Garson, Walter Pidgeon, Dame May Whitty. Running time: 134 minutes.

1943 *Sherlock Holmes Faces Death*, Universal, produced by Roy William, directed by Roy William, starring Basil Rathbone, Nigel Bruce, Milburn Stone. Running time: 68 minutes.

1944 *Mrs. Parkington*, M-G-M, produced by Leon Gordon, directed by Tay Garnett, starring Greer Garson, Walter Pidgeon, Edward Arnold, Agnes Moorehead, Dan Duryea. Running time: 124 minutes.

1944 *The White Cliffs of Dover*, M-G-M, produced by Sidney Franklin, directed by Clarence Brown, starring Irene Dunne, Roddy McDowall, Dame May Whitty, C. Aubrey Smith, Van Johnson, Elizabeth Taylor, June Lockhart. Running time: 126 minutes.

1945 *Son of Lassie*, M-G-M, produced by Samuel Marx, directed by S. Sylvan Simon, starring Donald Crisp, June Lockhart, Nigel Bruce. Running time: 102 minutes.

1945   *The Picture of Dorian Grey*, M-G-M, produced by Pandro S. Berman, directed by Albert Lewin, starring George Sanders, Donna Reed, Angela Lansbury, Sir Cedric Hardwicke. Running time: 110 minutes.

1946   *My Brother Talks to Horses*, M-G-M, produced by Samuel Marx, directed by Fred Zinnemann, starring Edward Arnold, Charlie Ruggles, Spring Byington. Running Time: 93 minutes.

1946   *Two Sisters From Boston*, M-G-M, produced by Joe Pasternak, directed by Henry Koster, starring Kathryn Grayson, June Allyson, Lauritz Melchior, Jimmy Durante, Ben Blue. Running time: 112 minutes.

1946   *Cluny Brown*, Twentieth Century Fox, produced by Ernst Lubitsch, directed by Ernst Lubitsch, starring Charles Boyer, Jennifer Jones, Helen Walker, C. Aubrey Smith, George Kirby. Running time: 100 minutes.

1947   *Good News*, M-G-M, produced by Arthur Freed, directed by Charles Walters, starring June Allyson and Mel Torme. Running time: 92 minutes.

1947   *It Happened in Brooklyn*, M-G-M, produced by Jack Cummings, directed by Richard Whorf, starring Frank Sinatra, Kathryn Grayson, Jimmy Durante, Gloria Grahame. Running time: 104 minutes.

1948   *On an Island with You*, M-G-M, produced by Joe Pasternak, directed by Richard Thorpe, starring Esther Williams, Ricardo Montalban, Jimmy Durante, Cyd Charisse, Leon Ames, Xavier Cugat & his Orchestra. Running time: 107 minutes.

1948   *Easter Parade*, M-G-M, produced by Arthur Freed, directed by Charles Walters, starring Judy Garland, Fred Astaire, Ann Miller. Running time: 107 minutes.

1948   *Julia Misbehaves*, M-G-M, produced by Everett Riskin, directed by Jack Conway, starring Greer Garson, Walter Pidgeon, Cesar Romero, Elizabeth Taylor, Nigel Bruce. Running time: 99 minutes.

1949   *Little Women*, M-G-M, produced by Mervyn LeRoy, directed by Mervyn LeRoy, starring June Allyson, Margaret O'Brien, Elizabeth Taylor, Janet Leigh, Rossano Brazzi, Mary Astor, C. Aubrey Smith. Running time: 121 minutes.

1949   *The Red Danube*, M-G-M, produced by Carey Wilson, directed by George Sidney, starring Walter Pidgeon, Ethel Barrymore, Angela Lansbury, Janet Leigh, Louis Calhern. Running time: 102 minutes.

1951   *Please Believe Me*, M-G-M, produced by Val Lewton, directed by Norman Taurog, starring Deborah Kerr, Robert Walker, Mark Stevens, James Whitmore, J. Carrol Naish, Spring Byington. Running time: 95 minutes.

1952 *Royal Wedding*, M-G-M, produced by Arthur Freed, directed by Stanley Donen, starring Fred Astaire, Jane Powell, Sarah Churchill, Keenan Wynn.

1952 *Kangaroo*, Twentieth Century Fox, produced by Robert Bossler, directed by Lewis Milestone, starring Maureen O'Hara, Richard Boone. Running time: 115 minutes.

1953 *You for Me*, M-G-M, produced by Henry Berman, directed by Don Weiss, starring Jane Greer, Howard Wendell, Gig Young. Running time: 95 minutes.

1953 *The Hour of 13*, M-G-M, produced by Hayes Goetz, directed by Harold French, starring Dawn Addams, Roland Culver, Derek Bond. Running time: 107 minutes.

1953 *Just this One*, M-G-M, produced by Henry Berman, directed by Don Weiss, starring Janet Leigh, Lewis Stone. Running time: 103 minutes.

1954 *Rogue's March*, M-G-M, produced and written by Leon Gordon, directed by Allan Davis, starring Richard Greene, Janice Rule, Leo G. Carroll. Running time: 105 minutes.

1954 *It Should Happen to You*, Columbia Pictures, produced by Fred Kohlmar, directed by George Cukor, starring Judy Holliday, Jack Lemmon, Michael O'Shea. Running time: 86 minutes.

1959 *Never So Few*, Canterbury/M-G-M, produced by Edmund Grainger, directed by John Sturges, starring Frank Sinatra, Gina Lollobrigida, Steve McQueen, Paul Henreid, Brian Donlevy, Dean Jones, Charles Bronson. Running time: 124 minutes.

1960 *Ocean's Eleven*, Warner Brothers, produced by Lewis Milestone, directed by Lewis Milestone, starring Frank Sinatra, Dean Martin, Sammy Davis, Jr., Angie Dickinson, Red Skelton, George Raft, Cesar Romero, Joey Bishop, Akim Tamiroff, Shirley MacLaine. Running time: 127 minutes.

1960 *Exodus*, Preminger/UA, produced by Otto Preminger, directed by Otto Preminger, starring Paul Newman, Eva Marie Saint, Lee J. Cobb, Sal Mineo. Running time: 212 minutes.

1960 *Pepe*, Columbia Pictures, produced by George Sidney, directed by George Sidney starring Cantinflas, Dan Dailey, Ernie Kovacs, Shirley Jones, Carlos Montalban, William Demarest et al. Running time: 195 minutes.

1962 *The Longest Day*, Twentieth Century Fox, produced by Darryl F. Zanuck, directed by Andrew Morton, Ken Annahim, Bernhard Wichi, Gerd Oswald, starring John Wayne, Robert Mitchum, Henry Fonda, Robert Ryan, Rod Steiger, Robert Wagner, Mel Ferrer, Jeffrey Hunter et al. Running time 180 minutes.

1962 *Sergeants 3*, Essex-Claude/UA, produced by Frank Sinatra, directed by John Sturges, starring Frank Sinatra, Dean Martin,

Sammy Davis, Jr., Joey Bishop, Henry Silva, Buddy Lester. Running time: 113 minutes.

1962 *Advise and Consent*, Columbia, produced by Otto Preminger, directed by Otto Preminger, starring Henry Fonda, Charles Laughton, Don Murray, Walter Pidgeon, Gene Tierney, Franchot Tone, Lew Ayres, Burgess Meredith. Running time: 140 minutes.

1964 *Dead Ringer*, Warner Brothers, produced by William H. Wright, directed by Paul Henreid, starring Bette Davis, Karl Malden. Running time: 115 minutes.

1965 *Harlow*, Paramount, produced by Joseph E. Levine, directed by Gordon Douglas, starring Carroll Baker, Martin Balsam, Red Buttons, Angela Lansbury. Running time: 125 minutes.

1965 *Sylvia*, Paramount, produced by Martin H. Poll, directed by Gordon Douglas, starring Carroll Baker, George Maharis, Joanne Dru, Viveca Lindfors, Edmund O'Brien, Aldo Ray, Ann Southern. Running time: 115 minutes.

1966 *A Man Called Adam*, Trace-Mark/EM, produced by Ike Jones and James Waters, directed by Leo Penn, starring Sammy Davis, Jr., Ossie Davis, Cicely Tyson, Louis Armstrong, Frank Sinatra, Jr. Running time: 103 minutes.

1966 *The Oscar*, Greene-Rouse/EM, produced by Clarence Greene, directed by Russell Rouse, starring Stephen Boyd, Elke Sommer, Milton Berle, Eleanor Parker, Joseph Cotton, Jill St. John, Tony Bennett, Eddie Adams, Ernest Borginine, Ed Begley, Walter Brennan, Broderick Crawford, Edith Head, Hedda Hopper, Bob Hope, Merle Oberon, Frank Sinatra, Nancy Sinatra. Running time: 103 minutes.

1968 *Salt and Pepper*, Chrislow-Trace-Markua, produced by Milton Ebbins, directed by Richard D. Donner, starring Sammy Davis, Jr., Michael Bates, Robert Dorning. Running time: 103 minutes.

1968 *Buona Sera, Mrs. Campbell*, UA (Italian), produced by Melvin Frank, directed by Melvin Frank, starring Gina Lollobrigida, Shelly Winters, Phil Silvers, Telly Savalas, Lee Grant. Running time: 111 minutes.

1969 *Hook, Line and Sinker*, Columbia, produced by Jerry Lewis, directed by George Marshall, starring Jerry Lewis, Anne Francis. Running time: 91 minutes.

1969 *The April Fools*, Jalem/National General, produced by Gordon Carroll, directed by Stuart Rosenberg, starring Jack Lemmon, Catherine Deneuve, Harvey Korman, Sally Kellerman. Running time: 95 minutes.

1970 *One More Time*, Chrislaw-Trace-Mark, produced by Milton Ebbins, directed by Jerry Lewis, starring Sammy Davis, Jr., Maggie Wright, Leslie Sands, John Wood. Running time: 95 minutes.

1972 *They Only Kill Their Masters*, M-G-M, produced by William Belasco, directed by James Goldstone, starring James Garner, Hal Holbrook, Harry Guardino, June Allyson, Tom Ewell, Edmund O'Brien. Running time: 97 minutes.

1975 *Rosebud*, Universal, produced by Otto Preminger, directed by Otto Preminger, starring Peter O'Toole, Richard Attenborough, John V. Lindsay. Running time: 126 minutes.

1976 *Won Ton Ton, The Dog Who Saved Hollywood*, Paramount, produced by David V. Picker, directed by Michael Winner, Arnold Schulman, starring Bruce Dern, Madeline Kahn, Art Carney, Phil Silvers, Terri Garr. Running time: 92 minutes.

1980 *Angels Brigade*, Arista, produced by Greydon Clark, directed by Greydon Clark, starring Jack Palance, Jim Backus, Neville Brand, Pat Buttram, Arthur Godfrey, Alan Hale. Running time: 87 minutes.

1981 *Body and Soul*, Cannon, produced by Menaham Golan and Yorman Globus, starring Jayne Kennedy, Perry Lang, Muhammad Ali. Running time: 109 minutes.

Television series in which Peter Lawford appeared:

Dear Phoebe, Produced by Chrislaw Productions, (1954 through 1956).
The Thin Man, (1957 through 1958).
The Doris Day Show, 1971.

Television films in which Peter Lawford appeared:

How I Spent my Summer Vacation, 1967
Step Out of Line, 1971
Supertrain, 1979 (Movie of the Week).
The Mysterious Island of Beautiful Women, 1979 (Movie of the Week)

Peter Lawford's television guest appearances:

Ford Theatre, 1953
G. E. Theatre, 1953
Schlitz Playhouse of Stars, 1954
Ford Theatre, 1954
Ford Theatre, 1954
Fireside Theatre, 1955
Alfred Hitchcock Presents, 1955
Screen Directors Playhouse, 1955
Schlitz Playhouse of Stars, 1956
Playhouse 90, 1956
Ruggles of Red Gap, 1957

Climax, 1957
Goodyear Theatre, 1959
Theatre 62, 1962
Profiles in Courage, 1965
Alfred Hitchcock Theatre, 1965
Patty Duke Show, 1965
Bob Hope Chrysler Theatre, 1965
Wild Wild West, 1956
Run for your Life, 1966
I Spy, 1967
Men from Shiloh, 1971
The Deadly Hunt, 1971
Ellery Queen, 1971
Bewitched, 1972
The Bold Ones, 1972
The Phantom of Hollywood, 1974
Born Free, 1974
Fantasy Island, 1977 (Series Pilot)
Hawaii Five O, 1978
Fantasy Island, 1979
Love Boat, 1979
Fantasy Island, 1980
Fantasy Island, 1982
Matt Houston, 1982

In addition to the above, Peter Lawford appeared on innumerable TV game shows throughout the last decade of his career.

Index